GOD VS. GAY?

OTHER BOOKS BY JAY MICHAELSON

Everything Is God: The Radical Path of Nondual Judaism

Another Word for Sky: Poems

God in Your Body: Kabbalah, Mindfulness, and Embodied Spiritual Practice

GOD vs. GAY?

The Religious Case for Equality

JAY MICHAELSON

QUEER ACTION/QUEER IDEAS
A Series Edited by Michael Bronski

Beacon Press, Boston

Queer Action/Queer Ideas—a unique series addressing
pivotal issues within the LGBT movement

Beacon Press
25 Beacon Street
Boston, Massachusetts 02108-2892
www.beacon.org

Beacon Press books
are published under the auspices of
the Unitarian Universalist Association of Congregations.

14   13   12   11   8   7   6   5   4   3   2   1

This book is printed on acid-free paper that meets the uncoated paper
ANSI/NISO specifications for permanence as revised in 1992.

Text design and composition by Wilsted & Taylor Publishing Services

Library of Congress Cataloging-in-Publication Data

Michaelson, Jay.
  God vs. gay? : the religious case for equality / Jay Michaelson.
      p. cm.—(Queer action/queer ideas)
  Includes bibliographical references and index.
  ISBN 978-0-8070-0159-2 (hardcover : alk. paper)
  1. Homosexuality—Biblical teaching. I. Title. II. Title: God versus gay?
  BS680.H67M53 2011
  261.8'35766—dc22   2011012336

For God shall be between me and you, and between my seed and your seed, forever.

—1 Samuel 20:41–42

The facts which will cure this prejudice belong to the ordinary talk of ordinary people.

—Iris Murdoch, "The Moral Decision about Homosexuality"

Contents

A Note from the Series Editor

Religion is a part of every American's life, whether she or he is a believer or not. It shapes how we make laws, who receives tax exempt status, and even how we establish national holidays. Most important, it informs how we think not only about sex but about love and intimate relationships. The United States was not "founded" on Christianity; it was established on the principles of human equality articulated by the Enlightenment.

Yet for the past half-century, a battle has been raging across America that has placed the scriptures at the center of the culture wars. This battle has shaped numerous aspects of American culture—often around issues of sexuality and, in particular, same-sex desire, identity, and activity, including same-sex marriage, laws regulating adoption, and the formation of gay-straight alliances in schools. This struggle between traditional believers and those with a more secular vision about sexual freedom often reaches a standstill fueled by antagonism and misunderstanding.

In *God vs. Gay? The Religious Case for Equality,* Jay Michaelson offers a solution to this problem that has the potential of moving us—as a culture and as individuals—to a new level of personal and social acceptance. Arguing that Jewish and Christian scriptures do not condemn same-sex love and intimacy, but, when read carefully, actually command an acceptance of them, Michaelson challenges us to rethink traditional paradigms of religion and society—and in doing so, gives us a new way to think about our own lives.

Michael Bronski
Series Editor, Queer Action/Queer Ideas

Introduction

"God versus Gay" is a myth. It is untrue, unsupported by Scripture, and contradicted every day by the lives of religious gay people. Yet it is also among the most pervasive and hurtful untruths in America today, and people all across the ideological spectrum believe it. Religious conservatives, secular liberals, and millions of people across the gamut of American political and religious opinion talk past one another, in heated agreement that it's either "gay rights" or traditional religion, the Constitution or the Bible. Pro-gay folks can't see how anyone could be opposed to equality, while opponents can't see how anyone could change thousands of years of tradition. The conversation goes nowhere.

Worse, this conflict is an *internal* one as well—inside each of us who has ever wrestled with sexuality and religion. I've worked in gay religious communities for over a decade, and in that time, I've met thousands of people wounded by what they see as the conflict between religion and homosexuality. I have counseled families who have been torn apart, people whose parents see them in the grocery store but won't acknowledge their existence. And before I came to reconcile my own sexuality and spirituality, I felt the conflict myself and wondered why God had cursed me. So long as the false choice between God and gay persists, our brothers, sisters, cousins, and friends will continue to struggle, continue to torment themselves, and continue to be excluded from their families and communities.

All of this is unnecessary. Religious people should support equality, inclusion, and dignity for sexual minorities *because* of our religious traditions, not despite them. Not only does the Bible not say what some people claim, but the Bible and centuries of religious teaching in Christian and Jewish traditions argue strongly for what sometimes gets called "gay rights." You read that right: *for* gay rights. While there are half a dozen verses that may say something about some forms of same-sex behavior, what they have to say is ambiguous, limited, and widely misunderstood. Meanwhile, there are hundreds of *other* verses that teach us about the importance of love, justice, and sacred relationships. I know it may sound unusual or even heretical to say so, but after substantial research (both within my Jewish tradition and, as a scholar of religion and an interfaith religious activist, in multiple Christian ones as well), years of soul-searching, and years of working with religious gay people, I sincerely believe that our shared religious values call upon us to support the equality, dignity, and full inclusion of sexual and gender minorities—that is, of lesbian, gay, bisexual, and transgender people.

So, if you are someone who struggles with the question of religion and homosexuality; if you are questioning your sexuality; if you are trying to reconcile your faith with the sexuality of a friend or family member; if you are a pastor trying to remain true to your ideals but compassionate to your parishioners; or, whatever your own religious or nonreligious views, if you are concerned about the hurtful, polarizing tone of political conversations about homosexuality, I hear you. I was like you. And this book is for you.

Admittedly, this book is for *me,* too. Before I came out, I was certain that being openly gay would spell the end of my religious life. I was an Orthodox-practicing Jew, and my religion gave meaning and shape to my life. But I repressed my sexuality, acting out occasionally but regretting it afterwards, and I tried, for years, to change. Eventually, after ten years in the closet—an all-too-cozy metaphor for lying to yourself and others, and hating yourself for doing so—I had had enough. The pain, isolation, loneliness, and shame had grown so great—the futile relationships with women, the arguments with God, the hatred of myself for being unable to change—that I was ready to forsake my religion for the sake of my happiness.

But what I found was a shock: coming out was the doorway to true love, faith, and joy. My relationship to God and to my religious community grew stronger than ever before. My spiritual path began to unfold, my prayer life began to awaken, and my love for other human beings slowly unfurled itself and expanded. "God versus Gay" had very personal consequences for me, and I have written this book both to save other people from the hell I lived through, and to clarify and crystallize what I have learned over the years. "God versus Gay" isn't just a false dichotomy. It's a rebellion against the image of God itself.

But this is not only a personal story; it is a political one as well. After all, the "equality" in this book's subtitle means not only that all of us are equal before God, or that same-sex love can be of equal holiness as opposite-sex love—although it does mean that—but also that this religious value has political consequences. Today, in most states, I can be fired from my job simply for having written this book and stating that I am gay. I can't visit my life-partner in the hospital. In many countries, I could be jailed for even telling the truth about myself. And there are many churches and synagogues where I have to lie in order to fit in. Yes, the gay rights movement has made remarkable advances, and studies suggest that within a generation, struggles for LGBT (lesbian, gay, bisexual, and transgender—the acronym is strange at first, but one gets used to it) equality will look like ancient history. But as far as American politics may have come on these issues, parts of American society are being left behind. And whether you're for gay rights or against them, you have to be concerned about the way our conversation has been taking place. It's been bitter and contentious, with little understanding or generosity on either side.

    This is a shame, and a risk. Consider, for example, the contrasting cases of two national conversations—on civil rights and on abortion. In the long and continuing struggle for civil rights, Dr. King and other leaders successfully and authentically framed the case for equality in religious as well as political terms. Remember, only a century ago, the Bible was used to enforce segregation as much as to oppose it. God placed the races on different continents, segregationists said. God sanctioned slavery in the Bible. And Africans were doomed to serve Caucasians as punishment for Ham's sin ("Cursed be Canaan! The lowest of slaves will he be to his brothers," says Noah in Genesis 9:25).[1] Dr. King and many others so succeeded in their reframing of civil rights that these arguments may strike us today as musty, even bizarre. But just fifty years ago, they were preached from pulpits around the country.

    What Dr. King and his allies knew was that religion must become an ally of social change if that change is going to take root in people's hearts. And so he preached as well as picketed. He didn't just make constitutional arguments but appealed to conscience, and spoke in the language of Scripture. He didn't spend much time explaining why racist readings of the Bible were false—he focused on why liberating readings were true. As a result, while we still have a long way to go in terms of civil rights for everyone, few people today would argue that equality is an affront to God's will—even though many would have a century ago.

Contrast that with our national "conversation," if that's what it is, about abortion. Here, the left makes secular, constitutional arguments, and the right makes religious ones. Not surprisingly, they talk past one another, and get angrier and angrier as time goes on. It's a battlefield, not a conversation. Whatever one's views on this contentious issue, surely we can all agree that sloganeering, political scheming, and lots of angry shouting are not the best ways to engage with an issue with so much religious and political significance.

Now, gay rights are not the same as African American civil rights. The struggles of LGBT people and African Americans are similar in some respects, but different in others. But the lesson I take from Dr. King and other heroes of the civil rights movement is that if we are to be responsible citizens of American democracy, we must engage with religious values, because these political questions are ultimately religious ones as well. We must have the religious conversation—not to win arguments, but to speak heart to heart with the millions of Americans who are not bigots or homophobes, but who are sincerely troubled by equality for gay people.

We have only barely begun this conversation today. So far, except for a few outliers, religion has been used on only one side of the argument. The Bible forbids homosexuality, we are told. Heterosexual marriage is at the core of God's design for the universe. Most liberals, in response, simply deflect these points, talking instead about separation of church and state. This has been a tragic mistake. Dr. King did not succeed in changing hearts because he invoked the Fourteenth Amendment; he opened hearts, and changed minds, because he invoked God.

As with "God versus Gay" itself, the consequences of this failure to speak religiously about gay rights are personal as well as political. It perpetuates a kind of spiritual schizophrenia, one that is deeply wounding and painful. Now, it's unsurprising that many gay people have given up on religion—religion gave up on them first. But to perpetuate this despair alienates family members from one another, forfeits the opportunity for religious growth and conversation, and ignores the millions of gay people who have *not* given up on religion. By perpetuating "God versus Gay," secular rhetoric alienates gay people from themselves.

Yet as John 8:32 says, the truth will set you free. The Bible does not forbid homosexuality, a concept invented in nineteenth-century Europe. But it does preach the centrality of love and relationship in God's design of the universe. It teaches how God loves us, and wants us to be happy, ethical, just, and fulfilled human beings. It demands that we create a just and compassionate world. And in both the Hebrew Bible and the New Testament, it demands that we sanctify physical intimacy, and open our hearts to love. (Incidentally, because I am writing for people of all faiths, I use each tradition's name for its sacred text. What Christians call the Old Testament, Jews call the Hebrew Bible.)

This is the conversation *I* want to have, because it connects me to my values, and to the values I share with other religious communities. Christian and Jew, progressive and conservative, Protestant and Catholic—we differ on many important details, but our shared fundamental values lead us to a different kind of conversation than the noisy shouting of TV talk shows and radio call-ins. If, like me, you have wrestled with the conundrum of how a loving God could possibly ask gay people to repress and distort themselves, then this book is about the good news that the God of Christianity and Judaism wants no such thing. If, like me, you despair of dialogue between religious and secular people on this divisive issue, then this book offers a way forward into meaningful, heartfelt, and sincere conversation. And if, like me, you are searching not only for tolerance but for authentic, spiritual, and respectful affirmation, then read on, because once the closet doors are opened, light comes streaming in.

I want to be clear about what this book is, and what it is not. It is a religious case, not a political one. It is affirmative, not negative. It is neither biblical apologetics nor an apology for acceptability of sexual diversity. And it embraces hard truths, not easy answers.

First, for political liberals, sexual behavior is a matter of personal liberty: what we decide to do with our bodies is our own business, and the state should not discriminate on the basis of our decisions. This is a strong, time-honored argument, and the dominant one among gay rights advocates. I am sympathetic to it myself. But this book does not make it. In making a *religious* case for equality, I can't say "that's an individual's choice," because religion often tells us which choices are right, and which are wrong.[2] To say so may seem offensive to some political liberals, but this is not a book about secular, constitutional values—it is a book about religion. And that means everything is on the table.

Second, I want to make an affirmative case for the religious and political equality of LGBT people. By "affirmative" I mean something more than simply saying that Leviticus, Romans, and Corinthians don't prohibit homosexuality. I mean that our shared religious values support full inclusion of gay people. To repeat: religious people should not be for equality despite their religions' teachings; they should be for equality *because* of them. Now, what about the "bad texts"? As we'll see in part 2, these texts are ambiguous, limited, and unclear. They are not nearly so straightforward as some people would have us believe. They can be interpreted in many different ways. And so we have to decide which interpretations are more in accord with our fundamental values.

By way of analogy, the Ten Commandments states very clearly, "Thou Shalt Not Kill." Does that mean that if someone is coming at you with a knife, you can't kill them in self-defense? Does that mean that no war is ever justified? Well, clearly, it can't mean those things, because other biblical texts talk about the rules of war and self-defense. Moreover, our fundamental religious values regarding the dignity of every human being would imply that you can act morally and still take another human life, if you have good reason to do so. So, what seems like an unambiguous text—much less ambiguous than the ones we'll look at—actually isn't.

This is why I discuss the "good" texts before the "bad" ones. In part 1, I explore some central religious values that we glean from the Bible: how being alone is not good in the eyes of God, how love is central to religious life, how God does not want us to harm ourselves, and how justice is a core religious value. This is the "positive" religious case: that unless there's some reason not to do so, religious values support inclusion and equality for gay people.

In part 2, I turn to the half dozen verses that some people believe prohibit homosexual behavior, and make the "negative" case: i.e., they don't. The language of the verses is ambiguous, their contexts (purity, idolatry, natural law) are totally different from our contemporary ones, and their meanings have nothing to do with contemporary claims about them. Wherever religious anti-gay sentiment comes from, it doesn't come from the Bible. The point of parts 1 and 2 together is that we can read these verses in an anti-gay way or a pro-gay way, but only the pro-gay way is compatible with fundamental Jewish and Christian values. To put it another way, the pro-gay readings don't need to "win." They just need to "tie." Because in the case of a tie between competing interpretations, we are compelled to take the reading that aligns with our fundamental values.

Finally, part 3 looks at the positive consequences of the pro-gay position for the religious life of ordinary Americans. Far from spelling the end of religious and family life, equality for gays and lesbians leads to more common ground, more valuing of the family, more societal stability, and more opportunities for growth as religious adults. Pro-gay turns out to be pro-God.

Throughout, I want to favor hard truths over easy answers—beginning with the reality of sexual orientation. Why, we might ask, should our attitudes change now, when for hundreds of years homosexuality was condemned by so many religious authorities? The answer is simple: we know something they did not. We know about the science of sexual diversity, and we have begun to listen to voices that were silenced or marginalized for hundreds of years. Thus, we see our sacred texts with new eyes, and reinterpret them in light of this new information—just as we did when we learned the Earth is a sphere and not a pancake. Like many other cultures, we may even come to see sexual minorities as having sacred roles within religious life. As long as we remain true to our values, science is not a threat to religion but an ally of it. New information has come to light. The question is: how do we maintain our core commitments in the face of it?

Now, I know many religious people would like to pretend that sexual orientation simply doesn't exist. Fully one-third of Americans, according to recent studies, believe that homosexuality is a "lifestyle choice." But what about heterosexuality? Is being attracted to a member of the opposite sex a "choice"? Is it a "lifestyle"? No—just as straight people never chose to be attracted to members of the opposite sex, so gay people never chose to be attracted to members of the same sex. Now, it is certainly true that many people (and, in particular, many women) experience their sexuality as being on a continuum, or as fluid, not as a set of clear-cut, binary choices. Yet even a fluid, evolving sexuality is obviously not a choice in the simple meaning of the term; we'll explore this more in chapter 1. And it's just plain insulting to call an aspect of one's soul a lifestyle. As Rev. Candace Chellew-Hodge put it, "We don't have lifestyles. We have lives."[3]

Sexuality is part of who we are as human beings. In chapter 4, we'll review some of the science of sexuality. But as religious people, we are also called to listen to one another, to really hear their stories and try to stand in their shoes. Just recently, I had someone tell me that my love for my partner is the same as someone's lust for a sheep or a goat. I asked him how he knew that, and I tried to describe the depth of our love. But he wouldn't listen. He had made his mind up that homosexuality was just lust, like bestiality, and that was the end of it. This is a failure of religious reasoning. Religious life has never meant sticking your head in the ground or pretending that the world is still flat. Religion lives when it grows, when it is able to maintain its core values while adapting to new facts and understandings. We should welcome this new understanding of sexual diversity, which is a natural part of God's creation, found in every culture around the world and in hundreds of animal species as well. We are able to encompass more truth in our religious teachings than our ancestors were. Yes, this new scientific information is challenging, just as it was challenging to learn that the Earth is not at the center of the universe. But this challenge makes our spirituality stronger, not weaker.

Similarly, I'm not interested in oversimplifying complicated texts and traditions. Most of the values we will explore together are recorded in the Bible. But the Bible says a lot of things. Some texts support my view about sexual diversity, and some oppose it. Some are, I think, illuminating and liberating, and others are, I think, sexist and awful. I'm not interested in whitewashing the parts that either disagree with my overall position, or which I find personally offensive. There are some people, I know, who think that religion should provide simple answers to complicated questions. I've never been one of those. For me, religion comforts the afflicted and afflicts the comfortable. It challenges us to be more than our base selves, and calls us to our highest ideals. At the same time, there is no getting around the fact that religion has been used as a tool of oppression, and has helped violent, evil people be even more violent and evil. I see nothing anti-religious about admitting that. On the contrary, precisely because I value religion, I welcome critiques of it. My writing gets better when people tell me where it fails. My spirituality does too.

Naturally, I have had to make choices to limit the extent of this exploration. I focus on the teachings of Christianity and Judaism, since the "Judeo-Christian tradition" remains the predominant one in American civil life, and my own experience is that of a religious Jew who has spent close to two decades studying and teaching in Jewish and Christian communities, as well as in academic settings, where I wrote my master's thesis on the New Testament. Fine treatments of sexual diversity in other religious cultures are listed in the bibliography. For similar reasons, I have tended to focus more on sexuality than on gender, that is, more on people our society calls gays and lesbians than on transgender people. Obviously, sexuality and gender are closely related—as we'll see, male homosexuality was often condemned because it involved men "acting like women"—and most of the arguments I make apply to gender minorities as well as sexual minorities. However, many of the theological and Scriptural questions involved are different, and I have focused on sexuality primarily. Moreover, I have tried in this book to speak from my heart and my experience, which does not include the experience of being transgender. Make no mistake: the subtitle of this book may be "The Religious Case for Equality" but it is really *a* religious case—one among many.

Our historical moment may seem like one of great crisis, but it is also one of unique opportunity. Like previous generations called to conscience on questions of slavery, fascism, sexism, and affronts to personal liberty, our generation is called to reflect upon the proper nexus between sexuality and the spiritual life. We have a mixed record so far. Ours is indeed a culture of vulgarization, tawdry sex, and the fraying of personal bonds. Yet an alternative is possible—and I believe that embracing the reality of sexual diversity will be an important step toward sanctifying sexuality and combating its degradation. We can do better, and we will.

For too long, we have allowed confusion, fear, and, occasionally, outright greed, to distort our religious teachings. But I will not allow them to alienate me from the God who loves me—and neither should you. Politically and personally, ethically and spiritually, the battle between "God versus Gay" must end.

GOD VS. GAY?

PART ONE

Why our fundamental values support, rather than oppose, equality for sexual minorities

CHAPTER I

"It is not good for a person to be alone"

Intimate relationship heals the primary flaw in creation

Imagine lying to everyone you know, all the time. Imagine feeling that your soul is distorted, evil, and broken. And imagine believing that, because of something you cannot change, God hates you. What would you do?

If you're like me, you'd do everything you could to change this awful part of yourself. You'd hide from everyone, constructing ever more elaborate masks that concealed (you would hope) the dark truth inside. And when all else failed, you'd consider ending your life.

Where do these feelings come from? Whose fault is it that 40 percent of gay teenagers consider suicide—four times as many as straight kids?[1] Are they all just confused—or is it possible that they're hearing *our* message, the message of "God versus Gay," all too clearly?

I was one of those statistics myself. Now I am married, successful, happy, and active in my religious community. But before I came out, I was as miserable and suicidal as the kids on the TV news. I just wasn't as courageous. If I had been, maybe I wouldn't be here today.

There are those who somehow believe that such self-hatred and contradiction is required by a loving God, a God who cares for human beings and nurtures them. They believe that God wants 5 percent of human beings to hate themselves, repress themselves, and consider killing themselves—all because of a trait, an aspect of their souls. The paradox is searing: you're making the wrong choice, because homosexuality is a sin, but you're so sick, you can't make the right one.

This cannot be so, if we take seriously the fundamental values of our religious tradition. On the contrary, those values—the sanctity of relationship, love of God and of our neighbors, the holiness of life, the importance of justice and compassion—demand that those of us who are gay or lesbian live full lives, and those of us who are not become supportive, loving allies. "The fruit of the Spirit is joy" (Gal. 5:22). How, then, could the Spirit lead to the tyranny of the closet and the threats to safety still experienced by gay people around the world and throughout history? Surely this is not "joy" but its opposite.

Before I came out, I was sure that doing so would spell the end of my religious life. Raised in a Conservative Jewish household, I absorbed the message that being gay was about the worst thing in the world. I thought it meant I could never have a family, and could not be gay and Jewish. Ironically—tragically—accepting and celebrating my sexuality was the beginning of my religious life, not the end of it. What we call in our popular culture "coming out" is a powerful spiritual experience, a gateway to the holiness of love. I was able to stop being dishonest, with myself and with God. Instead of sex being furtive and shameful, it became an integrated part of my emotional life.

In spiritual communities, bearing witness is a sacred act. We testify to the truth of religious teaching, we tell stories about the operation of grace in our lives—and what we say has meaning because it is our experience and it is true. So, let me bear witness to the reality of sexual orientation—not as a choice (though some may experience it that way, I do not), and not as a deviant pathology, but as a fiber of the soul. My story is not everyone's story; it's a male story, it's a Jewish one, and it's by no means universal. But the truth of my experience, and that of millions of other people, is that homosexuality exists as a trait, and it can be, like heterosexuality, a gateway to holiness or its opposite. Our testimony has provoked uncertainty and reflection among many sincere believers in different faith traditions because it seems to contradict what some of our traditions say about sexuality. It is new information that we must now take into account. We do need to reexamine what we thought we knew and reflect upon beliefs that seemed certain. Then again, isn't that a consummate religious act as well?

"It's Adam and Eve, not Adam and Steve."

We've all heard the cliché, and we all know its meaning: that male and female are at the heart of God's plan for the world, that heterosexuality is the only natural sexuality. No matter what a few other verses may or may not say, many people point to this irreducible fact of nature as proof that only procreative, "natural" heterosexuality can be part of God's plan.

But not so fast. Actually, homosexuality is natural too—it's present in hundreds of animal species, and in every culture in the world. Sexual diversity is the rule, not the exception—the plan, not the deviation. And even the story of Adam and Eve isn't as simple as it sounds.

The pairing of Adam and Eve, after all, was the solution to a problem. In the detailed version of the Creation story, they don't just appear on the stage; human coupling is the result of Divine dissatisfaction. God creates the human being, but then has to tinker with the original plan because of the first flaw God finds with all of God's creation. What is that problem?

Loneliness. "It is not good for the human being to be alone," God says in Genesis 2:18. In context, this is a shocking pronouncement. Six times God has remarked how good everything is: light, heaven and earth, stars, plants, animals—all of these are "good." The entirety of creation is "very good." Yet suddenly something is not good. Suddenly, God realizes there is something within the world as we find it that is insufficient, something all of us experience in our own lives and strive to transcend: the existential condition of being alone.

I invite you to set aside, for the moment, whatever preconceptions you may bring to this ancient biblical text. Perhaps you don't believe in God, or perhaps you understand the word differently from how I do. Or maybe you view the Bible as inerrant, not only on its surface but as interpreted by tradition. On the other hand, maybe, like many biblical scholars, you interpret the first two chapters of Genesis as comprising not one but two literary strands. Or maybe you've had the heavy books of the Bible thrown at you so many times that you have no interest in picking them up and opening them.

All of these views are just fine. Hold on to them for now. The invitation is to look afresh at these early few verses of the Bible on their own terms, because they tell us something crucially important about human relationships and their value in Christian and Jewish traditions. This matters even if you are not personally religious because these traditions have shaped how we live and continue to inform the moral judgments of a significant majority of Americans. These words retain an immense power to inform and inspire.

So again: loneliness is the first problem of creation, and love comes to solve it. The biblical writer (or writers, or Writer) looks around the world and finds a natural environment filled with radical beauty— a world that is good for one chapter and seventeen verses. Until verse eighteen.

Notice, too, that Eve is not the first solution God attempts to the problem of Adam's aloneness. God first presents Adam with every animal in the world, but none suffices. Only human companionship solves the existential problem of aloneness, the first problem our religious traditions set out to address. Eve is not created, in this narrative, to make children with Adam: this story is about loneliness and love, not procreation and progeny. Indeed, Eve's femininity is not even essential for her to be an *ezer kenegdo*—a "help-meet," someone able to be with Adam on equal terms and be a companion to him. Of course, procreation is also a central value, and it is articulated later in the text, but this story, on its own terms, is about companionship.[2]

The story of Adam and Eve has been used as a weapon against gay people (and women) for centuries, but I read it as validating the importance of human love and companionship in all its forms. If one has had the experience of love (of a partner, of a community, of God), then what is read in Genesis becomes inscribed in the heart: that human relationship is the bridge across existential loneliness. For most people, this love is experienced in a relationship between a man and a woman. For some, it may be found in many kinds of relationships. And for about 5 percent of people (we can argue about the numbers—the range is 3 to 10 percent), this love is found in a relationship between two men, or between two women.

I am part of that 5 percent. During my teens and twenties, as I struggled with my sexuality, I had relationships with women, and, as much as I was able, fell in love. But something was always off, even though at the time I couldn't quite identify it. (Maybe I knew, deep down. I don't know.) It took me ten years of wrestling, cajoling, self-hating, and self-judging—and finally a serious car accident in 2001, which shook up my body and soul—to finally admit the truth: if I wanted true love, the kind that the Song of Songs sings about, my Eve would have to be a Steve.

It was not an easy thing for me to admit. As I mentioned, I was raised a Conservative Jew but had taken on Orthodox Jewish practice in my twenties, like many young people searching for a more holistic and committed form of Jewish life. And I thought that coming out would spell the end of it. There was no way to be gay *and* Jewish—not religiously, anyway. I thought my family would disown me, and my friends would disdain me for having lied to them all this time. For years, I prayed to God to make me straight.

What some folks don't understand about the closet is that it's not just a set of walls around sexual behavior. It's a net of lies that affects absolutely everything in one's life: how you dress, who you befriend, how you walk, how you talk. And how you love. How can anyone build authentic relationships under such conditions? And if you're religious, how can you be honest with yourself and your God if you maintain so many lies, so many walls running right through the center of your soul?

Anti-gay politicians and preachers like to say that homosexuality is just about sex. But sexuality is about much more than sex—it's about *love*. How we love, whom we love, how open we are with the channels of love in our lives—these affect much more than the gender of the person we're embracing. And when those channels are blocked, the blockage affects everything. In my case, it stopped me from being a writer and pursuing my professional dreams. Even the novels I wrote alone in my apartment at night had to be carefully hidden from view, since they might be interpreted as gay and tarnish my perfect reputation. In the last several years, as I've worked on behalf of gays and lesbians in religious communities, I sometimes feel like closeted people are like the dead people in the movie *The Sixth Sense*: they don't know that they're half dead; they don't know what they're missing. And yet according to current statistics, fewer than half of LGBT people are living openly today.[3]

All this matters, religiously speaking. Certainly, celibacy may well be part of a spiritual path for some people, but not when it is compelled by shame. We are not speaking here of priests, monks, and those who take on vows of celibacy voluntarily. We are speaking of laypeople, for whom human relationship is sanctified when it includes an embodied element and the blessing of a religious community. This is what religion does: it takes the realities of our human lives and connects them to our deepest values. Birth and death, eating and drinking, commercial life—all of these are grist for the religious mill, because religion and spirituality are meant not as Sunday hobbies but as ways of life. A spirituality that has nothing to say about hospital wards, bedrooms, forests, and shopping malls is not a real spirituality.

So what do we do, then, with the problem of aloneness and the reality that, for 5 percent of us, the solution comes only within a same-sex relationship? Well, if Genesis 2:18–25 were all that our religious traditions had to say about human relationships, the answer would be fairly simple. For most people, "a man . . . shall hold fast to his wife." In some cases, a woman shall hold fast to hers. And in some others, a man shall hold fast to another. But of course, it's not so simple, because many people sincerely believe that certain other verses— Leviticus 18:22, Romans 1:27—rule out the possibility that Adam and Steve can experience grace, love, and holiness. In part 2, we will see that these few verses are obscure, ambiguous, and certainly do not contemplate loving, committed relationships. But first we need to build a larger context in which to understand them. In reading biblical text, we do this all the time. In the introduction, I mentioned the most basic of ethical norms: not to kill. These words—*lo tirtzach* in the Hebrew—do not admit of any exceptions. Yet we all know that, for better or for worse, there *are* exceptions: self-defense, for example. No verse exists in a vacuum, even when it is as unequivocal and clear as "thou shalt not kill." How much more so, then, for a handful of biblical verses that are ambiguous in their wording and intent.

So, yes, we will look at the "bad" verses, and there will be plenty of ink devoted to etymology, cultural context, Hebrew, and Greek. But none of that has any grounding without our fundamental religious values. A talented biblical commentator can twist words to mean whatever she wishes them to mean; "the devil can cite Scripture for his purpose."[4] What differentiates a linguistic game from a sincere engagement with sacred text is how much is at stake, how sincere we are in our intention, how careful we are in our process, and how connected we are to our fundamental values. The question is not whether gay people can find a way to weasel around Romans and Corinthians, or whether anti-gay people can use them as a brickbat. The question is what our deepest shared values—such as "it is not good to be alone"—tell us about the nature of same-sex relationships. That is an inquiry of value to us all.

None of that healthy reexamination of values can proceed, though, if we continue to deny the existence of gay and lesbian people.[5] Even in the twenty-first century, this is still a frequent tactic: to simply deny the existence of sexual orientation as a category, or pathologize it as a kind of deformity of character. No matter the existence of sexual and gender variance in every culture on the planet, and among hundreds of animal species. No matter the four-decades-old scientific consensus, never seriously contested, that homosexuality is not a mental disorder but a normal variation of human sexuality. Despite all this, there are still those who insist that homosexuality is a "lifestyle," a choice, or a pathology—and that all of us who feel it in our souls are deluded, perverted, or worse.

Fortunately, if religion provides much of the impetus for this willful ignorance, it also provides a remedy. Personal experience, personal testimony, and meaningful communication within one's faith community are part of every Western religious tradition. In chapter 4, we will look at the science of sexuality—but for now let's focus on the *witness* to it. Evangelicals offer their life stories as witness to the operation of grace in their lives. Rabbis base their legal decisions on both the weight of precedent and the tenability of law in people's actual lives. Mainline Protestant denominations and many in the Catholic Church have wrestled with the reality of gays and lesbians in the pews. All this is based on lived experience, on meeting the "other" and acknowledging him or her. The common denominators are openness, honesty, and conversation—all sacred religious values themselves, now applied to the sacred task of understanding Scripture, tradition, reason, and experience.[6] To deny the testimonies of millions of people is an aberration, an unjustified departure from the norm of religious conversation.

Nor can we adopt, as some have tried to do, an attitude of "hate the sin, love the sinner." Such subtleties don't hold when the same word—"homosexuality"—can mean both an activity and an identity. The sinner *is* the sin.[7] Sexuality is not just sex; sexuality is at the essence of who we are as human beings. In the words of theologian James B. Nelson, "sexuality always involves much more than what we do with our genitals. More fundamentally, it is who we are as bodyselves who experience the emotional, cognitive, physical and spiritual need for intimate communion, both creaturely and divine."[8] To hate an essential part of a person is to hate the person.

Sexual diversity is real. The question is how religious people are to respond to this reality. Authentic religion never hides its head in the sand. Just as religious communities have capably revised their doctrines regarding non-European people, women, and other formerly marginalized groups in light of clearer understandings of them, so too are we invited to engage with the reality of sexual diversity and bring to bear our fundamental values on the questions it occasions.

At the same time as we recognize the reality of sexual diversity, two qualifications are important to bear in mind. First, to reiterate what was said in the introduction, sexuality is not a simple binary. While most people (including myself) do experience their sexuality as essentially homosexual or heterosexual, many others do not, and every study of human sexuality, from Kinsey to the present, reveals it to be more like a continuum than a duality. Many people either identify as bisexual or experience their sexuality in some other fluid way—and many more women do than men.[9] Several scholars and theorists have suggested that our tendency to focus on sexual intercourse may, itself, be part of the problem. For example, Adrienne Rich, in her influential essay "Compulsory Heterosexuality and Lesbian Existence," argued that we should focus less on genital acts among women, and more on how romantic or affectionate pairs of women formed a kind of "lesbian continuum" and created alternatives to "compulsory heterosexuality."[10] And Lillian Faderman has persuasively shown how "romantic friendships," which may or may not have had a sexual component, were often women's primary emotional—and in the general sense, erotic—ties.[11] So it is more fruitful, and does less violence to women's experience, to recognize and appreciate instances where women are able to construct alternatives to compulsory heterosexuality, rather than try to fit women's intimacy into artificial binaries that privilege male experience. However, even for those who experience their sexuality as being on a continuum, "choice" is surely not the right word to convey the essence of sexual identity. I choose what clothes to wear and what to eat for lunch. Bisexuals and those of more fluid sexuality do not choose to fall in love, and do not choose their sexual identities. Thus even where there are aspects of volition and ranges of possible partners there are also elements of depth, essence, and soul.

Second, as I have remarked already, our current sexual categories are of relatively recent coinage. In the academic world, there exists a raging debate about whether sexuality is socially constructed or whether it is an essential, transhistorical fact of life.[12] Surely, though, this long and vociferous debate yields more heat than light. We know from visual and textual evidence (including pottery, paintings, poetry, and historical records) that same-sex behavior has existed around the world since the dawn of human expression. And yet we also know that it has been construed differently by different societies. To take but one example, as recently as two hundred years ago, men in many cultures would not consider themselves "gay" simply because they engaged in sexual relations with other men as long as they took the insertive, "active" role, because sexual identity was defined not by the gender of one's partner but the role one took in intercourse. So, as certain as we are that same-sex behavior has taken place everywhere across time, we are equally certain that it has been understood in terms very different from our own. Thus, as we turn to our religious traditions for information regarding homosexuality, we must do so with the understanding that "homosexuality" and "heterosexuality" do not even exist as categories until relatively recently. Even the term "sodomy" wasn't invented until the eleventh century. To say "the Bible forbids homosexuality" is as ridiculous as saying "the Bible forbids the Internet." Neither term would have made any sense to those for whom the Bible was originally written, as neither concept is part of the biblical worldview.

All this does not mean that we can have no recourse to sacred text, however. Its categories are different from our own, and that is an important part of the point. But even if "homosexuality" has not existed since time immemorial, people we would today call gay or lesbian have. Sexual diversity is, as we'll see later, one of the great gifts of human experience—a great gift that God has given us, if you will.

Nor is sexuality the same as lust. Matthew 5:28 teaches that someone who has a sinful thought has already committed adultery in his or her heart. Intent matters. The same physical act may be one of love or lust, passion or violence. What's religiously significant isn't how anatomies bump up against one another, but how the souls of lovers intertwine. What differentiates homosexuality from bestiality, incest, and the rest? Well, love, of course; the presence of mutuality, kindness, and caring in relationship; the holiness of sacred companionship. If doubts as to the reality and validity of sexual orientation still remain, there are plenty of sources to consult in the appendix to this book, as well as the discussion in chapter 4. But the real sources must be your own soul and the testimonies of people in your community, the family members, coworkers, and people who sit next to you in church or synagogue who are lesbian or gay. To explore how the mainstream Jewish and Christian traditions validate and celebrate the existence of same-sex love, we must first acknowledge its existence.

Love is fundamental. When we see two people in love, or if we are lucky enough to experience love for ourselves, we know this to be true. Somehow, even the poetic heights of a Shakespeare or a Sappho (neither one of whom was heterosexual) cannot convey the immanence of love itself, the lightness it brings to the heart. Perhaps definition is best left to the neuroscientists, with their materialism of hormones and chemical reactions. But if Genesis is any guide, and if our conscience is any guide, then we must see that having people in love with one another, building homes and perhaps families together, is religiously preferable to its absence. Nor is the result of an open and liberated life the sleaze of the lowest common denominator—on the contrary, sleaze comes from repression. The alternative to squelching, repressing, and distorting is, after much trial, openness, awakening, and the possibility of sanctification.

Now, with regard to the sexual expression of love, there exists a range of perspectives among religious traditions. Mainstream Judaism, for example, strongly emphasizes the holiness of love between people as expressed in sexuality. The seven blessings recited at marriage, for example, specifically thank God for creating joy, gladness, and sexual pleasure.[13] Some teachings within the Catholic tradition, on the other hand, regard sexuality as a species of carnality, and thus as a kind of necessary evil to be indulged in as little as possible. (Indeed, the original medieval proscriptions against same-sex behavior regarded it as a form of *luxuria,* which roughly means an overindulgence in sensual pleasure.[14]) Nor can the many praises of love found in the New Testament be read as praises of sexuality. As has been observed since a seminal 1939 book by Anders Nygren, the Greek word used in the New Testament for love is *agape,* not *eros.*[15] Generally, *agape* refers to selfless love—the benevolence of a Mother Teresa, for example. *Eros* refers to a love born of desire—not necessarily sexual desire but desire for love, passion, or companionship.[16] (Ironically, agape is closer to what is today called "Platonic love" even though Plato praises eros.)[17] Because of this distinction, it would be wrong to read sexuality into statements about Jesus's love for his disciples, for example.

Yet, as a century of theologians have tried to point out, the distinction is an imperfect one.[18] Repressed sexuality, particularly when it is covered over with lies and prevarications, distorts the entire soul, not just the libido. For years, I remember waxing poetic about unrequited love and yearning for friendship with straight male friends, connections I blocked by my own insularity. Yet for all these pretensions, what I really was experiencing was tension, frustration, and a longing for what I could never have. Yes, eros and agape are different, but the stifling of the former leads to a distortion of the latter. One is forever wishing for things to be other than they are—the exact opposite of gratitude, blessing, and appreciation of What Is.

And eros repressed is eros distorted. I am not surprised when I read of scandals among closeted rabbis, priests, preachers, and politicians. Of course George Rekers, cofounder of the Family Research Council, hired a prostitute from rentboy.com to accompany him on a trip to the Caribbean. Of course anti-gay preacher Eddie Long is being sued by four young men for sexually seducing them. Of course the New Life Church's pastor, Ted Haggard, had a long-term relationship with a drug-dealing erotic masseur. So long as people believe their sexuality to be dirty and sinful, they will act out accordingly.

Obviously, all of us are invited to curb our sexual appetites some of the time, as ethical human beings. But not *all* of the time. This smashing down of the saplings that God has planted runs counter to every religious teaching about the importance of love, intimacy, and human connection. There is no conflict between homosexuality and the Bible. The Bible exhorts us toward love and human intimacy; an open, honest sexuality does as well. The Bible warns us against aloneness; and the experience of aloneness accords. The Bible has a handful of verses condemning a narrow band of sexual behaviors, and so long as that band is kept as narrow as the text allows, there is no conflict between a religious life and a gay or lesbian one. On the contrary: the real conflict is between religion and repression.

What we are really talking about is the most fundamental message of Western religion: "Choose life" (Deut. 30:19). We are not like the death-obsessed culture of ancient Egypt, with its mummies and pyramids. We are blessed with the capacity to drink from the well of life for some short period of days. And, as the Song of Songs tells us, love is stronger than death. To choose life is to say yes to the world that religious people believe God has created. Eros is a key to unlock the spiritual life.[19] When we open our hearts to love, including love that is expressed in the body, the channels are open for the love of the transcendent, the ineffable.

CHAPTER 2

"I am asleep but my heart is awake: the voice of my beloved knocks"

A loving God could never want the "closet"

I have been blessed with a long and winding spiritual journey. I was born into a fairly conventional, Conservative Jewish family and was brought up within the mainstream of American Judaism. I went to Jewish summer camp, to Jewish day school—and my life, growing up, was shaped by Jewish holidays and the weekly rhythm of the Sabbath. For many years, I lived as an Orthodox Jew, strictly observing the minutiae of Jewish law. But I have also wandered far from my roots. I have spent many weeks on silent meditation retreats in Buddhist traditions—traditions in which I now teach as well. I have studied the New Testament extensively, both as a graduate student and as someone deeply involved with ecumenical and interfaith dialogue. And I have sat at the feet of teachers from Protestant, Catholic, Islamic, Sufi, Hindu, and several nonaligned spiritual traditions. I consider all this journeying to be fortunate—to be a blessing.

At the same time, I have often doubted my intentions, questioned the veracity of religious belief, and reflected on whether the benefits of religion outweigh its many costs. On the one hand, religious and spiritual practice offer technologies of personal transformation, gateways to the sacred, challenges to live ethical and moral lives, and the building blocks of community. On the other hand, religious fervor invites sectarianism, particularism, and a desperate clinging to belief that often blinds us to the very things religion is meant to reveal. Indeed, I have come to see that these "costs" and "benefits" are interrelated. Precisely because religious practice can transform a life, it becomes so precious that we want to own it for ourselves. Precisely because spirituality sanctifies time, space, love, family, and life, it has a tendency to get under our skin, into our guts—and it hardens into something fixed and immovable. Many times, I have asked myself what it all means.

The answer that I have found, the one I keep coming back to whenever doubt arises, is so simple that it has become banal: love. Scripture is full of pronouncements of God's love: "And so we know and rely on the love God has for us. God is love. Whoever lives in love lives in God, and God in him" (1 John 4:16). "I love those who love me, and those who seek me find me" (Prov. 8:17). But for me, even more persuasive than the evidence of Scripture are the experiences of love that I have been blessed to have, throughout all my spiritual wanderings. I have even begun to take it for granted that chanting *zikr* with Sufis, or attending Mass, or practicing lovingkindness meditation can awaken so much love inside of my heart.

Love is more than the solution to the conundrum of aloneness. Throughout the Bible, it is celebrated as the consummate human activity and a gateway to holiness. "Anyone who fails to love can never have known God, because God is love" (1 John 4:8). As Cardinal Basil Hume wrote, "every experience of love gives us yet another glimpse of the meaning of love in God himself. Human love is the instrument we can use to explore the mystery of love which God is."[1] When we speak of human dignity, or "the transcendent nature of the human person and the supernatural vocation of every individual";[2] when we speak of human beings created *b'tzelem Elohim,* in the image of God; when we say these things, we point to our capacities for thought, creativity, and intimacy, and toward our capacities for love. Sexuality is not simply lust. It is an expression of that which makes us most human.

Sexual diversity is also spiritual diversity, because how we love one another shapes how we love God. The Song of Songs, whether read literally or allegorically, is a beautiful, erotic love song that may at once describe earthly and Divine affection.[3] Of course, the Song of Songs is written in heterosexual terms. However, it is also, in scholar David Carr's words, "a forbidden love that risks discovery."[4] The Shunamite woman is dark-skinned, but insists on her beauty despite the conventions of the times; the love affair is basically an interracial one. And there is a remarkable equality between the man and the woman in the poem. Finally, contrary to the various theories of complementarity (the pop notion that men and women "complete one another"), the partners in the Song of Songs are equals to, not complements of, one another.[5] This is the human love that echoes the love of God.

What do we really mean when we use the word "God," after all? We have different interpretations of the word, different textual traditions, different theologies, different conceptions of what God is or isn't, whether we believe or not, whether it's all a grand delusion or whether it's the most important truth there is. But beneath these many differences, to have God in one's life is to say "Yes" to the world as an expression of love. All of us experience the world as a series of "it"s—books, chairs, mountains. Some of us experience the world as one big "it." But the religious experience You. This personalization, this ascription of You-ness, and the love that naturally flows from it—this seems to me the essence of the religious life.

Love, like God, is unprovable. Human beings experience love, and no doubt our neuroscientists will soon be able to tell us exactly where it occurs in the brain. No doubt our pharmacologists will be not far behind in synthesizing it. But whatever love is, it has little to do with external realities. Our beloved isn't *really* more wonderful, beautiful, and kind than every other person on the planet—it just seems that way, when we are in love. So too, the inanimate objects we casually say we "love" are not *really* special or precious; we make them so.

Likewise with what religious people experience as the love of God. Perhaps this "higher love" is, like its earthly corollary, but a movement of the brain, a dance of neurons and synapses. It may have no factual basis. But the subjective experience is available, if one wishes to seek it. This is how I interpret the theological statement that "God loves us": that the experience of love, untethered from an apparent earthly cause, is available.

This experience has nothing to do with theologies, proofs, stories, myths, arguments—indeed, these latter seem beside the point. I don't think religious people care primarily about the age of the Earth or the theory of evolution; we care about love, and some of us associate it with this or that belief about the world. This is why religious dogma is so "sticky"—because it is bound up in knots of love. But the religious experience is primary; the verbal articulations, secondary.

To experience this love requires from the religious person an openness to love—infinitely, inchoately, perhaps even indefinably—and to receive love in return. "You shall love the Lord your God with all your heart and with all your might" (Deut. 6:5). This is what Jesus calls "the first and greatest commandment" (Matt. 22:38). And in response to this devotion, the religious person finds, absurdly, that her love is returned in kind. "For God loves the just and will not forsake his faithful ones" (Ps. 37:28). Indeed, in the drama of the Passion, such love reaches its apotheosis, when "God so loved the world that he gave his one and only Son" (John 3:16).

Thus there is, for religious people, a further aspect of love, beyond and within the love among people: something boundless, unconditional, undeserved, and seeming to drip from every leaf in the forest and every particle of air. The spaciousness of this most transparent love is the texture of religious life itself. In the merest chime of a bell, in the briefest movement of wind, mystics of all faiths find the deepest of mysteries.

And I have learned this: If God loves us, then God could never want the closet. If there exists a loving God, I know in my heart that this God could not wish for human beings to lie, to repress their emotional selves, and to distort that aspect of the soul which leads to the highest of human satisfactions into a dark force of evil and objectification. It is inconceivable to me; the contradiction is too great. There is no reconciling a loving God and the tyranny of the closet. Whatever seven verses in Old and New Testaments mean, they cannot possibly mean this. It is unthinkable, obscene.

Obviously, I do not mean to suggest that human relationships must be the same for everyone. Again, there are those who feel called to celibacy, whether out of a religious calling, or the dictates of their hearts. But to be *compelled* to such abstinence—or, worse (and more likely), a life of furtive encounters, deceptions, tawdry dalliances, lies, and endless self-recriminations—is fundamentally incompatible with the concept of a loving God, of whose service is it written "her ways are ways of pleasantness, and all her paths are peace" (Prov. 3:17). In Jewish law, this principle is interpreted to mean that following God's commandments should not cause pain. As Rev. Candace Chellew-Hodge says, "Misery is God's way of telling you that this isn't the path you should follow."[6]

I want to share with you some words I wrote almost a decade ago, as I was just coming out of the closet. The occasion was Conservative Judaism's reconsideration of the question of homosexuality. I gave a speech at the movement's flagship institution, the Jewish Theological Seminary of America (JTS) in New York, in support of ordination of gays and lesbians. Ten years later, JTS now ordains gay rabbis, so the original purpose for these words is now, thankfully, history. But I want to share some of these words because they illustrate, better than I could today, what it means to be gay and religious, and how the love of and from God is not some abstract concept, but a very real force in the lives of LGBT people like myself.

What we are talking about today is something which causes great suffering. It causes deep and ongoing pain—in my case, pain so deep that it endures even today, even after I have spent years wrestling with it, and even though I have adopted a public rhetoric of acceptance and confidence. It made me hate myself, in a powerful and fundamental way. It hurt my family, which is why some members of my family aren't here to hear me speak today. It legitimizes and supports deep pain.

So the issues we're talking about today do matter. They are not abstract. For many years, knowing that I was gay and believing that there was something fundamentally wrong with that—and no theoretical niceties, no subtleties of "hate the sin, love the sinner," and no equivocations of *halachic* reasoning disguised the heart of the message for me—knowing these things made me want to die. Nothing less. I tried in my own impotent ways to kill myself. I failed. I experienced, for about ten years, a self-loathing that I hope none of you ever know, a wish to disappear and destroy myself that was too intense for tears and which cut me off from everyone I knew. Ultimately, thank God, I chose life over death. . . .

My community excluded me without even knowing it was doing so. I didn't come out until a couple of years ago, so my rabbi had no idea that by telling me that being gay was a sin—and I don't remember if he said being gay, or having gay sex, but I know what I heard—he was cutting me off from the community. He did it without even knowing, and I'm sure this goes on all the time today. Hearing these words just pushed me further into the closet, because I loved God, and here were God's representatives telling me—not even able to know before whom they stood—that God hated this. It wasn't only self-hatred; it was intense fear also. For years, I was horrified that my secret might be found out—by some of the people sitting here today—and that everything would be ruined.

What I learned from my rabbis and teachers was that something was essentially evil about myself. I would try to deny the compulsion I felt, or suppress it, but I knew it was there: evil, inside of me, impossible to eradicate. Imagine that: Something fundamental about yourself is evil. . . . This is what I learned in Sunday school.

I also learned that this one impossible shortcoming was somehow worse than all of the *lashon hara* [gossip], theft, usury, dishonesty, sectarianism, racism, *sinat chinam* [baseless hatred], hypocrisy, all of the self-satisfied contentment that we see . . . at so many synagogues around the country. I might rail against these things, but I was worse. You know, there are a lot of gossiping people who go to rabbinical school, and a lot of rabbis who engage in *sinat chinam* pretty openly. They have their *smicha* [ordination]. But not me.

And I was told by my rabbis that sexual orientation was a lifestyle choice. That if I wanted to, I could be straight, or at least celibate. This I knew was false, because if I could have done anything—anything—to stop being gay, I would have. I hated being gay. . . . And I tried everything. Abstinence, negative reinforcement, fantasizing about women. I was even in a loving relationship with a woman for over a year, trying all the while to be straight. I tried immersing myself in *ahavat hashem,* the love of God, only, focused only on Torah and learning, sublimating my sexual tension, I was a *kovesh et yitzro*—one who mastered his inclination—and I was miserable.

What do you wish for when you blow out your birthday candles? I wished only to be straight. What do you pray for when you pray to God? I prayed to God, for ten years, with a broken heart, which our tradition teaches is the purest prayer there is: to make me straight.

You cannot change your sexual orientation. You cannot. I tried. You cannot . . .

The worst is what it did to my *ahavat hashem*. Why would God make me this way? How could I be so evil? I couldn't make sense of it. One thing I know—and I know other people have other opinions, but, in my experience, from ten years of what I have lived: it is impossible to love God in denial. You hate yourself, you hate God for doing this to you, and you see the world as fundamentally, irreparably broken . . .

All this, when we could read Leviticus narrowly—only one kind of sex, only between men, maybe only in the context of *avodah zara* [idolatry]. You know, we have *halachot* [laws] that construe some *mitzvot* [commandments] narrowly simply to avoid ordinary unpleasantness. Yet here we are causing some people to kill themselves, to hate themselves, and to turn themselves away from God, for one particular interpretation of two verses. Can this possibly be the right reading? Is this really the truth? That some people should be shut off from Hashem, and enclosed in self-hatred?

The Talmudic sages knew many things that I do not know, but they didn't know about sexual orientation. It's a very new category—200 years at the most . . . They didn't know this truth: that because of the way some of us are, intrinsically, that this kind of love is the only way we can love, and thus the only path to fully knowing and loving God. . . .

Today, when I grow closer to God, I grow closer to accepting who I am. I return . . . to the reality of God in this moment, in this place. And I remember that God made me perfectly, and that loving a man is a pathway to loving Hashem. Particular love to universal love. That is my fundamental truth, and it is beautiful and it is holy, even if sometimes it is laced with tears.

I am different now from how I was years ago; I no longer wish to be anything other than who I am, and am grateful that I have been able to find love, both human and Divine, precisely by accepting, rather than rejecting, the traits of my personality and soul. Yet as I work with people still struggling with their sexuality, I am struck by how similar their stories are to mine. So many people believe that to come out, to accept one's sexuality and be open about it with others, would be the end of their religious lives—just as I once believed. They cannot conceive, as I could not, that coming out is the beginning of the authentic spiritual life, not the end of it. Once I was honest with myself, I could be honest with God. Once I started loving myself, I could start loving God. And once I allowed my heart to open, it opened in all directions.

This is how I, as a Jew, understand Paul's statement in Romans 8:38–39: "For I am sure that neither death, nor life, nor angels, nor principalities, nor things present, nor things to come, nor powers, nor height, nor depth, nor anything else in all creation, will be able to separate us from the love of God." To believe that God hates you if you're gay is to make a mistake about God's love: to think that it is conditional on something, that you're only okay if you act a certain way. This is not so. The love that the mystics, poets, and prophets describe flows unconditionally, and though it may take enormous faith to believe it, I have found that such faith is rewarded. God's love does not depend on anything.

Now, of course, this does mean that everything we do is perfectly okay. Indeed, it's because God loves us, some traditionalists say, that God does not want us to do what is wrong. I can offer many Scriptural, traditional, and theological replies. But my testimony, my experience, is what I can offer the most. I lived a decade being religious in the closet, and have lived a decade being religious out of the closet. I know the difference for me. And of this there is no doubt: openness to love is openness to God. Living in the closet, repressing my desire to love, I felt alienated from God, desperate to obey Divine command but powerless to do so. I channeled that repression into stricter observance of the commandments, but it didn't work. Inevitably, I would lapse. This one sin, this one failure, eclipsed all others in my heart. When I finally gave up, came out, and quit trying to be someone I was not, the fear, pain, and anxiety vanished— and was replaced by a consciousness of love that allowed me to grow spiritually.

I know that many people think God's love is expressed precisely by curbing our sexual desires and eradicating all sin. But homosexuality is not a sin; it is an inclination of the heart that can tilt toward holiness or perdition, health or depredation. And so, if we value opening to love, expressing love, and being in a relationship with a God who is said to love, we must want people to be able to be honest, intimate, and loving according to the characteristics of their souls.

Indeed, as much as religious love derives its terms and conditions from those of human relationships, so too are our human relationships meant to reflect and embody the everlasting love that is present in every moment. We do not render unto Caesar one form of love, and unto God another; in the currency of affection, the two are intertwined. How we love God and how we love one another are two movements of the heart which, themselves, are woven in embrace.

CHAPTER 3

"Love your neighbor as yourself"

Love demands authentic compassion for others

In nearly every religious tradition, God's love is the beginning, rather than the end, of one's religious work. To be authentically religious does not mean that God loves us, and that is the end of the matter. Rather, if God loves us, we are commanded to love one another:

> We love because God first loved us. If anyone says, "I love God," yet hates his brother, he is a liar. For anyone who does not love his brother, whom he has seen, cannot love God, whom he has not seen. Whoever loves God must also love his brother. (1 John 4:19–20)

> Jesus replied: "Love the Lord your God with all your heart and with all your soul and with all your mind." This is the first and greatest commandment. And the second is like it: "Love your neighbor as yourself." (Matt. 22:37–39)

> The whole of the Law is summarized in a single commandment: love your neighbor as yourself. (Gal. 5:14)

Love of other people may take many forms, from brotherly love between members of a faith community to the love that inspires us to mete out justice fairly, clothe the naked, and feed the hungry. When an earthquake strikes, it is an act of love to give of our time and resources to those who are suffering. When injustice takes place, it is an act of love to shout in protest. And when a population is vilified, subjugated, and despised; when the members of that group are mischaracterized and slandered; when selective teachings of religious faith are used as cudgels—then the mandate to love compels us to learn more, engage more, and finally to stand up for those who have been wronged.

Now, the feeling of love is not, itself, enough. After all, people have killed one another out of "love." And there are some who would argue that if one loves a gay person, then the best thing to do is to help that person stop being gay. So, how do we know when love is authentic, and when it is deluded? Scripture offers guidance:

> Love is patient, love is kind. It does not envy, it does not boast, it is not proud. It does not dishonor others, it is not self-seeking, it is not easily angered, it keeps no record of wrongs. Love does not delight in evil but rejoices with the truth. It always protects, always trusts, always hopes, always perseveres. Love never fails. (1 Cor. 13:4–8)

> Love does no harm to its neighbor. Therefore love is the fulfillment of the law. (Rom. 13:10)

Does anti-gay activists' "love" of gay people pass these tests? Is it patient, or does it rush to judgment based on stereotypes? Does it "do no harm to its neighbor," as it sends kids off to psychologically abusive, and totally ineffectual, "ex-gay" quack therapies? Is it "not easily angered"? That hasn't been my experience.

Humility is a crucial part of any mature love. To reach simplistic judgments is easy, but doing so does not honor the dictates of love as it operates in the world. Part of being a religious person is knowing what we do not know—even what we cannot know. This is one reason the encounter with the other is so important: because it is a form of revelation. We come to every experience with our ideas and faculties intact, but the other interrupts them, demands that we reconsider that which we think we understood.

This is how you can "love your neighbor as yourself." "As yourself"—not as you would like to love the other person, but as you yourself would like to be loved. The authentically religious person must engage in a form of sympathetic reasoning. As a necessary corrective to the egoic impulse toward selfishness, religious teachings demand an imaginary exercise in being someone else. What would I want, if I were standing in this person's shoes? What would I loathe, need, love, desire? Can I understand this person's life not merely according to my values, but in such a way as to *examine* my values in light of their experience? Can I open my heart to the possibility that love may require something greater than what I can presently understand? In this way, Western religious traditions cultivate compassion—literally, "feeling with."

Compassion rejects the imposition of my preconceptions onto other people, and invites a willingness to reexamine those preconceptions in light of what the other reveals to me. Perhaps this is why God is described in Exodus 34:6–7 as being "compassionate, gracious, patient, and abundant in loving-kindness and truth." Compassion depends upon patience and loving-kindness; it is the opposite of a snap judgment, the antithesis of generalization. As applied to gays, lesbians, bisexuals, and transgender people, the enterprise of compassion requires each of us to imagine ourselves in a subjectivity that may be quite different from our own. It is not a small request. I understand that some people find homosexuality difficult to comprehend, even disgusting. This is part of what it is to be human: people have a wide variety of sexual tastes and appetites, and what brings delight to one may cause disgust to another. But this is what is asked: to rise above one's own preferences, with patience and loving-kindness, to truly see from the perspective of the other.

Here's an interesting experiment. When you see a man and a woman holding hands on the street, what do you see? Most people answer "love," or relationship, or some variation on that theme. When you see two men or two women holding hands, what do you see? Most people answer "sex." See the difference? A man and a woman are telling us about their love life, but two men are telling us about their sex life.[1] No wonder so many people are still uncomfortable seeing such displays of affection in public—and no wonder people like me think twice before holding hands with our partners.

But imagine that too, if you will—imagine being reluctant to take the hand of the person you love in public.

I have faced this challenge myself. In my work, for example, I have tried diligently to understand the stories and sentiments of transgender people, whose experience of their own gender identity is so different from my own. How can I really "stand in the shoes" of someone who felt male their whole life but was born with typically female anatomy? Compassion requires it. But how can I do it? What has worked for me has been a lot of openness, a lot of direct listening, and even more benefit of the doubt.

Unless we are willing to be open to the truth of another person's experience, we cannot progress past the childlike opinion that what is right for us is right for everyone. This is how I understand the admonition to "judge not, lest ye be judged" (Matt. 7:1). If we sit in judgment of another, our compassion is incomplete. Jesus physically reached out and touched a leper to heal him (Mark 1:41). Did this compassion come from an abstract principle? From conventional wisdom? Or was it precisely the rising above assumptions and judgments, to the higher ground of empathy?

Of course, true compassion is not what contemporary Buddhists call "idiot compassion," which is simply indulgent. If a young boy is about to touch a hot stovetop, it's not compassionate to let him, even if he insists that he wants to do it. But gay people are not asking for indulgence or blanket approval; we are asking for the same mature compassion that religious life demands, and asking that such compassion govern our decision making. The love a straight woman feels for her husband, I feel for mine. It may be hard to believe or understand, without knowing me and my partner, but it is the case.

What about Leviticus, Romans, and Corinthians? Love demands that we read them narrowly, just as we read narrowly the commandments to stone rebellious children to death, or sell people into slavery. They are already marginal texts—homosexuality never appears in the teachings of Jesus, or the Ten Commandments, and love does not erase them. But it does limit them.

Love, in other words, tells us how to read. When I am offered competing accounts of what a text or teaching means, love sways the balance. In academic contexts (in which I have spent many years, as a law professor and professor of religious studies), competing interpretations may be evaluated on a level playing field, perhaps according to hermeneutical virtuosity, etymological evidence, or literary merit. But in religious contexts, love tilts the balance in favor of those readings that engender more love, more holiness, and more justice. For example, Jewish interpreters of Scripture have read literal commandments such as "an eye for an eye" allegorically, since the literal reading would be too cruel. They have said that almost all commandments are to be set aside in cases of *pikuach nefesh,* saving a life. And despite the many calls for the death penalty in the Bible, they have said that a court which metes out a single such penalty in seventy years should be regarded as being a bloody court.[2] In the Christian context, Jesus often chose compassion for people over literal rules. He healed a sick person on the Sabbath, in violation of the letter of the law (Luke 13:10–17). He ignored biblical rules on stoning an adulterous woman (John 8:1–11). He ate with people who hadn't washed before the meal (Mark 7:1–22). Indeed, so wide is the gulf between Christ's compassion and anti-gay legalism that one evangelical writer has asked, "When was it that we started resembling the Pharisees more than the one we call 'Lord'?"[3] Put simply, love demands the reading of text that allows for more love in the world.

Leviticus does not shape the boundaries of compassion; compassion shapes the boundaries of Leviticus. Our engagement with religious tradition, dogma, and biblical text is always shaped by our fundamental values, and those values have always evolved as our capacity for compassion grows. Just as men have begun to listen to the voices of women, and engage with religious traditions informed by compassion, so too are all of us now invited to listen to the voices of sexual and gender minorities, and act in kind. As that same evangelical writer put it, "Searching Christians often ask: 'Why have scholars, preachers, and teachers been mistranslating and misunderstanding these pages for so many years?' The answer lies in the fact that people have a natural tendency to care most when their ox is being gored."[4] Exactly—now we have the opportunity to hear these suppressed voices, and we do this not despite our religious values, but because of them.

One New Testament scholar has written that "any interpretation of scripture that hurts people, oppresses people, or destroys people cannot be the right interpretation, no matter how traditional, historical, or exegetically respectable."[5] This is a crucial point. If we approach "the question of homosexuality" as a legal, academic, or hermeneutical enterprise, we will get nowhere religiously. All the arguments work, and the anti-gay ones are just as clever as the pro-gay. No—to be responsible members of a faith tradition, we must first open our hearts, allow them to be broken by the heartrending stories of gays who have suffered from exclusion, plague, and self-loathing, and uplifted by inspiring stories of integration, love, and celebration. This is the evidence that we must admit in our deliberations—and if it is not immediately available, then we must seek it out. Any pretense of theological disposition that does not include in its procedure a long period of listening is morally bankrupt and borders on the blasphemous.

No religious tradition tells us to close our eyes, harden our hearts, and steel ourselves against the demands of love. Though it may occasionally offer us shelter in an uncertain world, rigidity of spirit is not the way to salvation. On the contrary, our diverse religious traditions demand that we be compassionate, loving, and caring toward others, even others whom we may not understand. The Golden Rule demands reciprocity and compassion, and basic equality. Do unto others as you would have them do unto you; give them the same privileges, civilly and religiously, that you would want for yourself. These are core religious principles, found over and over again in the Bible and in thousands of years of religious teaching. Compassion demands that we inquire into the lives of gay people, and discover if the "other" is like us or not. Look for the truth, and you will find it. Indeed, it will find you.

CHAPTER 4

"By the word of God were the heavens made"

Sexual diversity is natural and part of God's creation

Homosexuality is natural. The sentence is simple, honest, and supported by science—and yet, to many religious people it may seem surprising, even blasphemous, at first. Yet sexual diversity is part of the fabric of nature, and if we believe that fabric to have been woven by God, then it is part of the mind of God as well. Same-sex behaviors are found in over one hundred species, from apes to elephants, guppies to macaques.[1] Put in stark religious terms, sexual diversity is part of God's plan.

Often, when one asserts the naturalness of homosexuality, a second question immediately arises: what purpose does it serve? We can speculate as to such reasons, but let's first be clear that the question of *why* there is homosexuality in nature is a different question from *whether* there is. Let's be clear, too, that our attempts to answer the "why" question will, indeed, be speculation: As the book of Job says, "Where were you when I laid the foundations of the Earth?" (Job 38:4). Moreover, our answers to questions of purpose will be entirely dependent on which frame of mind we bring to bear on the question. Evolutionary biologists, for example, ask what benefit a trait brings to the survival of a species, whereas traditional theists might ask what purpose it serves in God's plan. Which facts one chooses will depend on which theory one is trying to prove. And some traits remain mysterious even within a given cognitive frame. We cannot pretend to know the "mind" of evolution, let alone the mind of God. So let's start with whether, and get to "why" later.

Let us begin with human beings. There exists a spectrum of human sexuality—the Kinsey scale is the most famous model—and men and women experience it differently. Most men experience their sexuality as relatively fixed and relatively binary, whereas women tend to experience sexuality as more fluid, and less cut and dried into categories of gay and straight. In studies conducted in the United States in the early 1990s, about 3.1 percent of men and 0.9 percent of women reported solely or mostly homosexual attraction, though presumably these rates are low since some people are reluctant to admit being gay.[2] More women than men report bisexuality.

In the last two decades, considerable evidence has been amassed for the biological basis of sexual orientation, research summarized in the recent book by Simon LeVay, *Gay, Straight, and the Reason Why*. LeVay's studies have shown that the structure of the hypothalamus— the region of the brain most responsible for sexual behavior[3]—is different in gay men and straight men, with gay men's more closely resembling those of women.[4] According to these findings, "gay men are gender shifted in the size of INAH3, the sexually dimorphic cell group in a region of the hypothalamus concerned with male-typical sexual behavior."[5] The evidence suggests that a combination of genetics, birth order, and the levels of sex hormones circulating during fetal life causes this different brain structure to develop.[6] (Brain structure among transgender people has not yet been studied as fully, but preliminary results are similar.)[7] Sexuality is a physical characteristic with psychological effects. It's a function of brain structure, determined by genes and hormones.

Nor are its effects limited to sexual choice. Secondary physical characteristics that generally distinguish gay people from straight, also attributable to the quantity of androgens during fetal development, may even include finger length.[8] Indeed, the differences between gay and straight children manifest well before puberty; retrospective studies have shown that children who later turned out to be gay "participated less in gender-typical activities and more in gender-atypical activities,"[9] a result borne out by anecdotal evidence, and generations of fathers' fears that their sons might turn out to be "sissies" (a word that historically referred to homosexuals, and only later to any "effeminate" man).

Homosexuality is widely found in other animal species, as set forth in exquisite detail in Bruce Bagemihl's *Biological Exuberance* and

Joan Roughgarden's *Evolution's Rainbow: Diversity, Gender, and Sexuality in Nature and People.* Many animals display homosexual behavior, and many have durable preferences for same-sex partners.[10] In Paul Vasey's study of macaques, for example, female pairs were shown to exist and endure for years.[11] Farmers have known that some rams prefer other rams since time immemorial;[12] we now know that the rate of homosexuality among sheep is about 10 percent, and the rams have the same type of difference in brain structure found among gay men.[13] And the omnisexual behavior of the bonobos, among our closest genetic relatives, has been known about for decades.

Now, it's very easy to oversimplify all of this evidence into trite claims about the "gay gene" and "gay animals."[14] No one has yet identified a gay gene, and, again, a combination of factors seems to be responsible for the incidence of homosexuality. And not every instance of homosexual behavior among animals is evidence of "true" homosexuality—often (though not always), it is simply because of a lack of opposite-sex partners around.[15] In any case, "gay" is a term of recent coinage. It doesn't apply to other human cultures, let alone to nonhuman animals.[16] This is why I use the term "sexual diversity"—it says more, and less, at the same time.

What might be the biological benefit of homosexuality, if indeed it is partially determined by genetics? Some scientists have suggested that perhaps homosexuality exists in nature because it is advantageous for communities to have some members more concerned with care of other individuals' children (or with the community as a whole) than with their own. In this model, called "kin selection" and first put forth by E. O. Wilson in 1975, "homosexual" animals fill in the gaps left by dead or incapable parents and tend to the needs of the community as a whole.[17] This scientific theory accords with the practices of some human communities, which have given special roles to gender-variant people, such as the 157 Native American tribes that regard them as sacred "third-gendered" people with special abilities as healers, shamans, or warriors.[18] (Indeed, some of these cultures have myths that specifically relate gender diversity to gender-variant animals.)[19] Other models suggest that male homosexuality is actually an enhanced sexual attraction to males, which may be of biological advantage to females,[20] or that some percentage of homosexuality among animal populations helps promote group cooperation and cohesion.[21]

Still other scientists have observed that, in animal species close to our own, sexuality performs many functions other than reproduction. Bonobo apes, for example, engage in sexual behavior to build all kinds of relationships, to establish power, and, apparently, for fun.[22] They also have one of the most peaceful of primate cultures. In this context, sexual variance could serve as an ordering mechanism for societal structures.

Now, I can sense a certain objection forming: we're not apes and sheep. No, we aren't, but remember that this whole inquiry begins from the question of whether homosexuality is natural or not. Opponents of equality can't have it both ways. If nature matters, here's the evidence. If it doesn't, then let's stop using the word "unnatural," which also applies to clothing, eyeglasses, and cooking, in connection with sexuality.

Some latter-day crusaders against homosexuality have pretended to play scientist with far-fetched claims like this rather colorful statement by the Family Research Council's Robert Knight: "Just look at the human body. . . . You can't fool nature. The rectum was not made for sexual activity. . . . It is an exit ramp, not an entry ramp."[23] Actually, pardon me for being graphic, but it happens that there is a high concentration of nerve endings in the anus and prostate, which can be stimulated only by massage or sexual activity. If Mr. Knight is serious about extrapolating behavioral norms from the design of the human rear end, then human anatomy makes the opposite argument from the one he puts forth. And women's bodies are even more wired for pleasure and delight, which is no doubt why people with Mr. Knight's views have engaged in female genital mutilation for thousands of years. Besides, is not the birth canal an "exit ramp" as well as an "entry ramp"? It's fine to say that the human body is not designed for nonprocreative sexual pleasure—except that it is.

The lesson here is to be cautious when mixing religion and science together. If we are to be scientific, we must admit of all the evidence. And if we are not, we should admit that we are basing our claims on religious opinion, and not on scientific fact. There is nothing wrong with that, of course; it is the charade that is disingenuous. This is true on both sides of the issue. Many in the LGBT community, for example, shy away from any conversation about science,[24] arguing that our dignity as human beings should not depend on hypothalamus size, and noting that science has been used to pathologize and medicalize sexuality for hundreds of years. On the other side of the issue, during the years of the AIDS plague many religious leaders arrogantly concluded that AIDS was a Divine punishment for "gay liberation." Of course, one doesn't hear such cluck-clucking anymore, now that AIDS kills far more straight people than gay people—including over 330,000 children per year.[25] The cruel irony is that while supposedly pious people watched suffering from afar, the gay community in the United States came of age in the 1980s and 1990s as it cared for its sick and set up massive health institutions while the government did nothing. No, God was not behind the AIDS crisis. But as when Jesus healed the leper, God was present in the gay community's response to it.

Notwithstanding all these concerns, I personally appreciate the scientific evidence of the physical nature of homosexuality in humans, including its common appearance among other animals. As someone who cares deeply for the natural world, I like knowing that my sexuality is connected to the rhythms of life around me. It is useful to me that scientists can now measure the structure of my brain to verify the inclinations of my heart. Useful, though perhaps not essential.

But what about Adam and Eve? If homosexuality is natural, then why does the Bible seem to specify an opposite-sex couple as reflective of the Divine order?

Many answers to this question are possible. One is simply to state that the Bible speaks in the language of human beings, and of general types; most people are predominantly heterosexual, and just as the creation story does not mention meerkats and ferrets, but only mammals in general, so too does it not discuss every permutation of human sexuality. Another reply is to recall that the original audience of the Bible lived in a time in which life was uncertain, and short. As a small nation surrounded by larger, more populous ones, the Israelites were greatly concerned with procreation and population growth, so naturally the Bible puts forth being fruitful and multiplying, and filling the earth with human beings, as the ideal condition. This made sense in the Bible's ecological moment but may require reinterpretation today. And finally, it is important to remember that for the Bible, the norm was not heterosexual monogamy but polygamy, not to mention prostitution, arranged marriage, and marriage to young children. So

Adam and Eve were not even normative for the Bible itself. And, of course, we should be cautious before we import too directly from the Bible's norms to our own. Do we really want to return to a world in which girls were married off at age eleven to teenage boys just entering puberty? Do we want to return to polygamy? If not, then we should be cautious about how we read the Bible's instructions on human relationships.

And what about Romans, which seems to define homosexual behavior—along with other forms of sexuality—as "unnatural"? We will explore this text in part 2. There, we will see that, for Paul, "natural" (*physin*) does not mean "according to biology" but rather "according to the proper hierarchy of male and female," in which women must always be passive and men must always be active. As in his many other uses of "unnatural," this is not a scientific term but a moral one, and a contingent moral one at that.

By moral measures, homosexuality is the most natural thing in the world. Same-sex couples are no more and no less functional, happy, stable, and capable of goodness than opposite-sex ones. (I review the sociological evidence for this in chapter 14.) Writer Joe Perez puts it simply in his book *Soulfully Gay*:

> To reject my same-sex orientation . . . I would need to have compelling and persuasive evidence that it was fundamentally incompatible with living with good health, happiness, love, and integrity. I have seen no evidence of that. Instead, I am constantly amazed by the richness, beauty, and deep spirituality I find in the lives of many gay men who have fully embraced their sexual orientation. . . . I haven't always seen it, not in every bar and bathhouse anyway. But that's because I was looking in the wrong places.[26]

Perez's last point is an important one. It's easy to say that all gay people are wild, promiscuous, diseased, and sinful. But it simply isn't so. Judging gay people on the basis of a few sensationalistic photos from gay pride parades is like judging straight people on the basis of Las Vegas strip clubs.

Speaking of which, I've been to many gay pride parades over the years, and in nearly every one, the marching bands, moms and dads, and church groups outnumber the guys in drag or leather.[27] Yet how many times have you seen the Gay Rotarians featured on the news? The media reports what's sensationalistic. In fact, there is a wide diversity of expressions, identities, and lifestyles within the LGBT world, and pride parades celebrate that diversity, as well they should. But in forming our own opinions, we need more than sound bites and media clips. Sexuality really is, like the flag suggests, a rainbow of identities, genders, lifestyles, and expressions. (This, by the way, is why many LGBT people prefer the word "queer." Formerly an insult, "queer" is at once a self-assertion by LGBT people, taking ownership of a word once used to stigmatize us, and an attempt to better capture the spectrum of identities, constructions, and languages that constitute sexuality.[28] I will use the word throughout this book, where appropriate.)

Some people are tall, some are short. Some are straight, and some are gay. It's really that simple. We do not know *why;* but we do know *that* sexual diversity is entirely natural, healthy, and reflective of the unknowable will of the Divine.

In recent years, some people have suggested that homosexuality is a disorder that can be "cured" with a variety of quack therapies.[29] If you have ever considered such "therapy," for yourself or for someone else, I have only one piece of advice: get the facts. Ex-gay organizations like NARTH, JONAH, and Exodus International are led by nonlicensed amateurs—and, in the case of JONAH, by a convicted felon. Most important, while their websites often tout success stories, *none of the organizations are willing to share actual success rates.* Obviously, this is because the rates are so low. No wonder so-called reparative therapy has been discredited by every scientific community that has examined it.[30]

And keep researching. Read about ex-ex-gays, including ex-gay activist John Paulk, photographed leaving a Washington, D.C., gay bar by activist Wayne Besen; or Michael Bussee, one of the founders of Exodus International, who is now one of its most vocal critics, and a well-adjusted gay man;[31] or numerous ex-gay leaders who now apologize for their mistakes.[32] Read the testimonies, and watch videos online, of actual ex-ex-gays, who talk about their experiences firsthand

and what it did to them.[33] Ex-gay propaganda offers little information about what actually transpires behind closed doors, which often includes wacky personal-growth techniques and highly dubious forms of aversion therapy (the sort of brainwashing depicted in *1984* and *A Clockwork Orange*). Stories of abuse abound: young men forced to strip naked in front of unlicensed, supposedly-ex-gay "coaches"; deprivation of sleep and food; weird New Age ceremonies (often conducted naked) designed to increase masculinity; and all the usual trappings of cultic brainwashing. Plus a whole lot of money flowing to the ex-gay "therapists" themselves.

Ex-gay documentation often cites "scientific" studies about the possibility of change—but, as monitors such as "Ex-Gay Watch" have exposed, most simply cite one or two long-discredited articles. There are no more two sides to the scientific evidence regarding human sexuality than there are two sides to whether the sun revolves around the Earth. The American Psychological Association has thirty-five thousand members, all of whom must pass stringent tests for admission. NARTH has fewer than fifteen hundred, none of whom do. These are not "two sides."

In addition, contrary to ex-gay claims about homosexuals being pathologically unhappy, every medical association in the United States that has examined the issue—the American Medical Association, the American Psychiatric Association, the American Psychological Association, the American Academy of Pediatrics, as well as the National Association of Social Workers—has determined that homosexuality is not a pathology, but a natural variation in human sexuality, and that gay people can be just as happy or unhappy as straight people. Ex-gays will claim that all these organizations are infested with pro-gay elements—but are we talking about "science" here, or conspiracy theories?

And finally, if you read the statements of the "conversion therapy" experts, they admit that all they are really capable of doing is getting men to perform sexually with women. Nearly all ex-gays are actually still gay: they still feel sexually and emotionally attracted to men. They just manage to have sex with women. Now, I am sure that for some small minority of extremely desperate people, "reparative therapy" can achieve this result. But is this really a success? Sexual orientation isn't just about sex; it's about love. Could you imagine being married to someone who could never truly love you, who is only able to "make it work" through careful visualizations, aversion therapy, and negative reinforcement? Is that really the kind of loving relationship anyone would want? As Rev. Michael Piazza has written of his meetings with ex-gays, "every one of them eventually came to realize that the only thing removed by all those 'transformations' was their integrity."[34]

None of the wacky ex-gay theories about the origins of homosexuality hold water either. I know plenty of happy, masculine gay guys who were athletic in high school, affectionately loved by their fathers, and didn't experience any sexual or emotional abuse—all of which are claimed by ex-gay theorists to be the causes of homosexuality. (Incidentally, have you noticed how little attention ex-gay ministries devote to women? It's like lesbians don't even exist. Maybe it's because women don't fit their neat patterns—or because women aren't important to them at all.) Really, gay people have heard this before. A century ago, we were told that we were gay because of failing to complete some Freudian stage of sexual maturity.[35] Now, it's supposedly because we had distant fathers. You know, this is America; if every man with a distant father turned out gay, our flag would be pink, beige, and teal.

We've also seen these "cures" before. Today, gay men are sent to boot camps so they can "man up." Half a century ago, we were sent to shock treatment. Gay people have been trepanned, lobotomized, hypnotized, and told to take cold showers and eat graham crackers.[36] And none of it has worked because there's nothing to cure in the first place.

Why would anyone subject their loved ones to such horrible, weird, and ineffective mistreatment? Largely, no doubt, because of ignorance. This is why I urge you, if you or anyone you know is considering such treatment, to do your own research. Get a sense of where scientific opinion really is, and what the rates of success really are. I know that many parents who send their children to such abusive pseudotherapies do so out of love. They want their children to be happy and cannot imagine them being happy and lesbian or gay. Unfortunately, the ex-gay story is a myth. Fortunately, so is "God versus Gay."

Wise religious people do not impute "ought" from "is" without careful consideration. We don't look to animals for moral guidance, and we don't derive ethical teachings from anatomical possibilities. We curb our natural instincts all the time—like the ones to kill, fight, and grab as much stuff as we can. But there are at least two important religious consequences of this evidence from nature, apart from knocking down the claim that homosexuality is unnatural.

First, all religious systems adapt to new scientific knowledge. This is what keeps religions resilient. When Earth was found to rotate around the sun, instead of the other way around, the church originally resisted—but eventually it adapted its timeless ethical teachings to this new scientific information. Likewise with what we now understand about sexual diversity. This new information may impact how we read a few problematic verses of the Bible, but so has our understanding of gender, the germ theory of disease, and space travel. Religious values have endured precisely because they are able to adapt in this way.[37]

The details of how this works in practice depend on one's religious tradition. In the Catholic tradition, for example, the doctrine of natural law refers to those principles that are readily discernible from nature. Historically, natural law has often been used against gay people, because of its focus on reproduction. But now we have new information about how sexuality in nature extends well beyond procreation, and our understanding of natural law may follow suit.[38] Likewise in Jewish law, where science informs how we understand and interpret legal precedent. For example, when electricity was discovered, there was, at first, uncertainty as to whether or not it could be permitted on the Sabbath. Eventually, it became understood that while electricity was not "fire," its use contravened certain norms of Sabbath observance, and legal decisions were reached on that basis. So too in the case of homosexuality. The Bible clearly understood same-sex behavior in terms of acts, not identity, and Jewish law tended to follow suit. Now, we understand that, for some people, sexual orientation is a trait. Thus the law evolves, reading precedent narrowly instead of broadly, because of what we now understand, to the best of our ability, to be true. Basic ethical principles do not change with the times, but the application of those principles does.

There is one final consequence of the naturalness of homosexuality: the appreciation of the complexity and beauty of nature, with sexual diversity being part of it. "The heavens declare the glory of God, and the firmament tells of the work of God's hands" (Ps. 19:1). "Lift your eyes and look to the heavens: Who created all these? God, who brings out the starry host one by one, and calls them each by name" (Isa. 40:26). "Since the creation of the world, God's invisible qualities—God's eternal power and Divine nature—have been clearly seen, being understood from what has been made" (Rom. 1:19). Appreciating the beauty and diversity of nature humbles and inspires us. And nature loves diversity, including sexual diversity.[39] Monoculture, binaries, and conformity are aspects of human invention; they, for better and for worse, are unnatural. The natural world is a place of shifting gender lines and multiple gender roles.[40] Sexual diversity is yet another aspect of the remarkable diversity of nature.

God is described in the Jewish tradition as the *meshaneh habriyot,* the one who varies creation, and sexual diversity is as much a part of the variety of nature as are mountain vistas and snowstorms and sunshowers. Some flowers are red, others yellow; some feathers are brown, others blue. Nature loves variety, diversity, and plenitude. And just as the heavens declare the glory of God, so too do the infinite permutations of intimacy. We inhabit a sensual universe filled with delight, and capable of great sanctity. That sexual diversity is natural does not mean that it is merely okay; it means that it is part of something wondrous, something beyond the capacity of the mind to frame, beyond the capacity of speech to articulate. It is a mystery, why we humans love the way we do, and all the more wondrous for being so.

CHAPTER 5

"Thou shalt not bear false witness"

Honesty and integrity are sacred; "coming out" is a religious act

When I lived in fear of being gay, I was afraid that I would die of AIDS, that I would never be able to have a family, that my parents would disown me. But above all, I feared losing my connection to God—as the pop song says, losing my religion. I was certain that religion and homosexuality were incompatible, because I had been taught that way, because I had no gay role models, and because the images I had of gay people were negative ones. All this took place in the 1980s and 1990s, not the fifties or sixties. All around me, in Florida, there were gay rabbis, lesbian ministers, and LGBT people of all spiritual and religious bents sincerely integrating their spiritual and sexual selves. But I didn't know it. Even in the age of the Internet, it's possible to believe, as I did, that being gay is the worst thing in the world, especially if you're religious.

So I lied. Chiefly, I lied to myself, willing myself to believe that I was bisexual, or that I could master this evil inclination, as my religious tradition taught me. But I also lied to girlfriends, family members, friends, and teachers. I lied to employers, to students, and to casual acquaintances. I lied all the time, to everyone. Even on the rare occasions when I would sneak out of my life and into the seedy gay underworld of secrecy and sex, I would lie, making up fake names and backgrounds so no one could identify me later.

Somehow, I believed that all this lying was in the service of God. From where I sit now, the proposition is preposterous. "He that works deceit shall not dwell within My house: he that tells lies shall not tarry in my sight" (Ps. 101:7–8). Surely the "seal of God is truth," as the Jewish rabbinic saying has it (Shir Hashirim Rabbah 1:9). Yet from where I hid for a decade of my adult life, I thought telling the truth would end my religious life. So I took on a weight of lies, invisible and omnipresent. Catastrophe was always around the corner—as close as a flit of the hand or gaze of the eyes. Locker rooms, cocktail parties, football games, college dorms—all of these were places of fear, because, with their casual conversations and erotic temptations, all were traps that could undo years of careful self-presentation. Of course, as we know from formerly closeted politicians, musicians, and clergy, the deception is never as perfect as one hopes it to be. Some of my family and some of my friends were surprised when I came out to them—but others said they knew all along.

Homosexuality is not a lifestyle, but the closet is a death-style. It's a slow, painful draining out and drying up of all that makes life worthwhile—even for those of us fortunate enough to live in places where gay bashing and state-sanctioned violence are comparatively rare. This is true even for those closeted people who seem to be happy and successful. In my work, I have met hundreds of them—mostly men, successful, often married, and with varying degrees of self-awareness. Many have children, careers, and lives that are filled with joy. Yet I almost always recognize in them the same tentative anxiety I once knew in myself—a certain illness-at-ease with life as presented, as if they are wearing clothing a size too small or too large. To suppose that such a life is what God wants of us is to be gravely mistaken either about the closet, or God, or both. Yet this is exactly what I used to believe, which is why I try not to rush to judgment of those who believe it still.

Coming out is thus a religious act. Indeed, the coming-out narrative may be familiar not just to many other gay people, but also to anyone who has been "born again" or experienced religious conversion. The patterns are similar: the struggle, the surrender, the renewal; the move from one world to another. Perhaps it is for this reason that many LGBT theologians have described coming out as a narrative frame that the gay experience provides for all of us, regardless of sexuality or gender.[1] "Coming out is a personal epiphany, a revelation," writes Olive Elaine Hannant.[2] It is "a rite of vulnerability that reveals the sacred in our lives—our worth, our love, our lovemaking, our beloved, our community, our context of meaning, and our God," writes Chris Glaser.[3]

Religious people should support equality for LGBT people because more openness leads to more honesty, more holiness, and more authentic spirituality. "Let them make me a sanctuary, and I will dwell within them," God says of the Israelites in Exodus 25:8. That is our charge, and we fulfill it whether deliberately or not. Build a sanctuary, a community, that excludes and demonizes our cousins and siblings, and they will get the message we send, choosing to leave, hide, or lie. Build a sanctuary that welcomes people of all sexual orientations and gender identities, and they will make freer choices, undistorted and unimpeded. Once shame lifts, gay people are not different from straight people. Some are wild and some straitlaced; some pious and some irreverent; some devoted to building families, and others uninterested in doing so. It is only the presence of shame that distorts sexuality into something dark and sleazy. The excess for which some people judge gays is the product not of homosexuality, but of homophobia.

In the Jewish tradition, there's a concept called *chillul hashem*—the profanation of God's name. Anytime a religious person does something odious and it becomes public, it's a *chillul hashem*: rabbis committing adultery, religious Jews convicted of bribery, and so on. Having spent a decade of my adult life in the closet, and a decade out of it, and having spent many years witnessing the effects of religiously justified hatred of gay people, I feel certain in my heart that the anti-gay distortion of religion is a great *chillul hashem*. Out of ignorance, and often unwittingly, we as religious communities are doing grievous harm to the very traditions we seek to uphold. With the force of moral condemnation and superiority, religion can be a powerful weapon—and it has bludgeoned, burned, and tortured gay people, literally and figuratively, for centuries.

For this reason, some of my friends have questioned the wisdom of my writing this book, arguing that religion cannot be saved, or should not be. Leave religion to the bigots, they say, and stop trying to apologize for who you are. Stop trying to make everything fit, to accommodate a twenty-first-century sexual identity within a Bronze Age text. Often, these arguments resonate with my heart, but I refuse to cede my spiritual heritage to those who do not even know of what they speak. The pretenders to religious certainty do not know the geography of my soul. They do not know the etiology of sexual identity, or the phenomenology of desire. And while they may know some interpretations of sacred writ and practice, I will not allow them to occupy the territory of religion on the basis of force alone. Am I to turn my back on my devotional practice, my community, simply because of other people's ignorance? No—just as I refuse to choose God over gay, so too do I refuse to choose gay over God. The dichotomy does not hold up under scrutiny, and having revealed itself to be false, I refuse to reinforce it.

Andrew Sullivan has written that, while some may read a passage in Leviticus as prohibiting homosexual behavior, the ninth commandment is unambiguous about not bearing false witness.[4] Surely all of us who consider ourselves followers of a religious or spiritual path know this to be true. Whether under oath or not, it is the height of hypocrisy to pretend religiosity while practicing dishonesty, especially with friends and families. Yet consider this: you might be on the other side of such a relationship right now. Some friend or family member you think is straight (perhaps because that person hasn't told you otherwise) may in fact be hiding the truth from you for fear of your response. Is that really the kind of loving relationship conducive to the religious life? Is that the kind of relationship any of us really wants?

If the closet is the place where repressed gay people hide, the gutter is where they go for release. Consider, too, then, that you may be consigning your friend, your congregant, or even your child to the very depravity that you condemn. Give sexuality a place of honor in the community, and it will be sanctified. Relegate it to the gutter, and that is where it will stay. The belief that homosexuality is a sin is a self-fulfilling prophecy. The gay sex scandals that embroil closeted or homophobic celebrities are the natural result of the closet, because the closet and the gutter complement one another perfectly. Have you ever noticed that when gay celebrities come out, the scandals stop? When New Jersey governor Jim McGreevey was in the closet, he was having clandestine affairs with security guards. When he came out, he married and entered a seminary. Meanwhile, most of us in the gay community are just waiting for the next sordid scandal from Ted Haggard (who bought sex and drugs from his masseur for three years, and who now is calling himself bisexual) or "ex-gay" leader George Rekers (who hired a male prostitute as a "travel attendant"). This is not because of what the Family Research Council, in response to the Rekers scandal, called "the fallen nature of all people."[5] "All people" don't surreptitiously hire male prostitutes for Caribbean getaways while preaching against homosexuality. Closeted people do.

The religious mandate for honesty falls upon all of us—and that includes those who would prefer to deny the truth about sexual diversity. We discussed the scientific data in the last chapter. But my emphasis now is not on the facts themselves but on every religious person's requirement to learn them before making judgments about other people. Pope John Paul II once said that "we need heralds of the Gospel who are experts in humanity, who know the depths of the human heart, who can share the joys, the hopes, the agonies, the distress of people today, but who are, at the same time, contemplatives who have fallen in love with God."[6] Are we fulfilling this ideal today, in our public religious rhetoric? Can people who deny the reality of my love, or liken it to the lust for an animal, be said to "know the depths of the human heart" or "share the joys" of people who find themselves to be gay or lesbian?

Quite the contrary, it seems to me. Rather than read the testimonies of faithful LGBT people, the findings of reputable scientists, or the histories of LGBT people around the world, many people are content to rest undisturbed in their ignorance. They say that homosexuality is a choice, even though teenagers are killing themselves because they cannot "choose" otherwise. Or they say homosexuality is some kind of curable pathology, even though there are millions of perfectly happy LGBT people, and almost no happy "ex-gays." Nor, as we will see in part 3, has there been any evidence that acceptance of sexual diversity would lead to erosion of the family, loss of sexual morality, or any of the other bogeymen often dangled about our heads like threats of disaster. These scare tactics are just that tactics. They are window-dressing covering up a discomfort, or perhaps a prejudice—and if we are honest, we should confront those truths directly as well.

We cannot, if we consider ourselves people of faith, hide our heads in the sand and pretend that what is so, is not so. The sun does not revolve around the Earth. God did not separate the races on different continents, and intend them to remain separate forever. And homosexuality is neither a choice nor a changeable pathological condition.

The danger of dishonesty touches each of us who refuses, out of fear or love, to grapple with the difficult facts of what it means to be human. This is how I understand the name "Israel," given to Jacob after he wrestles with a man all night—that he is a God-wrestler, a truth-wrestler, someone who allows himself to be embraced, enveloped, even defeated by truth. His is a quintessentially religious story, and his is the challenge to which we must rise.

For me, the quintessential "coming out" story in the Bible is that of Joseph and his brothers. Joseph has miraculously survived being sold into slavery (twice) and falsely imprisoned. He has ascended to the highest position of administrative power in Egypt, second only to Pharaoh. Years have gone by, and now his brothers come to Egypt in desperation, as a famine has devastated their land. Joseph recognizes them immediately, but they do not recognize him. Joseph then subjects his brothers to a test, to see whether they would treat the youngest, Benjamin, as cruelly as Joseph had been treated years ago.

Finally, the brothers pass the test, and Joseph is unable to restrain himself any longer. Genesis 45:1 uses a new word to describe what happens next: *v'hitvadah yoseph et echav*—and Joseph "made himself known" to his brothers. This is a unique word, not found anywhere else in biblical text: *v'hitvadah*. It's in the reflexive form, since it's something Joseph does to himself. He discloses himself, he reveals himself. He finally tells the truth about who he is.

This is Joseph's coming-out story. He tells the truth, to himself, his brothers—and, not least, the Egyptians whom he governs. The Bible story does not indicate whether Joseph had revealed his humble origins to the Egyptians—that he had been an Israelite shepherd, sold into slavery by his brothers. It seems unlikely that he would have. And Joseph has concealed his true identity from the brothers until this climactic moment. Life is going to be different for his family, and for his native and adopted nations, from now on.

Life has also changed for Joseph. Coming out is a courageous act, because inherent in the process of self-transformation is the change into the unknown. One cannot know how one (or one's relationships) will change, and there is no going back. The process can be terrifying. Yet, as the Joseph story also relates, it often becomes irresistible. Joseph cannot hold himself back, he can no longer restrain himself—this, certainly, is how I felt, after years of postponement and denial. When at last the truth can be spoken, there is a lifting of an invisible burden, and as I have seen time and time again, its heaviness outweighs any of the challenges one fears in advance. Freedom does not mean paradise—coming out does not take one to the land of Oz, or Eden. But it does mean a deep relaxing of fear, constriction, and worry—and, perhaps for the first time, the possibility of integrity.

These are ineluctable religious values. We read Scripture honestly when our reading promotes honesty. We read Scripture plainly when we may live plainly and simply in its light, rather than twist ourselves into shapes we were never meant to take. On questions of how to interpret Scripture, there are good arguments on both sides. But deciding between the two is not a theological coin flip. We are compelled to take the interpretation that allows for more love, holiness, justice, compassion, and truthfulness. I cannot understand a loving God who wants human beings to lie, cheat, and be degraded. Whereas I can easily understand fallible human beings being confused about sexuality and Scripture. As much as the affirming readings of Leviticus, Romans, and Corinthians may seem at odds with the traditional ones, the repressive readings of those texts are far more at odds with traditional values.

After all the wrestling, we are blissfully defeated by simple truths. This is so: that life is precious, and fleeting; that moments of being and transcendence are possible; that cruelty is evil and compassion good; that there is a love accessible simply by resting in a truth that cannot be expressed.

CHAPTER 6

"Justice—justice shall you pursue"

Inequality is an affront to religious values

In most states, gay people can be fired from their jobs or denied housing because of their sexual orientation. They can be denied the right to visit their lifelong partners in the hospital, or celebrate their love in their communities. In other countries, they are forbidden to express themselves sexually and are targets of state-sanctioned and state-tolerated violence. And they are judged secondhand, unfairly, and cruelly, according to stereotypes rather than reality.

This situation is unjust, and flies in the face of our religious mandates to pursue justice and fairness for everyone. Whenever we see inequality, we ought to devote ourselves to eradicating it. Our religious values compel us to right these wrongs. "Justice—justice, shall you pursue," demands Deuteronomy 16:20. This is the Hebrew Bible's call: not to oppress the stranger, to set up just courts that judge people fairly, to "proclaim liberty throughout the land" (Lev. 25:10). And it is echoed by the prophet Isaiah, quoted by Jesus in Luke 4:18: "God has anointed me to preach good news to the humble, to bind up the brokenhearted, to proclaim freedom to the captive, and liberation to the prisoner" (Isa. 51:1). And by Micah, who tells us to "act justly and to love mercy, and to walk humbly with your God" (Mic. 6:8).[1]

Now, some have suggested that gays want "special rights" at the expense of straights. But what are those rights? I don't know of any. The rights I'd be interested in having are *equal* rights. For example, I'd like the federal government to recognize my Massachusetts marriage, just as it recognizes my straight friends' marriages, even when they contravene religious law and tradition (as in the cases of interfaith or interracial marriage, for example). This isn't "special"—it's equal. One also sometimes hears of a sinister "homosexual agenda" being advanced by some secretive, powerful cabal of gay activists. What is it? No one really knows that either. Representative Barney Frank, at a 2010 news conference following the repeal of the "Don't Ask, Don't Tell" policy, playfully described it this way: "it's to be protected against violent crimes driven by bigotry, it's to be able to get married, it's to be able to get a job, and it's to be able to fight for our country. For those who are worried about the radical homosexual agenda, let me put them on notice. Two down, two to go."[2]

In other words, the "radical homosexual agenda" is a myth based upon fear and ignorance. What most gay people want is to be treated equally and fairly. Indeed, the very language of "radical homosexual agenda" is itself part of the problem.

The Bible is exquisitely clear on how we are to relate to minorities in our midst: "The stranger that dwells with you shall be to you as one born among you, and you shall love him as yourself; for you were strangers once in the land of Egypt" (Lev. 19:34). "You shall not mistreat a stranger, nor oppress him: for you were strangers in the land of Egypt" (Exod. 22:21). What is asked of us, in such exhortations, is to recall that those we would demonize, those we would "other," are people like us, created in the image of God. It is understood that all of us have a tendency to favor the in-group over the out-group—lately scientists have measured this on a hormonal level.[3] Thus the mandate to justice comes from a reminder of our own shared experience of oppression. Israelites, too, were strangers once—persecuted and enslaved. We may be comfortable now, but we are commanded to remember that this was not always the case—and to act appropriately. Thus the biblical command to do justice merges with the mandate to feel empathy. We are called upon to remember what it is like to be oppressed, and to try to get to know the group that is being disfavored. Maybe we are not widows or orphans ourselves   but we are asked, by our religious traditions, to empathize with them and treat them justly. This is especially true in the case of minorities; it is precisely when a majority of people have a certain view that protection of minorities is most necessary.

These commandments apply to all the "strangers" who dwell among us, and indeed, many gays and lesbians have found common cause with other minorities in their struggles against interlocking and intersectional oppressions. But there is something unique about gays and lesbians: that the stranger may be within one's own family. Re-member, few gay people grow up with gay parents, so many gay peo-ple know what it is like to be strangers even within their own homes. As such, the mandate to love the stranger imposes a higher responsi-bility in this case, because the stranger may be within: In the church pew, as a preacher inveighs against homosexuality. Around the din-ner table, when someone makes an anti-gay joke. In the junior high school, where bullies pick on "sissies." LGBT people may be strangers even when we are among our families and communities. The stranger may be the person next to you, whom you don't yet know is gay.

Now, some might argue that unlike other strangers, gays and lesbians are defined by conduct. We are not innocent but are acting in ways that invite reproach, and so these calls for justice ring hollow. But this claim can only be made on the basis of ignorance. As we have already seen, our religious mandates for compassion and truthfulness require us to base decisions not on stereotype but on reality. Get to know gay or lesbian people. Read testimonies, memoirs, and stories—not slanders. See that sexual diversity is real, natural, and capable of holi-ness. Then the injustice of discrimination on the basis of sexuality will become clear. To objectify another person, or base judgments on stereotypes, is to harden one's heart against them. Deuteronomy 15:7 demands "do not harden your heart, nor shut your hand from your needy brother." If we are truly religious, we cannot look the other way, or pretend that suffering is something other than what it is.

Surely it is obvious what differentiates homosexuality from vices like gluttony or greed: same-sex intimacy can lead to love, con-nection, intimacy, and holiness. Gluttony can't. Yet this is precisely the kind of insulting analogy one finds in today's ex-gay literature.[4] Worse, I've seen the love I share with my partner compared to the lust someone might experience with an animal—or even a child. You've heard this before—the "slippery slope" argument that if we legiti-mize homosexuality, what's to stop us from legitimizing bestiality, or prostitution, or whatever? But of course there's an answer to this rhe-torical question. Bestiality, pedophilia, and prostitution cannot lead to love, commitment, intimacy, holiness, family, and durable emotional bonds. Same-sex intimacy can. Therefore there is a clear difference between those things and same-sex intimacy. These supposed analogies are scare tactics—nothing more. And when I look to either the Hebrew Bible or the New Testament, I never see language like that. On the contrary, "the wisdom that comes from heaven is first of all pure; then peace-loving, considerate, submissive, full of mercy and good fruit, impartial and sincere" (James 3:17).

Really, even if one were to maintain that some same-sex activity is prohibited by religious law, how could we justify singling it out for discrimination, when so many of us fall so short of the mark all the time? Consider the Sermon on the Mount, according to which divorce, except on the grounds of infidelity, is tantamount to adultery (Matt. 5:32). Should we shun "openly divorced" parishioners from our congregations? Should remarried people, who openly and flagrantly display their adulterous behavior, be shunned from church leadership positions? Perhaps we should amend the "Defense of Marriage Act" to forbid remarriage. And that is just the beginning. We should never swear oaths (Matt. 5:33), always turn the other cheek (Matt. 5:39), never allow charitable donations to be publicized (Matt. 6:2), and not think about what we eat or how we dress (Matt. 6:25). Even if homosexuality were sinful behavior, to single it out for opprobrium is to treat it unequally.

Surely this is why the crux of the Sermon's message is "Do not judge, or you too will be judged. For in the same way you judge others, you will be judged, and with the measure that you use, it will be measured to you" (Matt. 7:1). None of us sits in so lofty a perch as to be able to judge other people and not be found wanting ourselves. None of us can meet these standards, which is why none of us can sit in judgment of another. Jesus did not sit in judgment of the marginalized; he fought on their behalf, against the power structures that demonized them.[5]

As with love, which requires empathy and humility to "stand in the shoes" of the other, so too with justice. We can rise above gut reactions that circumvent moral reasoning. We can remember that none of us is above the sting of inequality, even if at the moment we are in a position of power and privilege. When any person is oppressed, none of us is truly free.

PART TWO

What the "bad verses" really say about homosexuality

CHAPTER 7

Leviticus

*One form of male intimacy is related
to worship of foreign gods*

Fine—but doesn't the Bible forbid homosexuality?

Very well, one might say: love is important, loneliness is profoundly "not good," justice and compassion are beloved of God. But
doesn't the Bible say, clearly and unambiguously, that homosexuality
is wrong?

Well, no—not at all. In fact, in the extremely rare cases where
the Bible does mention same-sex behavior, its statements are limited,
ambiguous, and seem to have nothing to do with what we, today,
understand as homosexuality. The sliver of biblical text that has been
interpreted against gays and lesbians—7 verses, at most, out of 31,102
in the Hebrew Bible and New Testament—has been twisted, distorted, inflated out of all proportion and out of context. It may seem
like a bedrock principle that the Bible forbids homosexuality, but it
just doesn't.

In this part, we'll look at the biblical passages that have been used
against gays and lesbians and have caused so many families and communities so much pain. We will take them apart word by word, often
in the original Hebrew or Greek, so you can decide for yourself what
the verses actually mean. This part of the book will be more technical and more hair-splitting than the previous and the following parts,
but I think it's important to look as closely and literally as possible
at these verses. Let's just remember what's at stake; over the years, I
have met with hundreds of LGBT people and their friends and family
members whose lives have been wrecked because of how the Hebrew
word *toevah* is translated. Imagine: lives affected by the translation

of a word! So, if the next few chapters seem overly detailed, or seem to miss the bigger picture, I invite you to step back periodically and remember just how much hangs on these technical details of word choice and vocabulary. No, bullies aren't throwing copies of Leviticus at the "fag" they taunt in the hallway. But they *are* learning what society thinks of gay people, and society bases those views, in part, on the Bible.

Many religious people feel the contradiction between the traditional readings of Romans and Leviticus and the deeper values of respect and love that the Bible teaches, but have felt there is little they can do about it. If you are one of those people, read on. There need be no contradiction between the commandment to love our neighbors as ourselves and the handful of biblical verses that have troubled us for so long. We don't even need to weasel out of the plain meanings of those verses, because their plain meaning reveals far more ambiguity and range than many suppose. All we need to do is read honestly and closely, and the verses themselves reveal interpretations that accord with conscience and courage. As I will say time and time again, it's not that these interpretations are the only ones, or even the most immediate ones. But they are authentic, honest, and plausible—and because of our shared religious values, they are necessary as well.

I want to reiterate a few "ground rules" before moving forward, so that our effort to un-distort these biblical verses is not, itself, distorted.

First, the reason this part comes second, rather than first, is that the core message of this book is about positive values, not negative ones. These few verses are far less important than the hundreds of verses and insights of conscience about the holiness of love, or human dignity, or honesty, or justice. *Those* are the important religious teachings about homosexuality. But it would be naive to ask those questions without also taking account of these problematic verses. Second, although it will become evident that these verses do *not* mean what some people claim, my intent is not to apologize for homosexuality, or for the Bible, or to manipulate biblical text in order to make everything fit. The text is what it is, and, as we will see, there are aspects of it that many readers will find disturbing. I find this honest approach to be more valuable to me, as a religious person, than sugarcoating the challenging parts or pretending that they do not exist.

Third, it bears recalling that the Bible does not comprise the entirety of religious teaching in any religious tradition. Jewish law is as much informed by the Talmud and later generations of rabbinic decisions as it is by biblical text. Catholic teaching is informed by natural law and church holdings. And Protestants work not only with text and the individual conscience, but with many generations of commentary as well. And of course, all of our traditions are informed by the teachings of our religious traditions, the knowledge we have gained from science and philosophy, and the promptings of conscience. As the late Rev. Peter Gomes wrote, "The Bible must be understood not as a thing in and of itself but as part of the whole teaching and practice of the Christian faith. The confrontation between our social and moral presuppositions is what we bring to the text, and what we find in the text and in its context is something we will have to face."[1] That being said, the Bible lays the common foundation for these teachings, and forms the oft-contested ground of our religious reasoning. For that reason, the Bible is my focus here.

Fourth, I want to be clear that I am offering literal readings of these biblical texts—not allegorical or spiritual ones. This distinguishes my approach from that of many others: I think the "pro-gay" readings are faithful to the actual, literal words of the text. Yes, context is important—as two evangelical readers of the Bible have said, "a text taken out of context is pretext."[2] But my approach is to read the texts literally, on their own terms. This does not mean that I am personally committed to biblical fundamentalism, inerrancy, or literalism. Nor am I taking a stand on how we *should* read. Rather, I am assuming what I take to be the most conservative of interpretive positions, because the liberating readings prevail even with that methodology.

Indeed, I often feel we don't read these texts literally enough. Daniel Helminiak, in his best-selling *What the Bible Really Says About Homosexuality*, points out that Jesus's famous statement in Matthew 19:24 that "it is easier for a camel to pass through the eye of a needle than for a rich man to enter the kingdom of God" is usually read as a metaphor for how it is impossible for a rich person to go to heaven. Actually, though, the teaching almost certainly refers to a narrow gate in Jerusalem that was called the "Eye of the Needle."[3] Camels had to be unloaded in order to fit through this particular gate, and in the same way, rich people must divest themselves of possessions in order to enter the kingdom of God. This is not some symbolic or spiritual reading—it is a literal one, even a hyper-literal one. Yet without this context, the literal meaning cannot be apprehended. Ignoring this information isn't fidelity to the text; it's a betrayal of it.

Finally, and most importantly, I am not pretending that my readings of biblical text are the only possible ones. Leviticus 18:22 can be read as forbidding all same-sex behavior on the part of men or women. It can be read broadly or narrowly or anywhere in between. However, only the narrow reading is in accord with our shared fundamental values. As I mentioned in the introduction, these readings don't need to "win"—they need to tie. If you showed Romans 1:27 to a Greek-speaking visitor from Mars, she might read it broadly or narrowly. But if you first taught her Genesis 2:18, or the way integrity opens the heart to the sacred, then she would conclude that, given various alternatives, the only ones that made sense were those that read these verses narrowly. In a purely academic context, all readings are equal and may be judged solely on their merits. But our reading of Scripture takes place in a context in which children are killing themselves because of the myth of "God versus Gay." Thus, all readings are not equal; those that accord with our fundamental values, promote life, and sanctify righteous living are superior to those that do not. Our guiding question must not be "which reading do I prefer" or "which reading seems the most likely" but rather "which reading is *plausible* and accords with our fundamental values."

Let's be honest. If we are clever enough, we can interpret texts in any way we want. Thus, intention is everything. If our intention is to seek the truth, as best as we can understand it, then the conscience is at ease; the excited tension associated with trying too hard to make a particular case subsides, and, in my experience, a calm clarity often emerges. Some call this the Holy Spirit, others just the faculty of discernment. But however we understand it, the simplicity of intention is the critical ingredient—simply to begin anew, without preconceptions, and let the text speak.

There are, at most, seven references to same-sex activity in the Hebrew Bible and New Testament. Jesus never mentions it. The Ten Commandments never mention it. It's not that sexual diversity wasn't in existence in biblical times—it was, and was well known. Yet the Bible is almost totally uninterested in it.

I am not the first to attempt these readings of sacred text, and for many LGBT religious people, this part of the book may seem a bit old hat. We've heard many of these arguments before, and, to be honest, many of us have grown tired of making them. Yet if there is one thing I have learned being an advocate for sexual minorities in religious communities over the last decade, it is that we are always at square one. Gay kids will always be born into families that have never paid much attention to these crucial texts, and so we will always need to begin again. Those interested in other interpretations of these texts may wish to consider sources such as John Dwyer's *Those 7 References* (Episcopal); Daniel Helminiak's *What the Bible Really Says About Homosexuality*; Rev. Peter Gomes, *The Good Book*; Rev. Jeff Miner and John Tyler Connoley, *The Children Are Free: Reexamining the Biblical Evidence on Same-Sex Relationships* (evangelical); Rick Brentlinger's *Gay Christian 101* (evangelical); Rev. Michael S. Piazza, *Gay by God* (evangelical/Methodist); and Rev. Mel White's *What the Bible Says— And Doesn't Say—About Homosexuality,* online at www.soulforce.org. There are literally dozens more—many are listed in the bibliography.

So what are those seven references?

The first and second are Genesis 19, the story of Sodom, and its literary echo, Judges 19.

The third and fourth—Leviticus 18:22 and 20:13—comprise the Hebrew Bible's prohibition on male anal sex as a ritual purity violation.

The fifth is Romans 1:26–27, which criticizes the Romans for "unnatural" sex acts.

The sixth and seventh are 1 Corinthians 6:9 and 1 Timothy 1:10, which say that licentious people, idolaters, and thieves will not inherit the kingdom of God.

For reasons that will become clear, we'll start with Leviticus.

Leviticus 18:22, which contains the Hebrew Bible's most notorious prohibition on homosexual behavior, is often read in a vacuum, as if it's floating in the air. Have you ever read it together with its preceding verse? See if this changes the flavor:

And you shall not give any of your seed to set them apart to
Molech, neither shall you profane the name of your God: I am
the Lord. And at a man you shall not lie the lyings of woman;
it is a *toevah*.

We'll explore this important context in a moment, but first, let's
analyze each word in turn.

The Hebrew word *et,* which I've translated here as "at," is actually
untranslatable; it's a grammatical signal that the next word is a direct
object. Often, you see this part of the verse translated as "Do not lie
with a man as with a woman," but "with" is not the meaning of *et*.
If the Bible wanted to say "with" it would use the word *im. Et* suggests something about the nature of the prohibited act: it's something
done to a person, or at a person. This has led some commentators to
interpret Leviticus 18:22 as being about sexual violence, or sexual
degradation: basically, about "making a man into a woman," which,
in biblical times, was a humiliating and degrading act.[4] That would
mean that this verse is no more about a loving same-sex relationship
than a prohibition on rape is about a loving opposite-sex one. This is
not my precise reading here, but it is certainly justified by the word *et*.
Just reading the verse literally tells us that this prohibition is not about
love, but about sexual objectification.

Second, and so hidden in plain sight that many people don't notice
it at all, there's the word "man." Leviticus 18:22 is only about men. It
was never, in Jewish or Christian law, expanded to include women.
The later Jewish prohibitions on lesbianism derived themselves from
an entirely different source, an obscure verse about not following "the
practices of Egypt," which was interpreted first by rabbinic legend,
then by medieval casuistry, to prohibit lesbian sexual activity.[5] Until the twelfth century, lesbianism was only as problematic as, say,
wearing a bikini. It was seen as immodest, perhaps lewd—but never
a violation of biblical law. In the Christian tradition, one statement
in the New Testament (Rom. 1:26–27) does mention women, but as
we'll see, it probably has more to do with women being dominant
sexually than with lesbianism. The story of Sodom is about male rape,
and Paul's words in Corinthians about men having sex with men. To
group gay men and lesbians together, in terms of religious values, is
a huge anachronism. At least half of the people we now call "homo-

sexual" are not covered by this prohibition. Leviticus 18:22 has nothing to do with lesbians at all.

The third important term in the verse is *mishkevei ishah,* which literally means "the lyings of woman." This may seem obvious—don't lie with a man as you lie with a woman—but its scope is not actually clear. The Hebrew words *tishkav* ("lie") and *mishkevei* ("lyings") are basically the vulgar words for sex. When the Bible refers to making love, it uses the word *yada,* as when Adam "knew" Eve his wife; *tishkav* is having sex, not making love. Moreover, biblical and Jewish law regard this "lying" as requiring penetration by a penis. That's what sex is for these sources, and without penetration, there isn't any sex. *Mishkav zachar* (the lying of a man) means penetration; *mishkevei ishah* means being penetrated.[6] Thus Rashi, perhaps the most well-known of the Jewish biblical commentators, states that there are two ways to "lie" with a woman (vaginally and anally). Since only one of those "lyings" is possible with a man, what is prohibited here is anal sex.

This is an important detail, and forms the basis for the current understanding of the verse in many religious Jewish communities. Anal sex is prohibited by the Torah, this view holds, but other forms of sex are not. Now, many sexual activities are prohibited for straight, married people too. For example, according to Jewish law, men and women may not have sex during the woman's menstrual period. But do rabbis go around inspecting the private lives of married couples, asking when women are menstruating? Of course not—that would be offensive. So, this opinion holds, just as we don't intrude on the private lives of straight people, so we don't intrude on the private lives of gay people. We assume that married gay couples are observing the law—i.e., not having anal sex—and we don't inquire any further. (Contrary to stereotype, about a third of gay men do not regularly engage in anal sex.)[7] That's between the couple and God. Since other forms of male sexual activity are permitted, this allows us to bless same-sex unions while maintaining a strict interpretation of Leviticus 18:22. We only need to read the verse according to its plain meaning: that *tishkav* means anal sex—and only that.

The last key word of the verse is, in my opinion, the most important: *toevah.* As I've lectured and taught across the country, I've been amazed at how everyone thinks they know the meaning of this obscure Hebrew word: Abomination, right? Isn't that what it says in the Bible?

No. Whatever *toevah* means, it definitely does not mean "abomination." Colloquially, abominations are things that should not exist on the face of the Earth: three-eyed fish, oceans choked with oil, and maybe Cheez Whiz.[8] The word "abomination" is found in the King James translation of Leviticus 18:22, a translation which reads, "Thou shalt not lie with mankind, as with womankind: it [is] abomination." Yet this is a misleading rendition of the word *toevah,* which actually means something permitted to one group and forbidden to another. Though there is (probably) no etymological relationship, *toevah* means taboo.[9]

The term *toevah* (and its plural, *toevot*) occurs 103 times in the Hebrew Bible, and almost always has the connotation of a non-Israelite cultic practice. The primary *toevah* is *avodah zara,* foreign forms of worship (often called "idolatry"), and most other *toevot* flow from it. The Israelites are instructed not to commit *toevot* precisely because other nations do so. Deuteronomy 18:9–12 makes this quite clear: "When you come into the land that YHVH your God gives you, do not learn to do the *toevot* of those nations. Do not find among you one who passes his son or daughter through the fire; or a magician; or a fortune teller, charmer, or witch. . . . because all who do these things are *toevah* to YHVH and because of these *toevot* YHVH your God is driving them out before you." Elsewhere, Deuteronomy 7:25–26 commands "you shall burn the statues of their gods in fire. Do not desire the silver and gold on them and take it onto yourself, else you be snared by it, for it is a *toevah* to YHVH your God. And you shall not bring *toevah* to your home." Six verses in Deuteronomy further identify idolatry, child sacrifice, witchcraft, and other "foreign" practices as *toevah.*[10] Deuteronomy 32:16 is typical: prophesying Israel's unfaithfulness, Moses said, "They provoked God with foreign things, angered him with *toevot.*" *Toevah* is serious, but it is serious in a particular way: it is an idolatrous transgression of national boundary. It is certainly not abomination.

Toevah is used four times in Leviticus 18—once to refer to male anal sex, and then three times as an umbrella term. As in Deuteronomy, the signal feature of *toevot* is that the other nations of the Land of Israel do them: "You shall therefore keep my statutes and my judgments, and shall not commit these *toevot* . . . because the people who were in the land before you did these *toevot* and made the land impure [*tameh*])" (Lev. 18:26–27; see also Lev. 18:29). The term is repeated with reference to homosexual activity in Leviticus 20:13.

Toevah is also culturally relative. For example, there are things that are *toevah* for Egyptians but perfectly acceptable for Israelites. Genesis 43:32 states that eating with Israelites is *toevah* for Egyptians. Genesis 43:34 states that shepherds are *toevah* to Egyptians—the sons of Israel are themselves shepherds. In Exodus 8:22, Moses describes Israelite sacrifices as being *toevat mitzrayim*—*toevah* of Egypt—although obviously Israelite ritual is not an abomination.

So, if (1) *toevah* is a culturally relative taboo related to boundary between Israelite and foreign, and (2) male anal sex is specifically called a *toevah,* unlike other prohibitions (e.g., incest), then: (3) male anal sex is a culturally relative taboo related to boundary between Israelite and foreign.

This isn't about abomination or nature, or even morality—this is about a ritual purity law that distinguishes Israelites from foreigners.

Other books of the Bible bear this out. The books of Kings and Chronicles use *toevah* nine times to refer to acts that other nations committed in the Land of Israel.[11] Ezra 9:1, 9:11, and 9:14 use the word in exactly the same way. In all these cases, *toevah* refers to a foreign cultic behavior. Jeremiah associates *toevah* with idolatry and unspecified transgression.[12] Malachi 2:11 uses the term to refer to the Israelites' having "married the daughter of a foreign god." The prophet Ezekiel uses the term *toevah* a record-setting thirty-nine times to refer to idolatry, usury, haughtiness and pride, heterosexual adultery, and violence, as well as a general term for foreign acts or transgression in a cultic context.[13] In one extended passage (Ezek. 8:1–18), Ezekiel is taken on a visionary tour of *toevot,* all of which have to do with idolatry, including women weeping for the goddess Tammuz and men worshipping the sun. This extended passage, with six mentions of *toevah,* links the term in every instance with *avodah zara,* or idolatry. In five instances, Ezekiel mentions *toevah* together with both idolatry and *zimah* or *znut,* lewdness,[14] strongly suggesting that the nature of sexual *toevah* is not mere sexual activity, and certainly not loving intimate expression, but sexuality in a cultic context. Likewise in Deuteronomy 23:19, which labels as *toevah* sacrifices bought through prostitution or "the price of a dog," a biblical euphemism for a male cultic prostitute.

In rare cases, *toevah* can also mean other things. Deuteronomy 17:1 uses it to refer to the sacrifice of a blemished animal. Deuteronomy 22:5 calls cross-dressing (which in Orthodox Jewish law includes women wearing pants) a *toevah,* though this may be connected to cultic sexual practices as well. Remarriage (i.e., of the same two people) is *toevah* according to Deuteronomy 24:4. The sole ethical use of the term in the Torah is in Deuteronomy 25:16, in which the use of unequal weights and measures is called *toevah.* Psalm 88:9 poetically invokes the term, by way of analogy, for being alienated from one's friend: "You have taken me far from my acquaintance; made me a *toevah* to him, put away, and I cannot come out." Isaiah uses it to refer to the sacrifices of hypocrites, as a taunt against earthly power, and, once again, idolatry.[15]

The only major exception to this biblical trend, and it is a unique case, is the book of Proverbs, where *toevah* is used twenty-one times to refer to various ethical failings, including the ways, thoughts, prayers, and sacrifices of the wicked, pride, evil speech, false weights, deviousness, lying, scoffing, justifying the wicked, and defaming the righteous.[16] Scholars have proposed varying theories as to why the references in Proverbs are unlike the overwhelming majority of other cases, though we may never know for sure.

Aside from Proverbs, though, *toevah* has nothing to do with ethics, and everything to do with cultic behavior, idolatry, and foreign ritual. However we may understand this type of transgression, it is certainly not "abomination" in the modern sense. (Incidentally, the King James Version uses the term "abomination" to translate not just *toevah* but also the related terms *sheketz, pigul,* and *nivash,* as well as six times in translation of New Testament texts.[17] One of these variant uses has led to the website godhatesshrimp.com, which makes posters that say "God Hates Shrimp" (Lev. 11:10–13) in the form of "God Hates Fags." Biblically, they are certainly correct; strange that we never see angry protests in front of Red Lobster.)

Finally, it is noteworthy how *toevah* is used in Leviticus 18:22. The chapter describes several sexual sins, then mentions Molech worship (a form of Canaanite idolatrous practice), then says specifically that male anal sex is *toevah,* then describes the whole list of sins as *toevot* that the Canaanites performed.[18] Now, imagine if a similar structure were used today. Imagine if someone said to you, "Don't Kill, Don't Steal, and Don't Eat the Cheese—It Is Spoiled." The first two instructions have no conditions; they are universal prohibitions. The third one, though, provides a reason for the ban, implying that when the cheese isn't spoiled, the ban would not apply. Likewise here. Leviticus says very clearly: no incest, no idolatry, no male anal sex because it is *toevah*. It's almost as if Leviticus is going out of its way to specify that male anal sex is prohibited because it is a Canaanite cultic practice.[19]

Which it was. We learn from Deuteronomy 23:18 and 1 Kings 14:24 that the Canaanites had *qedeshim,* sacred prostitutes, both male and female, who would enact the role of a god or goddess in an ecstatic, sexual ritual. Campaigns against cultic prostitution were undertaken by King Solomon and King Josiah.[20] Similar forms of cultic prostitution were found in Babylonia, as recorded by Herodotus,[21] and elsewhere in the Ancient Near East.[22] Especially since Leviticus 18:22 follows Leviticus 18:21, it seems clear that what's being forbidden here is what the Bible is always interested in forbidding: idolatry.

Indeed, as we'll see in the cases of Romans, Corinthians, and Timothy, what appear to be regulations of homosexuality are *always* about idolatry, and about demarcating a sharp boundary between lascivious, pansexual, idol-worshipping pagans on the one hand, and Jews and Christians on the other. (It's no coincidence that the primary Pauline condemnations come in letters to the Romans and Corinthians; Rome and Corinth were known as the most licentious places in the empire.) Israelites, and later Christians, are told not to do what the other nations do, which includes these idolatrous forms of sexual practice. Idolatry is the source of sin, especially sexual sin, in apocryphal books such as Wisdom of Solomon (see 12:23 and 16:4). And every one of the biblical texts supposedly about homosexuality is actually about idolatry and about boundary-making between communities.[23]

The view that Leviticus 18:22 is really about cultic prostitution also accords with the general context of the verse in the Book of Leviticus. Leviticus 18 is part of a large section of the Torah that describes the boundaries between pure and impure, Israelite and Canaanite, proper and improper worship, and which follows upon the death of Aaron's sons following their offering of "strange fire." In other words, not only does the language of *toevah* strongly suggest a connection to idolatry, but the overall context of the verse does as well.[24]

Now, taboos may still be important: as a religious Jew myself, I don't eat shrimp. But it helps clarify and limit the nature of the prohibition. Moreover, for most Christians, Levitical taboos (like not eating shrimp) were nullified by the coming of Christ. If this is just some ancient cultic taboo, then it no longer has applicability. More generally, understanding the nature of the prohibition as being against cultic prostitution certainly helps me understand how Leviticus 18:22 relates to my own life: it doesn't.

I think this literal reading of Leviticus 18:22 makes more sense than any other one. I think it "wins." However, even if it only "ties" with the anti-gay readings, that is enough. The point here is that it is *plausible,* and that such a reading is *necessary* based on our fundamental values. All this textual investigation doesn't take place in a vacuum. It takes place in a context in which children are killing themselves because of "God versus Gay." If I had to take a tortured, roundabout reading of Leviticus, I would do that, because a tortured reading of one verse makes more theological sense than the torture of young gay people.

But I don't even have to do that. All I have to do, to remove the false stigma of "God versus Gay," is read the verse closely, literally, and attentively. Leviticus 18:22 is a prohibition on male anal sex in the context of idolatry. Nothing more.

CHAPTER 8

Sodom

Cruelty and inhospitality are the "sins of Sodom"

Oh, so you're one of those sodomites.
You should only get AIDS and die, you pig.[1]

—Talk radio host Michael Savage

The most infamous story of homosexuality in the Bible—the story of Sodom—is not about homosexuality at all.[2] Indeed, not only was the "sin of Sodom" understood in biblical texts to be ethical rather than sexual, the association between Sodom and homosexuality does not begin in the Church until the fourth century, and the term "sodomy" was only invented in the eleventh century as a legal classification for specific sins of Catholic priests. Like the word "abomination," the term "sodomy" is a misleading part of the myth of "God versus Gay."

Most of us know the story, told in Genesis 19, well. God is preparing to destroy the cities of Sodom and Gomorrah, but will spare them if ten righteous people are found. Two angels (in the form of men) come to Sodom, and Lot meets them at the gates of the city, inviting them to stay with him overnight. They do so, and Lot makes them a feast. "But before they lie down," Genesis 19 continues, the men of the city surround Lot's house and demand that Lot "bring them out to us and we will know them," a phrase clearly understood sexually.[3] Lot goes out, begs "please, my brothers, do not do evil," and offers his own virgin daughters in place of the men. They refuse, saying "we will execute judgment on the one who has come to stay [with you], and now we'll do worse to you than them." They press Lot back against the door, and are on the verge of breaking through the door when the angels grab Lot, pull him inside, and smite the men of

Sodom with blindness. Quickly, the angels help Lot's family escape, and Sodom and Gomorrah are destroyed by fire and brimstone.

The Hebrew Bible almost univocally understands the sin the Sodomites committed in terms of ethics and hospitality, not sexual morality. But even before turning to those texts, if we were to read the story of Sodom with fresh eyes, it is obvious that homosexual rape is the means, not the ends, of Sodom's wickedness. Genesis 19 clearly contrasts Lot, who goes above and beyond the requirements of hospitality, with the Sodomites, who do the reverse. Lot insists that strangers dine and rest with him; the Sodomites seek to humiliate them. This emphasis on hospitality is entirely of a piece with what we know of the Ancient Near East, where hospitality was a core value. The Ancient Near East had no Holiday Inns; hospitality was essential for survival, and its presence or absence tells us much about the ethical character of people. Consider Luke 7:44–46 (where Jesus rebukes Simon that "I entered your house, you gave me no water for my feet. . . . You gave me no kiss. . . . My head with oil you did not anoint."), Hebrews 13:2 ("Be not forgetful to entertain strangers: for thereby some have entertained angels unawares."), and Romans 12:13 (Christians should be "given to hospitality."), as well as Titus 1:8 and 1 Timothy 3:2. Treating guests properly is no minor virtue; it is of paramount concern to the Hebrew and Christian Bibles.[4]

Moreover, the story of Sodom is in a section of the Bible where hospitality and ethics are central themes. Only one chapter earlier, Abraham had welcomed three men to his tent, and the text spends five verses on the details of the menu he prepares. (Indeed, after departing, these men "look toward Sodom," suggesting they may be the same messengers.) Right after Abraham's bargaining with God on behalf of Sodom comes the Sodom story and its aftermath, and right after that comes yet another story of hospitality, this time of Abraham and Sarah's visit to Gerar, where Abraham, fearing that King Abimelech will kill him in order to marry Sarah, tells the king that Sarah is his sister. These chapters of Genesis are about variations of hospitality: Abraham's and Lot's generosity, the wickedness of Sodom, and Abraham's fear of the king of Gerar. The male Sodomites' interest in men is incidental: if they were raging homosexuals, Lot would not offer his daughters in return. Homosexual rape is the way in which they violate hospitality—not the essence of their transgression. Reading the story of Sodom as being about homosexuality is like reading the story of an ax murderer as being about an ax.

This is even more clear in the "literary echo" of the Sodom story in Judges 19.[5] There, a Levite is traveling with his concubine, and staying at a house in Gibeah. As in the story of Sodom, the Levite is threatened by a Benjaminite mob that wants to "know him." His host offers his own daughter, the mob refuses, and finally the Levite hands over his concubine to the mob, who rapes and "abuse[s] her" all night long (Judg. 19:25). This horrible story, which concludes with the Levite dismembering the concubine, is meant to tell of the degradation of Israel prior to the institution of the monarchy. But in mirroring the story of Sodom, it also tells us that it is not the gender of the angels or the Levite that matters to the mob; it is the use of sexual violence to degrade and humiliate. The Benjaminites are neither "gay" nor "straight," and neither are the Sodomites. Both are predators, humiliators, dehumanizers.

Consider a recent example. In 1997, several New York City policemen viciously beat Abner Louima and "sodomized" him with the handle of a bathroom plunger. Do we think for one minute that the policemen were gay? Obviously not. Obviously, they were using anal rape as a means of degrading Louima. Likewise in the case of Sodom.[6]

Other texts of the Hebrew Bible interpret the story in this way.[7] Sodom's wickedness is connected to cruelty, injustice, and deceit—never homosexuality. Jeremiah 23:14: "I have seen also in the prophets of Jerusalem a horrible thing: they commit adultery, and walk in lies: they strengthen also the hands of evildoers, that none returns from his wickedness: they are all of them unto me as Sodom, and the inhabitants thereof as Gomorrah." Amos 4:1–11: "Hear this word, children of Bashan, that are in the mountain of Samaria, which oppress the poor, which crush the needy, which say to their masters, Bring, and let us drink. I have overthrown some of you, as God overthrew Sodom and Gomorrah." Repeatedly, Sodom is linked with oppression of the poor, crushing the needy, and ethical wickedness—never sexual immorality. Elsewhere, Sodom and Gomorrah are mentioned as placeholders for idolatry,[8] wickedness in general,[9] or for evidence of God's Divine wrath.[10] In the Gospels, Jesus mentions Sodom as an example of Divine punishment (Luke 17:29).

Had the story of "Sodom" been about homosexuality, would he not have mentioned that fact, even in passing?

Most convincingly, Ezekiel 16:49–50 specifically defines the sin of Sodom. "Behold," the prophet writes in God's voice, "this was the iniquity of your sister Sodom: pride, fullness of bread, and abundance of idleness was in her and in her daughters, neither did she strengthen the hand of the poor and needy. And they were haughty, and did *toevah* before me, and I took them away as I saw fit." Now, even if we assume that *toevah* here refers to the specific *toevah* of Leviticus 18 and 20, and not to the other 101 times the term is used in the Bible, then male anal sex is *one* of the six sins of Sodom. It is, at most, no more central to "sodomy" than are pride, gluttony, sloth, and economic injustice. Yet even this is a wild stretch of interpretation. As we saw in the previous chapter, the word *toevah* is used thirty-nine times in the book of Ezekiel. Twenty-nine times it refers to idolatry and other foreign cultic/ritual acts. Five times, Ezekiel mentions it in connection with both "whoredom" (*znut* or *zimah,* both used elsewhere in the Bible to refer to female prostitution) and idolatry (*avodah zara*). Twice it refers to heterosexual adultery, once to violence, and once to usury. Ezekiel never once mentions, alludes to, or even hints at homosexuality.[11] So, to read homosexuality into the description of Sodom's sin, when (a) Ezekiel uses the word *toevah* thirty-nine times and never once refers to homosexuality and (b) Ezekiel lists five specific injustices as the "sin of Sodom," has absolutely no basis in the text.

The sole biblical reference to sexual immorality connected with Sodom occurs in the short New Testament epistle of Jude, and even there, the reference is to licentiousness, not homosexuality. Jude, writing against "ungodly people, who pervert the grace of our God into a license for immorality and deny Jesus Christ our only Sovereign and Lord," recites several examples of Divine punishment, and then says: "In a similar way, Sodom and Gomorrah and the surrounding towns gave themselves up to sexual immorality and perversion. They serve as an example of those who suffer the punishment of eternal fire" (Jude 1:7). That's it—and since Jude's homiletical purpose is to preach against heretics, he is obviously not talking about homosexuality, but rather the heretical view that the coming of Christ had obviated the need to obey the law. (This is similar to other early Christian texts that link Sodom with various types of sexual misconduct, such as angels having sex with humans.)[11] To twist this linkage of Sodom and immorality into a condemnation of homosexuality simply doesn't make sense.

Classical Jewish sources follow the same pattern. The Babylonian Talmud, for example, associates Sodom with abuse of strangers, pride, envy, cruelty to orphans, theft, murder, and injustice (BT Sanhedrin 109a, BT Eruvin 49a, BT Ketubot 103a). And, as collected by Rabbi Steven Greenberg in his landmark book on Judaism and homosexuality, *Wrestling with God and Men,* there are many Jewish legends of Sodom that depict it as an extraordinarily rich, stingy, and cruel city.[13] Indeed, as Greenberg notes, only a single classical Jewish text, the *Avot de Rabbi Nathan,* links Sodom with homosexuality, and then only in one of the two extant editions of it. The rest discuss Sodom at length, but never make the association.

Where, then, does the common usage come from? The evolution is gradual. The first clear association of Sodomy and homosexuality comes not from a Christian source but a Jewish one: Philo, who uses the Sodom story to castigate Rome, characterizing both cities as places of "strong liquor, dainty feeding, and forbidden forms of intercourse."[14] The early Church fathers had various different views. Origen, for example, associates sodomy with inhospitality.[15] Chrysostom associates it with both inhospitality and homosexuality.[16] St. Jerome identifies the sins of Sodom with pride and decadence, but St. Ambrose says that Sodom's chief sins were luxury (*luxuria*) and lust (*libido*). Over the centuries, for reasons that remain unclear, the association shifted. By the time of St. Augustine, the sin had migrated to "debaucheries in men" (*stupra in masculos*). Eventually, as shown by Roman Catholic scholar Mark Jordan in his exhaustive book *The Invention of Sodomy,* the term "sodomy" (*sodomia*) was coined in the eleventh century as a new classification for certain clerical sins by theologian Peter Damian.[17] Over time, the term "sodomy" has come to be peculiarly slippery: on the one hand, it is a special vice of homosexuals, but on the other, it theoretically refers to any nonprocreative sex, and thus applies to many more straights than gays.[18]

Really, how could the tale of Sodom—a story about rape—have anything to do with a loving relationship of any kind? Does the story of David and Bathsheba, in which King David spies on Bathsheba and arranges for her husband to be killed in battle (2 Sam. 11:2–5), mean that all heterosexual relationships are similarly depraved? And what about the "echo" in Judges 19—since the men of Gibeah rape the (female) concubine, does that mean that all "heterosexuality" is forbidden by the Bible? Obviously not. Obviously, the evil of the Sodomites is rape, inhospitality, cruelty, and violence.

In any event, it should be quite clear that:

1. The Bible never links the story of Sodom with homosexuality. To use the Sodom story as evidence that the Bible condemns homosexuality is inaccurate.
2. Biblical sources, and the story itself, uniformly show that the story is about hospitality, cruelty, and so on.
3. Even if the story were about lust, it is about rape, not homosexuality. The Sodomites were not "gay." They were rapists. This is why Lot could offer his daughters as replacements, why the Judges version of the tale actually involves a female substitute.

As with *toevah,* which means not "abomination" but "taboo," the term "sodomy" is part of the problem—part of the myth of "God versus Gay." The Bible condemns many things in the story of Sodom. But homosexuality is not one of them.

CHAPTER 9

The Gospels

What Jesus didn't say about homosexuality

As we move from the Hebrew Bible to the New Testament, our consideration shifts in several ways. First, we move from what is sometimes loosely referred to as the Judeo-Christian tradition to Christianity specifically. Second, we change societies, languages, literary forms, and philosophical contexts. This is important for understanding the words of Scripture. For example, the way Paul uses words like *anomia* and *physin* is very different from how Ezekiel used Hebrew words that were translated as such. If we want to gain a close, literal understanding about what biblical texts have to say, we have to pay attention to those shifts. Finally, we move into a literary context in which not all texts are created equal. If Jesus said something recorded in the Gospels, that statement is more important than a single comment in the Epistle of Jude, or, for that matter, a superseded comment from one of the five books of Moses.

So let's start there. Here are all the statements Jesus Christ made about homosexuality:

Surprising, isn't it? Let's check again—nope, nothing, even though Jesus lived at a time when pederasty and other forms of same-sex activity were common. This silence speaks volumes. If homosexuality were an important part of Christ's message, why is it absent from it? It's not as if Jesus hesitated to critique his society, after all. If this widespread practice were so abhorrent to him, would he really be silent?

We cannot simply pass over this silence, or attribute it, as some have done, to a tacit acceptance of the Old Testament's existing rules. Jesus wasn't tacit about the values that mattered most. If regulation of homosexual behavior were one of them, the Gospels would not be silent. On the contrary, the silence indicates supersession. The Old Testament's proscriptions on male anal sex are connected to prohibitions on idolatry; they are about ritual purity, not ethical law. For Christians, the distinction is central. While the Hebrew Bible remains authoritative for moral teachings, it is not binding on Christians for ritual ones—if it were, Christians would have to avoid shrimp and lobster, wear fringed garments, and perhaps offer sacrifices instead of hymns.

The Old Testament's proscriptions on male anal sex are similar. First, as we saw in chapter 7, the Levitical rule is classified as a *toevah,* which everywhere except for the book of Proverbs has to do with ritual, cultic offenses. Second, the rule is surrounded by ritual purity codes, and is a part of ancient Israelite concerns about order and disorder, boundary and purity. Third—and this was a point originally made by John Boswell—most of the time the Septuagint translates *toevah,* it does so with the Greek word *bdelygma,* signifying a ritual/cultic violation (sixty-nine times—including Leviticus 18), rather than the word *anomia,* signifying a moral/ethical violation (seven times). By a factor of ten to one, the Septuagint understands *toevah* as a *bdelygma,* or ritual violation of Israelite monotheism.

Indeed, when it came time for the Church fathers to specify which Old Testament rules remained in force and which did not, the ban on male anal sex did not make the list. As Boswell notes, only a single early Church theologian, Clement of Alexandria, used it as a basis for his own prohibitions. All the other church fathers based their prohibitions on the texts of Romans, Corinthians, and Timothy, which we'll examine in a moment.

As we turn to the New Testament, then, we do so with practically a blank slate. In the Christian context, the prohibitions of Leviticus should be understood as superseded.[1] Like the other ritual requirements of the ancient priestly code, they should bother the faithful Christian no more than a shrimp cocktail.

Despite Jesus's silence, there are a few lessons we can glean from the Gospels regarding sexual diversity. Let's look at three of them.

The first is the story of the faithful centurion, told in Matthew 8:5–13 and Luke 7:1–10. In the story, a centurion comes to Jesus and begs that Jesus heal his servant. Jesus agrees and says he will come to the centurion's home, but the centurion says that he does not deserve to have Jesus under his roof, and has faith that if Jesus even utters a word of healing, the healing will be accomplished. Jesus praises the faith of the centurion, and the servant is healed. Obviously, the primary point of this tale is to illustrate the power and importance of faith, and how anyone, even a Roman soldier, can possess it.

Yet there is also an unmistakable same-sex subtext to this story.[2] The servant for whom the centurion pleads is more than just an ordinary servant; one would not expect a Roman centurion to intercede—let alone "beg" (*parakaloon*)—on behalf of a mere cook or housekeeper. Rather, as any contemporary reader would know, the relationship between a centurion and his favored servant is assumed to be a romantic one. The centurion's servant is a *pais,* a boy companion, not a *doulos,* a mere slave.[3] And it was common practice for Roman centurions to have younger male servants who acted as concubines as well. (The servant here is not so unlike the armor bearer in the model of David and Jonathan, which we'll explore below.) In other words, Jesus is being asked to heal not just the centurion's servant, but also his lover.

Now, the text does not record the nature of this relationship, so it is subject to interpretation. However, consider for a moment how crystal clear this relationship would have been to someone hearing the story in the first century, or witnessing it firsthand. And consider, too, the radical act of healing the centurion's servant/lover: Jesus is extending his hand not only to the centurion but to his partner as well. In addition to Jesus's silence on homosexuality in general, it speaks volumes that he did not hesitate to heal a Roman's likely same-sex lover. Like his willingness to include former prostitutes in his close circle, Jesus's engagement with those whose conduct might offend sexual mores even today is a statement of radical inclusion, and of his priorities for the spiritual life.

The second, and related, point to make is Jesus's general stance toward "family values" and the nature of his community. We are told by some religio-political pundits today that the nuclear family is the bedrock of all civilization. And indeed, I will argue in chapter 14 that full inclusion and acceptance of gays and lesbians will strengthen, not weaken, families. But as we ponder such questions, let's remember that Jesus and the apostles would, by the standards of their society, themselves be considered quite "queer," not in a sexual sense, but in terms of gender roles and societal expectations.[4] Think about it: this was someone who told people to leave their parents and follow him (Luke 14:16), to reject societal expectations of familial life and devote oneself to a different kind of community, a "family" marked by love and spiritual fellowship (Matt. 12:50). This is a savior who lived his life on the margins, and who deliberately flouted the conventions of his day. Jesus was a boundary crosser. He violated Israelite purity codes, accepted a former prostitute into his inner circle, spoke with women when others did not (John 4:27), and preached that precisely those who were most oppressed were most beloved of God.[5]

Third, let's consider Jesus's attitude toward eunuchs, who were also very queer in their societal context. Jesus identifies three types of eunuchs in Matthew 19: eunuchs from birth, eunuchs who were made that way, and "eunuchs for heaven." Now, we are not entirely certain what this means. The ordinary understanding is that a eunuch is someone who has been castrated. This practice was common in the ancient world, and eunuchs played important roles as guardians of harems and assistants to female royalty. However, Jesus is clearly not using the word in its ordinary sense, since those in the third category of eunuchs are not physically castrated but spiritually neutered, as it were, so that they can serve God. So what was meant by "eunuchs from birth"? This could mean men who are physically unable to make children, either because of impotence or birth defects such as crushed testicles.[6] But it may also mean men who are congenitally not attracted to women—people we might today call homosexual.[7] This may seem like a novel interpretation, but it is not; Clement of Alexandria, for example, believed that "some men, from their birth, have a natural sense of repulsion from a woman, and those who are naturally so constituted do well not to marry."[8] It may well be that Matthew 19:12 is referring to such men.

Even if it is not, however, it is striking that Jesus specifically recognizes, and does not judge, the presence of sexual/gender diversity among people. Some people are eunuchs, of whatever type, and they are able to refrain from marriage. Others are not, and they are permitted to marry, though it is still better not to do so: "The one who can accept [celibacy] should accept it" (Matt. 19:12). As in the story of the Ethiopian eunuch in Acts 8:26–40, God's emissary does not withhold the gospel from the gender-variant person who desires to hear it.

It would have been understandable, and perhaps more appropriate, for a Jewish teacher in occupied Palestine to emphasize ritual purity and conventional family structures. He could easily have rejected the centurion's probably sexual companion, not to mention Mary Magdalene; no one would've been surprised. Whatever Paul or the priestly writer of Leviticus has to say, let's remember that in addition to Jesus's silence on homosexuality, his actions send a clear, radical message of inclusion.

CHAPTER 10

Romans

Men not being dominant is a consequence of turning from God

The way we read the Bible's most notorious statement about homosexuality is a classic case of anachronism. In Romans 1:26-27, Paul uses a Greek word, *paraphysin*, to describe women and men violating gender roles. That word has been translated as "unnatural," and taken to mean that heterosexuality is natural and homosexuality is not. But Paul never had biology in mind—he was writing 1,500 years before the scientific revolution, and he was concerned with morality, not science. (Which is a good thing, since, as we saw in chapter 4, homosexuality is entirely natural and present in hundreds of animal species.) What's more, he isn't writing about homosexuality as we know it at all: he had no concept of sexual orientation, is actually talking about the proper hierarchy of men and women, and is critiquing lascivious sexuality, not stable relationships.

Let's take a closer look. Here is Romans 1:26–27, in the New International Version, situated in its context, beginning with verse 18:

> The wrath of God is being revealed from heaven against all the godlessness and wickedness of people, who suppress the truth by their wickedness, since what may be known about God is plain to them, because God has made it plain to them. For since the creation of the world God's invisible qualities—his eternal power and divine nature—have been clearly seen, being understood from what has been made, so that people are without excuse.
>
> For although they knew God, they neither glorified him as God nor gave thanks to him, but their thinking became futile and their foolish hearts were darkened. Although they claimed

to be wise, they became fools and exchanged the glory of the immortal God for images made to look like a mortal human being and birds and animals and reptiles.

Therefore God gave them over in the sinful desires of their hearts to sexual impurity for the degrading of their bodies with one another. They exchanged the truth about God for a lie, and worshiped and served created things rather than the Creator—who is forever praised. Amen. Because of this, God gave them over to shameful lusts. Even their women exchanged natural [*physin*] relations for unnatural [*paraphysin*] ones. In the same way the men also abandoned natural relations with women, and were inflamed with lust for one another. Men committed shameful acts with other men [*arsen*], and received in themselves the due penalty for their error.

Furthermore, just as they did not think it worthwhile to retain the knowledge of God, so God gave them over to a depraved mind, so that they do what ought not to be done. They have become filled with every kind of wickedness, evil, greed and depravity. They are full of envy, murder, strife, deceit and malice. They are gossips, slanderers, God-haters, insolent, arrogant and boastful; they invent ways of doing evil; they disobey their parents; they have no understanding, no fidelity, no love, no mercy. Although they know God's righteous decree that those who do such things deserve death, they not only continue to do these very things but also approve of those who practice them.

As biblical commentators have explained, Paul's purpose, here at the beginning of the epistle to the Christian community in Rome, is to explain that the pagan Romans, wealthy and powerful though they are, have no excuse for turning away from God. Though they did not have the particular revelation at Mount Sinai and did not have the direct witness of Christ, Paul insists that the Romans should know the basics of revelation because God's power and nature "have been clearly seen" in the order of nature itself. The Romans, who claim to be such philosophers, are in fact willfully ignorant of the truth of God, and worship idols and images. Because of the Romans' willful ignorance, God "gave them over" to shameful, unnatural lusts of the body—including some kind of homosexual desire—and also to a depraved mind, which is why they became filled with wickedness, evil, greed, and depravity.

This is not exactly a celebration of sexual diversity. However, even before we turn to the language of verses 26 and 27, their context should be clear. Paul is not preaching that homosexuality is a sin—he is preaching that some form of illicit homosexual behavior is a *consequence* of sin. Whatever sexual behavior Paul is writing about, it is the symptom, not the cause, of the Romans' failure: the Romans turned from God, and *therefore* (*dio*) God gave them over to sexual immorality (Rom. 1:24). This is like a parent telling a child, "If you don't wear your jacket, you'll get a cold." Obviously, getting a cold is not desirable, but it's not the sin. The real sin is not wearing a coat, or, more generally, not being careful. Likewise, it's not the sexual behavior that's the focus of Paul's attack; it's the failure of the Romans to recognize God.[1] Sexual immorality is one of many consequences that flow from that fatal error. It's not the sin; it's the consequence.

Does Romans 1:26 prohibit lesbianism, as some have suggested? We don't actually know. There was an awareness of lesbianism in the ancient world, and many Greek and Roman (male) authorities regulated, ridiculed, and even pathologized it, understanding it as women trying to be like men.[2] Paul may have drawn on these Greek and Roman concepts here. However, contemporary Jewish sources did not regard lesbianism as sex at all, because sex was defined, in that male-centered culture, as penetration by a penis. Indeed, St. Augustine interprets verse 26 as being about heterosexuality, not lesbianism.[3] But if Paul isn't speaking of women having sexual relations with one another, what does he have in mind?

The key here is the word *physin,* meaning "natural," and its opposite, *paraphysin.* To our twenty-first century eyes, "natural" probably means what happens in nature. And indeed, Paul's use of *paraphysin* —*contra naturam,* against nature, in the Latin—has given support to anti-gay writers who have called homosexuality "unnatural" in some scientific sense. Today, this interpretation poses a problem, because we now know that homosexuality is in fact quite natural, found in hundreds of animal species. But in fact, Paul never intended this sense of the word at all. Our use of the term "nature" derives from the scientific revolution—it's anachronistic to project it onto Paul. There are two alternatives we will explore here.

The first possibility is that the use of *physin* is like what later became known as natural law: the basic principles, observable from nature and reason, that teach us morality.[4] Paul did not have the rich concept of natural law that Catholic teaching has today, but he did set forth a clear schema in which the body is naturally to be subjugated to the spirit, the letter of the law is to be subjugated to the spirit of the law,[5] and women are to be subjugated to men (more on that in a moment). What this has meant, for most of Church history, is that any nonprocreative sex is "unnatural," because it elevates physical pleasure over spiritual and uses the body for something other than its intended use. Homosexuality, masturbation, oral sex, and sex with birth control are all equally unnatural in this sense.[6]

That being said, Paul obviously does single out some specific forms of behavior in Romans 1:26–27—and this brings us back to the roles of men and women. For Paul, as for two millennia of Christian theologians, part of the "natural" order is that men should dominate women. This view is not unique to Paul, of course. Many societies have held similarly lamentable views, including Paul's own Jewish and Roman contemporaries. In the Roman case, the proper hierarchy of gender roles even affected how homosexuality was regulated. As is well known, Roman culture encouraged certain forms of male homosexual behavior, but only when free, adult men were dominant. Adult free males could penetrate slaves (of any gender), and men could penetrate women. But, as scholar Bernadette Brooten writes, "free, adult males ought never be passive, and women should never be active . . . [and] should they transgress these boundaries, society deemed their behavior "contrary to nature" (*para physin*)."[7]

This, then, is what Paul means by "unnatural": when women are active, and men are passive. This is also why males having sex with males is "unnatural": because it involves a man taking the woman's role, which is a violation of how things are meant to be. Remember that in Paul's time, as in many cultures today, the real offense of male homosexuality is not that two men are involved, but that one man is taking on the "female" role in sexual intercourse. In fact, Paul's language is strikingly similar to that of the Jewish/Hellenistic philosopher Philo, who said that in Sodom (i.e., Rome), "they accustomed those who were by nature men to submit to play the part of women."[8] Contrary to popular clichés about ancient Rome, this was stigmatized even then: for example, Julius Caesar was relentlessly mocked for taking the receptive role in his relationship with Nicomedes, the king of Bithynia (one such jibe: "Caesar conquered Gaul, Nicomedes Caesar"), and the taking of the receptive role relative to a man of inferior rank was actually criminalized.[9] Here is Brooten again: "'natural' intercourse means penetration of a subordinate person by a dominant one."[10] That's what Paul is talking about—in the same words, in the same culture, at the same time. And this helps us understand what Paul means in the otherwise cryptic verse 29: "they received in themselves the due penalty for their error." The punishment not only fits the crime—the punishment, being penetrated, being "made into a woman," *is* the crime.

Now, in an age of female (vice) presidential candidates, do we still believe that for women to ever rule over men is unnatural? Of course not. Categories like *physin* are culturally specific, and most of us have already set aside this particular iteration of it. To put it simply, in the worldview of Romans 1:26–27, homosexuality is exactly as unnatural as Sarah Palin.[11]

It is also possible (though not certain) that Paul isn't condemning homosexuality in general, but has in mind the predominant form of homosexual behavior practiced in Rome, namely, pederasty. It's striking that Paul uses a particular Greek word, *arsen,* for his condemnation in verse 27. *Arsen* is a generic Greek word for "male." The word for "men," as in adult men, is *aner* (ἀνήρ). Thus Paul is specifically *not* using the term for men having sexual relations with other men. He is using the term for males having sexual relations with males. Given what we know about Roman sexual mores at the time Paul was writing, this predominantly meant adult men having sex with young adolescent males. Since, as we have observed, many other forms of male–male sexual behavior were already frowned upon in contemporary Roman society surely what Paul had in mind was not what the Romans disdained, but what they approved of: pederasty.[12]

John Boswell and other scholars propose an alternative reading of *physin* that is important to note as well. Boswell claims that, for Paul, one can only speak of "natural" in terms of "natural *for.*" It is natural for cows to eat grass, for example, but not for humans to do so. Likewise, what Paul is condemning is same-sex behavior (chiefly pederasty) engaged in by presumptively heterosexual people, for whom it is not natural. The principle Boswell relies upon is Aquinas's: "Because of the diverse conditions of humans, it happens that some acts are virtuous to some people, as appropriate and suitable to them, while the same acts are immoral for others, as inappropriate to them."[13] Paul does not discuss people for whom homosexuality is natural; to them, his condemnation simply does not apply.[14] In the words of Rev. Michael Piazza, "From dogs to dolphins, same-gender sexual attraction is a reality. What is 'natural' for one individual may be a direct violation of another's nature. We, who God has created, have an obligation to live out, as fully as possible, the nature with which God has created us. To do otherwise is unhealthy and an insult to God."[15]

This reading comports with the fact that, elsewhere, what is *para physin* can actually be good. In Romans 11:24, for example, Paul describes how God prunes the gentiles from a wild tree, and grafts them onto the cultivated olive tree of God's people. This kind of graft is "contrary to nature," but it is not a bad thing.[16] The moral valence of *para physin* depends on its effects. In Romans 1, it is part of a nation turning aside from God and doing what is not natural for them to do. In Romans 11, it is part of God's plan itself.

The key term in Romans 1:26–27, for Boswell's reading and my own, is *paradidomi*—meaning "gave them over." This is the same term used in Matthew 17:22 (and elsewhere) to describe Christ being given over to the Romans.[17] Gay people are not "given over" to homosexuality as a consequence of something else; they're just gay. Let me speak from personal experience. Like many gay people, my experience is that I was born this way. I am right-handed, I have hazel eyes, I am gay. All of these traits seem, in my experience, to be equally inherent in who I am. Nor was I given over to homosexuality because of something that happened to me. I was not abused as a child, I was not "recruited" into the "gay lifestyle." You'll search my biography in vain for any causes that gave me over to homosexuality.

But I do have experience of being given over to unhealthy forms of sexuality, what Paul might call "shameful lusts," as a consequence of my own turning away from God. Ironically, this was precisely when I repressed my sexual identity. I turned away from God for ten years when I was in the closet: I was lying to other people about who I was, I was repressing the parts of myself that should have led me to love, and I was throwing away the gifts God had given me. And sure enough, I was given over to lusts that caused me great shame. The only people I could have sex with were strangers, in fleeting, risky encounters that might work fine for some people but which left me feeling empty, fearful, and degraded. I couldn't form relationships. And I was a liar, like the countless closeted preachers and politicians who have been discovered to be carrying on illicit affairs with prostitutes, drug dealers, or even adolescents. Fortunately, I never sank to the depths of a Ted Haggard or an Eddie Long; I never abused my own students or parishioners, and never had sex with minors. But I do understand how someone can be given over to what many of us would agree are exploitative and harmful behaviors. Understood in this way, this passage from Romans makes perfect sense to me. Indeed, I lived it, until I finally came out.

I'm suggesting that Paul's meaning here is that the Romans turned their backs on God, and as a result were *given over* to various forms of immorality, including sex that Paul understood as unnatural (*paraphysin*) because it violated the natural roles of men (active, dominant) and women (passive, submissive). Paul is not singling out homosexual activity as a sin (it is a consequence, not a cause), not referring to gay people as we understand them today (who cannot be "given over" to homosexuality), not referring to loving and sacred forms of same-sexual expression (since he specifically describes the lusts as "shameful"), and possibly not referring to adult homosexuality at all (since pederasty was the predominant form of homosexuality in Rome, and Paul uses the general term *arsen*). That is the extent of the condemnation.

This reading accords with Paul's overall agenda and worldview, with the literary context of the passage, with the Roman context that he was addressing, with what we understand about the naturalness of sexual diversity, and with the lived experience of millions of gay people. Paul is attempting to draw a boundary between the Christian and pagan communities in Rome and using gender roles as the place to draw that boundary.[18] While today our understanding of what is natural for men and women has obviously evolved, the passage still has poignancy today, and warns how someone can be "given over" to troubling sexual behaviors as a result of turning away from truth and love. Paul makes sense.

One could also read Romans as prohibiting homosexuality of all kinds. But then one has to answer a host of difficult questions. First, why doesn't Paul explicitly prohibit it? If homosexuality is the sin rather than the consequence, why is it presented, to use the analogy from above, as the catching of a cold and not the failure to wear a jacket? Second, how do we square a blanket condemnation of homosexuality with the Roman context that Paul was addressing? Was he just misinformed? Third, if *paraphysin* means "unnatural" in some scientific sense, why doesn't Paul ever use the term in that sense anywhere else in the Bible? And how *do* we square a scientific meaning of "unnatural" with the scientific evidence about homosexuality in animals and the lived experience that sexuality is often not a choice? Fourth, how do we reconcile Paul's language about being "given over" with the experience of millions of people that their sexuality is a trait? Are millions of people so completely deluded? Fifth, how can we understand all homosexual behavior to be "shameful lust" when there are happy, stable same-sex people, couples and families, and grace so obviously operates in their lives? And finally, how can we square a blanket condemnation of all homosexual behavior with the fundamental religious values we explored in part 1?

The supposedly "plain" reading of Paul raises so many unanswerable questions that it is clearly not the plain reading at all. It raises more problems than it solves. In contrast, if we understand Paul according to both the details of Greek vocabulary and the larger context of Paul's overall project, everything makes sense. This is a condemnation of the ways in which Roman men were "feminized" in a "shameful" way, as a result of turning away from God. This has nothing to do with gays or lesbians as we know them today; it's about the consequences of turning away from God, for a population engaged in sex where men are "degraded." And let's recall that the real concern here is drawing a boundary between the Christian community and the general Roman one; *they* do these things, and so *we* do not. Not only is this reading of Paul more compassionate, and thus more in line with the values we explored in part 1; it makes more sense on its own terms as well.

We don't have to twist biblical texts into pretzels. If we simply read these verses on their own terms, they are far narrower and far less clear than we are sometimes led to believe. We merely need to look with new eyes at this old text, and the truth will set us free.

CHAPTER 11

Corinthians and Timothy

Christians should not mingle with a pagan,
idolatrous, lascivious society

There are two other mentions of possible same-sex activity in the
New Testament: 1 Corinthians 6:9 and 1 Timothy 1:10. As in Romans, homosexuality (if that's what it is) is mentioned only in passing
in these verses, which are part of larger sections about different subjects. We'll look at each one in turn.

First, here's the full passage from 1 Corinthians 6:1–11, in the
New International Version:

> If any of you has a dispute with another, dare he take it before
> the ungodly for judgment instead of before the saints? Do you
> not know that the saints will judge the world? And if you are
> to judge the world, are you not competent to judge trivial
> cases? Do you not know that we will judge angels? How much
> more the things of this life! Therefore, if you have disputes
> about such matters, appoint as judges even men of little ac-
> count in the church! I say this to shame you. Is it possible that
> there is nobody among you wise enough to judge a dispute be-
> tween believers? But instead, one brother goes to law against
> another—and this in front of unbelievers!
>
> The very fact that you have lawsuits among you means
> you have been completely defeated already. Why not rather be
> wronged? Why not rather be cheated? Instead, you yourselves
> cheat and do wrong, and you do this to your brothers. Do
> you not know that the wicked will not inherit the kingdom
> of God? Do not be deceived: Neither the sexually immoral

[*pornos*] nor idolaters nor adulterers [*moichos*] nor male prostitutes [*malakoi*] nor homosexual offenders [*arsenokoitai*] nor
thieves nor the greedy nor drunkards nor slanderers nor swindlers will inherit the kingdom of God. And that is what some
of you were. But you were washed, you were sanctified, you
were justified in the name of the Lord Jesus Christ and by the
Spirit of our God.

Here, Paul is writing to the Christian community in Corinth, a
city widely known to be among the lewdest, sleaziest places in the
Roman Empire; ancient Corinth would make Las Vegas look like
Disneyland. In addition, Christian Corinth was witnessing a "liti-
gation explosion," and members of the Christian community were
bringing their disputes before the secular courts. Paul inveighs against
this practice. First, it evinces a lack of faith; Christians should bring
disputes before saints. Second, believers should not have their cases
decided by unbelievers—they should settle matters themselves. Third,
true believers should prefer being wronged over settling a dispute
in court. The real reward and punishment are meted out not in this
world, but in the kingdom of God, and sinners—including four types
of sexual sinners and six types of non-sexual ones—will not inherit
the kingdom of God. Finally, Paul reminds the Corinthian Christians
that they themselves were once sinners before accepting the salvation
of Christ.

As in Romans, this passage is part of a larger sermon about the
boundaries between the Christian community and the wider world.
And as in Romans, the "wider world" is here accused of every form
of wickedness under the sun, including some forms of sexual lasciviousness. Now let's again look closely at the key terms in the passage.

First, whatever the *arsenokoitai* do, it is no better and no worse than
getting drunk, or gossiping. Not laudatory behavior, but hardly fire-
and-brimstone evil either. Second, women, unlike in Romans, are
totally absent from this condemnation. Both *malakoi* and *arsenokoitai*
are men, grammatically and definitionally. We may group gay men
and lesbians together—but in Corinthians, as in Leviticus, the only
targets of opprobrium are men.

Third, it is obvious that Paul is talking about sexual lasciviousness and immorality generally, not homosexuality. This isn't "God

versus Gay"—it's God versus sexual licentiousness.[1] This chapter of 1 Corinthians contains a laundry list of sinful behaviors. Obviously it's not about homosexuality, and certainly not same-sex relationships. Condemning a lesbian couple in church on the basis of Corinthians is like condemning a straight couple on the basis of a judgment about pornography or rape.

So, who are the *malakoi* and *arsenokoitai*? We don't really know.[2] As for *malakoi* (μαλακοί), the term has been translated as "effeminate" (King James Version), "weaklings" (Tyndale), and "boy prostitutes" (New American Bible). *Malakos* literally means "soft."[3] The term appears in some Roman contexts as referring (in a derogatory way) to people who wore makeup, acted effeminate, and habitually took the passive role in same-sex intercourse.[4] Surprisingly, however, according to Boswell, who cites a number of Catholic sources, "the unanimous tradition of the church through the Reformation, and of Catholicism until well into the twentieth century, has been that this word applied to masturbation,"[5] not homosexuality, since such indulgent behavior was seen as "soft" or "effeminate." Indeed, it is striking that many early Christian condemnations of homosexuality rely on Romans exclusively, not Corinthians.[6] Others have suggested that *malakoi* were not unlike the *qedeshim* of the Hebrew Bible: not ordinary prostitutes (*pornos,* a word Paul uses earlier in the verse) but sacred prostitutes connected to idolatry.

Unlike *malakoi,* the word *arsenokoitai* (ἀρσενοκοῖται) seems to be Paul's invention. It's a compound word made up of the word for "male" and "have sex," and scholars believe it was Paul's neologism for men who have sex with men, based on the Septuagint's translation of Leviticus 18:22. Yet the scope of the term is unclear. First, since *arsenokoitai* is derived from Leviticus, it means only as much as *mishkevei ishah* means: if Leviticus only refers to male anal sex, then *arsenokoitai* does as well. As for the people Paul is writing about, a variety of interpretations have been proposed. Based on one of the understandings of *malakoi* discussed above, Biblical scholar Robin Scroggs's reading is that *malakoi* are sacred prostitutes who take the receptive role, and that *arsenokoitai* are those men who take the insertive role in the same cultic practice. He says that "the words point to a very specific form of pederasty,"[7] and should be translated as "male prostitutes and males who lie with them."[8] Boswell, as noted above, says that *malakoi* refers to masturbation, and that *arsenokoitai* refers to "male sexual agents, i.e., active male prostitutes, who were common throughout the Hellenistic world in the time of Paul."[9] (Boswell observes that there need be no real connection between the two; after all, there is no particular connection between drunkards and slanderers either.) Or perhaps, if *arsenokoitai* does, as the etymological evidence suggests, refer back to Leviticus, then the term should be limited to male anal sex within a cultic context. Several scholars have suggested such definitions.[10]

Really, what is Paul writing about in these verses? He's critiquing an entire society, and "shaming" Christians for continuing to associate with it. Paul specifically mentions "idolaters" in between *pornos* (sexually immoral), and *moichos* (adulterers), *malakoi,* and *arsenokoitai.* Is. this just an accident? Surely not. Surely what Paul is talking about here is an entire "pagan" culture in which idolatry and lasciviousness went hand-in-hand. Paul was painting, with a broad brush, a society of depravity. People sinned sexually in every possible configuration: adultery, general immorality, general looseness of morals, and some kind of cultic homosexuality or prostitution as well. Just as in Romans, where these transgressions were the signs of a society that had turned away from God, here they are listed as signs of a society whose judges are not to be trusted and whose values are not to be emulated.

Certainly, in this litany of lusts, we do not see anything resembling stable, sanctified same-sex relationships. Here the situation is similar to that of the Sodom story. Whoever Paul is describing, they are lust-filled, immoral people who have turned their backs on God. Now, is that true of lesbians and gays today? Not all of them. Therefore, they can't possibly accord with these obscure Greek terms. As scholar Martti Nissinen has written, "the modern concept of 'homosexuality' should by no means be read into Paul's text, nor can we assume that Paul's words in I Corinthians 6:9 'condemn all homosexual relations' in all times and places and ways. The meanings of the word are too vague to justify this claim, and Paul's words should not be used for generalizations that go beyond his experience and world."[11]

Corinthians, then, resembles Leviticus and Romans. It is plausible to read both texts as condemning all (male) homosexuality—but it is not necessary to do so. And it is necessary *not* to do so if these verses are to coexist with hundreds of other ones that talk about love, companionship, holiness, family, justice, and compassion. Once again, the point is not that the more compassionate readings of these texts are absolutely, definitely correct. The point is that they are plausible, and because of our fundamental religious values, they are necessary.

In the case of Corinthians, (1) the text isn't about homosexuality, but about submitting to pagan law; (2) the listed sins aren't about sexual acts per se but the abuse of sexuality in the context of an immoral pagan society; (3) it's reasonable (though not conclusive) to read *malakoi* and *arsenokoitai* as being about idolatry, pederasty, and prostitution; (4) since *arsenokoitai* appears to derive from Leviticus, this is further evidence that the prohibition is on sexuality connected to cultic, idolatrous worship; (5) for the same reason, it is limited to male anal sex, and not homosexuality broadly; (6) *malakoi* may have nothing to do with homosexuality at all; and (7) even if *arsenokoitai* means "males who have sex with males" in general, the condemnation is only as severe as that against drunkards and swindlers.

The passage in 1 Timothy is similar in structure and in theme. There, Paul is depicted as again preaching on the validity of the law.[12] Once again, the crux of the argument has nothing to do with homosexuality, and *arsenokoitai* are again mentioned in a laundry list of sinners. The passage in 1 Timothy 1:8–10 reads as follows:

> The goal of this command is love, which comes from a pure heart and a good conscience and a sincere faith. Some have wandered away from these and turned to meaningless talk. They want to be teachers of the law, but they do not know what they are talking about or what they so confidently affirm. We know that the law is good if one uses it properly. We also know that the law is made not for the righteous but for lawbreakers and rebels, the ungodly and sinful, the unholy and irreligious; for those who kill their fathers or mothers, for murderers, for adulterers and *arsenokoitai,* for slave traders and liars and perjurers—and for whatever else is contrary to the sound doctrine that conforms to the glorious gospel of the blessed God, which he entrusted to me.

Readers of Paul will immediately recognize these themes. Grace, love, and faith are the essence of religious life; adherence to the law is not. Thus, while the written, external law can be used properly for good, it is "made" for the irreligious, and is to be transcended.

It is important that in Timothy, unlike in Corinthians and Romans, *arsenokoitai* are here paired with adulterers (*moichos*). This is a crucial juxtaposition. As in the language of Romans about being "given over to shameful lusts," the parallel structure between *arsenokoitai* and *moichos* suggests that it is extramarital lust that is being condemned here. Just as an adulterer is not a "heterosexual" but rather someone who violates the sanctity of marriage by having sex with a woman, so too *arsenokoitai* are not "homosexuals" but those who violate the sanctity of marriage by having sex with a man. The issue is less the physical act itself than the context: sex outside of marriage. The social context of an act changes the moral valence of an act. Killing a person is murder; killing in self-defense is not. Sex with a woman outside of marriage is condemned; the same sex act inside of marriage is celebrated. And sex with a man that stems from infidelity, or lust, or turning away from God earns Paul's condemnation; but the same act engaged in as part of a sacred, life-affirming relationship is simply not what he is talking about.

In a sense, 1 Timothy brings together the themes from Corinthians and Romans. Once again, this supposed condemnation of homosexuality is not actually about homosexuality at all. Romans is about turning away from God, Corinthians is about turning away from God's saints and toward pagan courts, and Timothy is about turning away from God's grace and backsliding toward the law. All have as their focus the boundaries between the Christian community and the outside world. In all three cases, there is no question that some men who have sex with men are condemned. But the condemnations come in roundabout, limited, and contextualized ways. Neither Jesus nor Paul nor anyone else in the New Testament preaches directly against gay people.

Now, some preachers act as if the only kind of gay sex is the lascivious, pornographic, or sleazy kind. But that's just patently untrue. Long-term, committed gay relationships are not so different from long-term, committed straight ones, in terms of grace, love, holiness, sanctity, passion, and spirituality. Yet can you imagine condemning all heterosexual relationships because of rape? We all know that sexuality is powerful, and can be used for good or ill. And we all reach judgments about what kinds of sexuality are harmful or beneficial for us. Yet the axis of distinction—the line between good and bad—surely is not the homosexual/heterosexual one. *Arsenokoitai* are lustful, lascivious, possibly idolatrous men who were ruled by lust. They have as much in common with a loving gay man as a rapist or an adulterer has with a loving straight man.

Causality is important too. Whatever Paul is talking about here, it is definitely not the modern notion of homosexual orientation, since the concept was unknown to him. Paul is talking about an appetite, not an orientation. Just as there is no "orientation" toward slander, there is no orientation toward whatever same-sex acts Paul is condemning here; the inclusion of *arsenokoitai* in the laundry lists of Corinthians and Timothy is proof that Paul is not talking about sexual orientation but about lustful acts, possibly in the context of idolatry. And in Romans, he even explains the reason why they take place: because the Romans have turned away from monotheism. The rejection of God is the cause of their behavior, not sexual orientation or for that matter any of the bogus pseudoscientific explanations proffered by contemporary ex-gay propagandists. The *arsenokoitai* are not men who weren't adequately loved by their distant fathers! They are men who rejected God and have fallen into depravity.

The only way that Romans, Corinthians, and Timothy can be read as blanket prohibitions on male homosexuality (let alone lesbianism) is to read individual phrases out of context, in translation, and without attention to what Paul is actually writing about. In all cases, the specific scope and language of the verses are unclear. As with Leviticus, where seemingly disconnected verses about Molech worship and male anal sex become comprehensible when understood in terms of Leviticus's larger themes, so too do these seemingly random references, scattered across three epistles and never addressed with any real focus, now begin to make sense. Paul isn't condemning homosexuality; he's doing what he usually does, which is to insist on the internal, natural law of love; the salvation of the spirit; the grace of the New Covenant. These are familiar themes, and Paul's inclusion of wanton male lasciviousness in that context makes perfect sense. Homosexuality is not a concern for Paul. Male lascivious sexuality is.

In case we have lost the larger picture in the details of Greek grammar, you are reading these words in the context of great suffering—

if not your own, if not within your family, then certainly within your community. There are people ashamed of who they are, or who their relatives are, and who believe that they are "glorifying God in the body" (1 Cor. 6:20) by lying, and by repressing and ultimately distorting their sexuality into forms that may be hideous even to themselves. Does God want this?

Could I have written this part of the book before the first part? As an academic enterprise, I think that my textual readings are intellectually sound and historically tenable. But who would care? The only reason we take this fresh look at Scripture is that faith and conscience demand it. We are called to love, and love calls us to look again at what we thought we knew. But when we do that, something remarkable happens. The miracle—and I often believe it really is just that—is that we don't need to read these verses out of the Bible, or twist them beyond recognition, because on close inspection, these "clobber texts" just don't mean what many suppose them to mean. The great conflict between God and gay, between fidelity to Scripture and the love of ourselves, our friends, and our family, doesn't arise. In a strange and unexpected way, these misused verses from thousands of years ago reveal the timeless truth that inspired them.

CHAPTER 12

David and Jonathan

Love between men in the Bible

One of the more painful aspects of growing up gay is invisibility. Fortunately, today, with the Internet and mass culture, few gay and lesbian kids are likely to grow up believing that they're the only people like them in the world. But there's still a myth that homosexuality simply appeared on the world stage when it was first named 120 years ago. As if the only people who ever lived were Adam and Eve, or Romeo and Juliet.

We now know this is not true. There are historical documents from all time periods and all cultures that attest to the existence of same-sex relationships throughout history. Some of this evidence was hiding in plain sight; after all, the author of *Romeo and Juliet* also wrote sonnets to a young man. Some of this evidence was deliberately buried; did you know the painters of the Sistine Chapel and the *Mona Lisa* would today be identified as gay? And some of the evidence, though ample, is still hotly contested—about American icons like James Dean, Abraham Lincoln, Eleanor Roosevelt, and Walt Whitman, for example. We'll look at a few of these cases in chapter 15.

Visibility is especially important within the Bible. That is why this part of the book would not be complete if we did not discuss the Bible's clearest expression of same-gender love, the story of David and Jonathan. No, David was not "gay." He had numerous love affairs with women (often troubled and ethically dubious), as well as one with a man. But labels are not the point; this is a tale of two men who were in love with one another, who expressed that love physically, and who are an essential part of the Bible's overall depiction of love between people.

Before turning to the story, two prefatory notes are important.

First, there are other stories of same-sex love in the Bible, but I have chosen to focus on this one because it is the one that most likely contained a physical component. I recognize that this choice is problematic, because it may exclude other, nonsexual forms of same-sex intimacy, particularly among women. The story of Ruth and Naomi, for example, is one of the Bible's rare explorations of love between women. Ruth is clearly devoted to her mother-in-law, and her poetic words—"Wherever you go, I will go"—have been an inspiration to lovers of all configurations over the centuries.[1] Likewise, the pairs of female emissaries in the New Testament, Tryphaina and Tryphosa (Rom. 16:12) and Euhodia and Syntyche (Phil. 4:1), indicate, at the very least, deep friendships between women. If we take seriously the notion of the "lesbian continuum" mentioned in chapter 1,[2] that may be enough, and many religious scholars have applied it to these stories.[3] In the case of Ruth and Naomi, "here we have two women who made vows, lived together for life, loved each other deeply, adopted each other's extended families as their own, and relied on each other for substance—as do many lesbian women today. Instead of condemning these relationships, the Bible celebrates them, giving them their own book in Scripture."[4] In focusing more extensively on David and Jonathan, I do not want to repeat the mistakes of many other male scholars who overlook, distort, or minimize these sacred, loving relationships among women.

Second, this telling of the story of David and Jonathan is not meant to offer any commentary on the meaning of Leviticus. The Hebrew Bible contains both legal and narrative material, and often the two contradict one another. For example, Deuteronomy 7:3 explicitly forbids an Israelite from marrying foreign women. Yet King Solomon did so, and the text does not judge him for it. The dietary laws of Leviticus seem in direct contradiction to the menu offered by Abraham to the angels in Genesis 18:8. Abraham and Sarah were half siblings according to Genesis 20:12, which means their marriage transgresses the incest laws of Leviticus 18:9–11. Likewise with Moses's parents, who were nephew and aunt (Exod. 6:20 vs. Lev. 18:12).[5] The Hebrew Bible does not speak with one voice, and we should not assume the writer (or Writer) of Leviticus has the same agenda as the book of Samuel. These are two voices in the biblical conversation. What the David and Jonathan story does tell us is that the Bible knew of, and presented affirmatively, a wide range of emotional and erotic possibilities for its male heroes—and that all of us have something to learn from them.

The story of David and Jonathan begins in the first book of Samuel, chapter 16. There, God rejects Saul as king of Israel and instructs the prophet Samuel to anoint a son of Jesse in his place. Samuel passes over all seven of Jesse's elder sons, finally coming to the youngest, David, a teenaged shepherd described in 1 Samuel 16:12 as "beautiful to the eyes and good to behold." David is anointed with oil, and "the spirit of God came upon David from that day forward." Yet just as the holy spirit comes to David, it departs from Saul, who is soon "troubled by an evil spirit from God." Saul's servants suggest that he find someone to soothe him by playing the harp—and eventually bring him David, now described not merely as a shepherd but "a skillful musician, valiant warrior, man of war, wise in speech, and attractive man—and God is with him." And so, "David came to Saul and stood before him, and he loved him very much, and he became his armor-bearer."

The term "armor-bearer" (*nosei keilim*) is an important one, and would be immediately recognized by a contemporary reader of the book of Samuel. In Mediterranean cultures of the time, the armor-bearer is essentially the hero's sidekick. Ancient examples of hero and armor-bearer include Achilles and Patroclus in the *Iliad,* and Gilgamesh and Enkidu in *The Epic of Gilgamesh.*[6] (For a contemporary analogue, if you like, you can think of Batman and Robin.) Moreover, as we noted in chapter 9, it was widely understood that the hero would be older, stronger—and generally in love with his younger companion. This love had a sexual component as part of the overall relationship. In Greece, the relationship was one of *erastes* (the older, dominant partner who would take the active sexual role) and *eromenos* (the younger partner who would take the receptive role), and it is immortalized on vases, in poetry, and throughout the culture that also gave us democracy, philosophy, athletics, and the dramatic arts.

The armor-bearer relationship appears several times in the book of Samuel. In chapter 16, Saul's son Jonathan has an armor-bearer who speaks to him in surprisingly amorous language: "Do all that is in your heart; turn, and I am with you as your own heart" (1 Sam.

16:7). Later, when Saul dies in chapter 31, his armor-bearer falls on his sword (1 Sam. 31:5). Clearly, the armor-bearer relationship described here is a close, personal bond. Now, whether it included a sexual bond, as it did elsewhere in the Mediterranean context, is not specified. But this was a familiar, conventional relationship at the time. Moreover, the erotic element of it is hinted at here by the fact that David's sole qualification for the job is that he's good-looking. After God's spirit descends on David, he is regarded in other ways, but before that, he seems to be chosen purely because he is attractive. But all this is prologue—let's get back to the story.

In the next chapter, the Philistines, the Israelites' great enemy, unveil their great hero, Goliath. All the Israelites are terrified of him, including King Saul, but David—who originally went to the front lines to deliver cheese to the Israelite warriors—is unafraid. David even rejects Saul's armor, and faces Goliath with just a staff, a sling, and five stones. Goliath is insulted that the Israelites have sent a mere boy to fight him—but, as we all know, David slays Goliath, and leads the Israelites to a routing of the Philistine army.

David returns a hero and is installed in the royal court. And now the story takes a new turn: "When [David] finished speaking with Saul, the soul of Jonathan was knit with the soul of David, and Jonathan loved him as his own soul . . . Jonathan and David made a covenant, because he loved him as his own soul. And Jonathan stripped himself of the robe that was on him, and gave it to David—and his sword, and his bow, and his girdle" (1 Sam. 18:1–3). Like his father, Jonathan has fallen in love with David—but unlike Saul's, this love is described in passionate terms. Jonathan's soul is knit together with David's, and Jonathan loves him dearly. And then, curiously, he strips naked. Why? Some readers of the story suppose this is a sexual reference, but it is not what they suppose. Saul has already adopted David as his armor-bearer—and now Jonathan has done the same thing. The text is setting up a love triangle between the three men but Jonathan's love of David is different from Saul's. David doesn't do anything for Jonathan, he's not being hired to play the harp—Jonathan loves him freely, and in a much deeper way than Saul does.

Meanwhile, Saul becomes jealous of David, who is being lauded as a hero by the Israelites, and begins to plot against him. Saul makes

David an army captain and promises his daughter Michal in marriage if David emerges victorious, all the while hoping that the Philistines will kill him. Yet David triumphs and marries Michal, who, like Jonathan, has fallen in love with him. (Michal's love is not described in similarly powerful terms; the text in 18:20 merely states, "And Michal, Saul's daughter, loved David.")

David's two lovers, Jonathan and Michal, each save his life from their vengeful father. First, Saul tells Jonathan that David should be killed, but "Jonathan, the son of Saul, delighted in David very much" (1 Sam. 19:1), and he pleads successfully on his behalf. Then, after Saul becomes enraged again, Michal helps David escape from the royal court—through a window, no less—into the wilderness. In chapter 20, Jonathan visits him, promising "Whatever your soul asks, I will do it for you." David is terrified, and, at David's request, the two make an alliance, Jonathan promising to notify David of any threats to his life.

Verse 17 then reads: "And Jonathan added, to swear his love to David, because he loved him as he loved his own soul." Jonathan and David have already sworn their military pact; this, the text specifies, is in addition to that. *V'yosif,* the text says: Jonathan added something extra. This is a pact of love. And notice, throughout, that it is Jonathan who is in love with David—not necessarily the reverse. Through this point in the story, David is obtaining various tangible benefits from Jonathan, but Jonathan is not gaining anything from David. Once again the text goes out of its way to describe Jonathan's love for David as something more than mere friendship and certainly more than an alliance.

Saul knows it too. When David fails to appear at court for a feast, Jonathan makes an excuse for him. Saul replies, enraged: "You perverse and rebellious son! Behold, I know that you have chosen the son of Jesse to your shame, and the shame of your mother's nakedness! For as long as the son of Jesse lives on the Earth, you and your kingdom shall not be established" (1 Sam. 20:30–31). The second line of Saul's admonition frames Jonathan's action in dynastic terms—but the first is clearly sexualized. Jonathan has chosen David to his shame—the Hebrew root is *bushah.* As if that weren't clear enough, Saul emphatically calls Jonathan "perverse" and adds that his love affair with David is to the "shame of your mother's nakedness," *ervat imecha,* a term that unambiguously refers to sexual sins. Back in Leviticus 18, the prohibitions on incest use identical language: *ervat imecha* appears in verse 7. There is no question, reading verse 30, that Saul is scolding Jonathan for a sexual relationship.

Jonathan and David's last meeting, as David is about to go into hiding, is recorded at the end of chapter 20: "David came up from the south and fell on his face to the ground, and bowed three times. And each man kissed one another, and each man cried with one another, until David gained composure. And Jonathan said to David: 'Go in peace, as the two of us have sworn in the name of God, saying God will be between me and you, and between my seed and your seed, forever'" (1 Sam. 20:41–42).

This is the last time the two would see one another alive. For the next ten chapters, the book of Samuel recounts David's flight from Saul, their occasional encounters, and finally Saul's and Jonathan's deaths in a battle with the Philistines. The scene is heartbreaking. Jonathan has risked his own life for the man he loves, and even David is moved to tears. But it is only when Jonathan dies that David finally realizes how much Jonathan meant to him. His lamentation, contained in 2 Samuel 1:18–27, is famous even today. It reads, in part:

> How the mighty are fallen, in the midst of the battle! Jonathan, gone upon your high places. I am grieved for you, my brother Jonathan, you were so dear to me. Your love for me was more wonderful than the love of women. How the mighty are fallen, gone are the instruments of war.

Thus ends the story, although the tale has a postscript, as David eventually honors the covenant he made, giving to Jonathan's son Mephibosheth the lands of Saul that came into David's possession during the Jewish civil war (2 Sam. 9:1–13). What do we make of this eulogy, and the tale it concludes? Certainly, religious traditions have appreciated the depth of David and Jonathan's "friendship." The rabbis of the Talmud said it was the epitome of selfless love, for example (Mishna Avot 5:1). But is there more than that?

As we have already seen, to simply export the concepts of "gay" and "homosexuality" from our period to the Ancient Near East would be ludicrous. Jonathan had a son (and thus an unnamed wife as well), and, as an Ancient Near Eastern prince, he would have understood his love of a handsome young lad very differently from how gay and lesbian people understand their love today. We may be fixated, today, on whether David and Jonathan "did it" or not, and we may search in vain for evidence one way or the other. But this fixation on one sexual act is our problem, not theirs. What is clear is that Jonathan loved David in an intense emotional way that is far more than mere platonic love or friendship, as those terms are understood today, and that both he and Saul had relationships with David that would conventionally have been understood as including an erotic element.

For this reason, the story of David and Jonathan has been used for centuries as a code for homosexual love affairs, such as those between Philip II and Richard the Lionheart, and Edward II and Piers Gaveston, both described in contemporary histories with allusions to David and Jonathan. Their love was also an inspiration for artists including Michelangelo and Donatello, both of whom had sexual and emotional relationships with men.[7] Oscar Wilde cited it at his trial.[8] Contemporary scholars including Theodore W. Jennings Jr., Tom Horner, John Boswell, David Halperin, Martti Nissinen, Rabbi Steven Greenberg, Susan Ackerman, and Jean-Fabrice Nardelli have understood the tale of David and Jonathan to include clear references to sexuality—with Nissinen even speculating that more overt references may have been edited out.[9] Some have even suggested that the "pact of love" between David and Jonathan should be considered a marriage. As Tom Horner put it,

> Cannot two men be good friends, without the issue of homosexuality being raised? Yes, they can. But *when* the two men come from a society that for two hundred years had lived in the shadow of the Philistine culture, which accepted homosexuality; *when* they find themselves in a social context that was thoroughly military in the Eastern sense; *when* one of them—who is the social superior of the two—publicly makes display of his love; *when* the two of them make a lifetime pact openly; *when* they meet secretly and kiss each other and shed copious tears at parting; *when* one of them proclaims that his love for the other surpassed his love for women—and *all* this is

present in the David–Jonathan liaison—we have every reason
to believe that a homosexual relationship existed.[10]

At the very least, surely we would all agree that what Jonathan felt
for David can be described as a *romantic* love with erotic overtones,
whether or not it blossomed into sexual activity. And surely that is
more important. As we explored earlier, the very notion that "homosexuality" can mean both an orientation toward romantic connection
and a physical sex act is part of the problem. It reduces love to sex, and
reduces gay people to what we do with our genitals. What matters
here is that Jonathan loved David, that this love was an essential part
of the story of David's ascent to kingship—and that, understood traditionally, this is part of God's plan. Jonathan's love for another man is
not some bit part in the drama of the Bible. If Jonathan had not loved
David as he loved his very soul, there would be no Messiah.

If we allow the Bible to tell its own story, what emerges is a touching and perhaps tragic tale of one man's love for another, a deep,
passionate, embodied love that ultimately shaped the most important
drama in human history: the line of David, leading to the messianic
redemption. David and Jonathan's romance prepares David for his relationship with God,[11] seals the transmission of the Israelite monarchy
to the Davidic line, models a relationship to God that all of us might
reflect upon,[12] and alters the very course of human history. What
also emerges is a biblical universe with multiple configurations of,
and approaches to, sexuality, homosociality, eroticism, and same-sex
romantic love. LGBT people find ourselves in history, and everyone
who has experienced love finds another prism through which this
universal human emotion can be refracted. The story expands our
horizons regarding the emotional capacity of human beings—and
that is of importance to us all.

This is the message with which we will soon transition to the final
part of this book: that the experience of sexual and gender diversity
isn't just of interest to gays or lesbians, but has something to teach all
of us. Just as the struggle for equality is everybody's struggle, so too
the gifts of being gay or lesbian are shared with friends, families, and
communities. And they are gifts. Our world contains infinite variations of love. Yet from a mystical point of view, we are far more than

a rainbow of sexualities—we are countless refractions of light, each with our own hue, yet each a mote on the same beam of sunlight. And the more of those tints we can become aware of, the more of That Which Is—the "I am that I am" that spoke to Moses from out of the fire—becomes cognizable. Not through limitation, but through endlessly astounding proliferation.

CHAPTER 13

Sexual diversity in Christian theology

How did we get here from there?

Before moving on from the biblical material, it is worth asking one question left open by the readings we have explored. If homosexuality was indeed of such marginal concern to biblical texts, then how did we get to where we are today, a world in which some people believe that an absolute ban on homosexuality must be part of the Ten Commandments? The story is not a simple one. John McNeill calls it "a cumulative process of development in which many diverse influences played a part: the post-exilic Jewish reinterpretation of the Sodom story, pagan and Christian developments of Roman law, the teaching of the Church fathers, the legacy of Church councils and synods, the penitential system, and so on."[1] This road is indeed long and winding, and there is not time to travel all of it here. But it is useful to chart some of it before we move to the consequences of liberated sexuality for religious values and communities.

For the Church Fathers, as for Paul, the problem was sexuality, not homosexuality. We today may regard homosexuality and heterosexuality as different moral/theological questions, but for most of church history they were not; sex acts, with whatever partners, were first and foremost sexual acts—not homosexual or heterosexual. And for the first millennium of church history, sexuality in general was sharply curtailed, especially for the clerical leadership, where celibacy was held as the ideal. Indulgence in sexual activity was seen as an inversion of physical and spiritual priorities—the "devil's gateway"—and the control of sexuality was part of how the early church defined itself amid the chaos of the declining Roman Empire.[2] The advent of Stoicism, which tended to identify nature with reason and to denigrate love and pleasure, may also have played a key role.[3] For these reasons, homosexuality was almost never singled out for special opprobrium; among the church fathers, only John Chrysostom seems particularly agitated by it.[4] The problem was sexuality generally.

This is also true in the writings of St. Augustine (345–430), who has come to be regarded as the primary source of the anti-sexual views that became church orthodoxy for 1,500 years. Augustine was initially a Manichean who believed that the world was sharply split into good and evil. He was also a highly sexual, passionate man who had affairs with both women and men.[5] When he converted to Christianity, he maintained his basic dualism, but now mapped it onto the spiritual (good) and physical/sexual (bad).[6] Celibacy was the ideal state, and sexual pleasure was a consequence of the Fall. Sexuality had only one function—procreation—and any deviation from that function was unnatural. (This leads to some bizarre consequences; at one point, Augustine advises having "natural" sex with a prostitute rather than "unnatural" sex with oneself or another man.)[7] Augustine is anti-eros, but not anti-homosexuality.

Likewise throughout the first millennium of the church, homosexual acts were classified as sins, but not as any worse than others. Rules against homosexuality are included in many early church counsels,[8] but nowhere in these documents is it singled out for special condemnation. John Boswell controversially claimed that there was "no general prejudice against gay people among early Christians" and that many early Christian figures were involved in relationships we today might label as homosexual.[9] He notes that Christian emperors taxed, rather than banned, male prostitutes,[10] and that the eventual rules against homosexuality are of Roman, rather than Christian, origin.[11] Indeed, many pagans used to say that Christians were lax in terms of sexual morals.[12] Boswell's work has come under attack, however. Bernadette Brooten has said that lesbianism was widely condemned even where male homosexuality was not, and that Boswell lumps women and men together, when in fact their situations were different.[13] Others have criticized Boswell for ignoring evidence that painted early Church attitudes in a less tolerant light.[14] What we can say is that, at the very least, the regulation of homosexuality was far less central a priority in the first millennium of Church history than in the second, and that, in Boswell's words, "even where such authorities explicitly condemned homosexuality, they also categorically rejected the majority of human erotic experience."[15]

When male homosexuality did eventually become of specific interest to the Church, it was originally because too many priests were engaging in it. The term "sodomy" originated not in the Bible but with eleventh-century theologian Peter Damian's attempts to eradicate clerical sin.[16] Sodomy was not a sin of the people; it was misconduct on the part of priests who were meant to be celibate. [17] Indeed, the evidence from the time is remarkable.[18] At least one bishop whose same-sex love affair was well known was accepted within the highest ranks of the Church hierarchy, even as a variety of other sins were zealously prosecuted.[19] Monks, priests, even archbishops (including Anselm) wrote passionate love letters to one another—not erotic in the sexual sense, but suffused with physical, erotic language: "wherever you go, my love follows you," "even if you sent every scent of perfume . . . still it could not make up to my soul for this separation," and the like.[20] We even possess a letter from one twelfth-century woman to another, reprinted in its entirety by Boswell and including lines such as "when I recall the kisses you gave me, and how with tender words you caressed my little breasts, I want to die because I cannot see you."[21] One monk in particular, the abbot Aelred of Rievaulx, bears particular mention.[22] Aelred writes that before his vow of celibacy, he had sexual relationships with other men. After he became a monk, and eventually an abbot, he elevated emotional, passionate friendship between men to the highest level, especially in his best-known work, *Spiritual Friendship,*[23] drawing in part on rich interpretations of the "beloved disciple" tradition in the New Testament, and the story of David and Jonathan.[24] Aelred had two long-term love affairs, first with a monk named Simon and then, after Simon died, with another monk whom Aelred does not name. In both cases, Aelred was committed to his vow of chastity, though he indicates that he may have fallen short at times. Aelred was perhaps the greatest expositor of same-sex love in the Christian world prior to the contemporary period, and may be considered its unofficial patron saint.

The tide turned at the end of the twelfth century, probably due to campaigns against Islam (where same-sex eroticism was widespread)[25] and heresy, as well as to a rise in conservatism generally.[26] The thirteenth and fourteenth centuries saw a significant increase in the severity of punishment for homosexual activity. According to Louis Crompton, "During the 200 years from 1150 to 1350, homosexual behavior appears to have changed, in the eyes of the public, from the personal preference of a prosperous minority, satirized and celebrated in popular verse, to a dangerous, antisocial, and severely sinful aberration."[27]

St. Thomas Aquinas (1225–1274) brought together this new understanding of sodomy with the concept of natural law, moral principles discernible from reason.[28] In the *Summa Theologica,* Aquinas discusses six sexual offenses, which he categorizes as *luxuria,* a term that (as the modern "luxury" suggests) previously meant anything from wearing soft clothing to taking hot baths.[29] Five of these are abuses of otherwise acceptable acts of intercourse: fornication, adultery, incest, "deflowering," and rape. The sixth is a category of acts that are "against nature" (*contra naturam*) because they cannot bring about conception: masturbation, bestiality, "unnatural" sexual positions, and same-sex relations.[30] In these codes, homosexual behaviour is no worse than masturbation—or, for that matter, lending money at interest, which was also called "unnatural."[31] Yet by the year 1300, homosexual activity was punishable by death.

Discerning the evolution of the church's attitudes toward women's sexuality is even more difficult. On the one hand, Judith Brown notes that the church's official penalties for what we would today call lesbianism were much lower than for what we call male homosexuality, and were identical to those for masturbation.[32] She theorizes that because women did not release semen, they could not pollute, and that lesbianism was seen as a mere substitute for sex with men. On the other hand, Bernadette Brooten, noting that early Christian sources adopted ancient stereotypes against lesbians, claims they considered female same-sex behavior as problematic as men's.[33] Often, church authorities didn't even know what to call lesbians: they use terms such as *fricatrices* and *tribades,* both derived from Greek words for "rub." (Similarly, Jewish authorities used the term *nashim mesolelot zoh b'zoh:* women who rub one another.)

In any event, the increase in persecution of women seems to have taken place later than that of men: around the sixteenth century, in the context of the pursuit of heresy. Since then, many women burned as witches were actually members of sexual and gender minorities.[34]

With only a few exceptions, the major Western religions remained hostile to homosexuality for the next seven hundred years. But LGBT people did not simply disappear. Many, doubtless, lived closeted lives.

Many entered the priesthood. And many found lives on the margins of mainstream society—as historians have shown, sexual-minority subcultures thrived in modern Europe, generally in cities, with complex systems of social organization and varying degrees of tolerance from governmental authorities.[35] Interestingly, panic about "deviant" sexuality has always been with us also. Whatever the time period, it was always the worst of times. Graham Robb's book *Strangers* gathers together some of the statements people have made over the years: "This sin is now so frequent that no one blushes for it any more, and many indulge in it without perceiving its gravity" (Anselm in 1102); "Buggery is now almost as common among our gallants as in Italy" (Samuel Pepys in 1663); "Sapphism and sodomy are growing at an unheard-of rate" (a doctor in 1884).[36] It is remarkable, really; every age has supposed that it is the first one in which sodomy is rampant. (Robb puts forth an interesting theory as to why this is the case: in every person's personal history, sexuality is "on the rise" simply because we grow from children into adults. We all remember a time when things were less sexual, because *we* were.)[37]

Today, the positions of different denominations vary widely. To bring our historical survey to a close, we will briefly survey the current state of church teaching.

Today's Catholic teaching on homosexuality follows directly from the earlier sources we have reviewed, but expands upon them more than the sources themselves require. The catechism of the Catholic Church[38] teaches that "homosexual acts are intrinsically disordered. They are contrary to the natural law. They close the sexual act to the gift of life. They do not proceed from a genuine affective and sexual complementarity. Under no circumstances can they be approved." [39] At the same time, the Church urges that "the number of men and women who have deep-seated homosexual tendencies is not negligible. This inclination, which is objectively disordered, constitutes for most of them a trial. They must be accepted with respect, compassion, and sensitivity. Every sign of unjust discrimination in their regard should be avoided." Many Catholic scholars have commented on these positions, and I will not add to their extensive critiques here.[40] It is worth noting that since these Church teachings are based largely on natural law at least as much as on Scripture, they leave the door open for further reflection as scientific knowledge improves (e.g., as we understand how homosexual inclinations do proceed from genuine affective complementarity, and do have a place in the order of nature). In addition, while "objective disorder" is a harsh judgment, the Church has used the same term to describe "degrading conditions of work which treat laborers as mere instruments of profit,"[41] conditions which prevail throughout most of the world. In addition, it has been observed that within the Catholic Church, a disproportionate number of clergy members—surveys suggest that between 28 percent and 48 percent of active priests, and 55 percent of seminarians—are gay.[42] (That being said, 93 percent of instances of sexual abuse of children are heterosexual.)[43] This simply stands to reason: to a gay young man, the church offers a life of prestige and mission, whereas the alternatives are grim. Thus, Mark Jordan has suggested that rather than see the Catholic attitude toward gay people as "them versus us," it's really us versus us: closeted gay people persecuting openly gay people. As he puts it, "many silent sodomites burned sodomites who started to speak. Many closeted homosexuals in the hierarchy now condemn open homosexuals in the pews."[44]

Of course, the Catholic Church does not have a monopoly on secretly gay clergy. As we have already mentioned, evangelical megachurch leader Ted Haggard (now making a comeback) had a multiyear relationship with a drug-dealing male prostitute. Rev. Paul Barnes, pastor of a Denver megachurch, had numerous affairs with men. Pastor Eddie Long has recently been accused of sexually abusing several teenage boys. And as we've already noted, George Rekers, cofounder of the Family Research Council, hired a male prostitute to accompany him on a trip to the Caribbean. Eros repressed is eros distorted, so it is no surprise that so many of the most vocal anti-gay voices are themselves . . . gay.

In contrast, there have been openly gay priests in the Episcopal Church since the 1970s, and surveys show that 75 percent of U.S. Episcopalians think that gays can be faithful Christians. The road has not been uniformly smooth: the 2003 ordination of Gene Robinson as the first openly gay bishop led to a rebuke from the Anglican communion, and threats of a schism within the movement, particularly as communities outside the United States are far less accepting, continue to this day. This break, however, has not happened, and thanks to the high degree of autonomy accorded to individual dioceses, there is a wide range of practice within the movement. Many dioceses perform same-sex weddings, for example, while many conservatives within the Episcopal Church remain committed to a formally anti-gay doctrinal position. Yet it is striking how relatively few sex scandals happen in the Episcopal Church; where sexuality is honored and clergy can be honest about who they are, they tend not to abuse parishioners and secretly hire prostitutes.

In May 2011, the Presbyterian Church (U.S.A.) voted to allow ordination of gays and lesbians, by removing a requirement that clergy be either celibate or heterosexually married.[45] This historic decision was the culmination of decades of progress on LGBT issues, beginning in 1978, when the church officially banned anti-gay discrimination, and thoughtful (often contentious) debate.[46]

The United Methodist Church, basing itself on the "Wesleyan quadrilateral" of scripture, tradition, experience, and reason, has taken a position of welcoming gays and lesbians into congregations but not ordaining them as clergy or performing same-sex unions. The UMC Book of Discipline still holds "the practice of homosexuality" to be "incompatible with Christian teaching." Activist groups within the Methodist community are working hard to shift these official positions.

In August 2009, the Evangelical Lutheran Church in America (ELCA) passed a statement called "Human Sexuality: Gift and Trust," along with resolutions permitting congregations to perform same-sex commitment ceremonies, supporting the ordination of gay and lesbian ministers, and taking further steps toward integration.[47] The organization Lutherans Concerned (www.lcna.org) works with Lutheran congregations of all streams, including more conservative ones, to become more inclusive and welcoming.

The most inclusive denominations are the Unitarian Universalists, which as early as 1970 passed a resolution condemning anti-gay discrimination, and which performs same-sex marriages as a matter of church policy; the United Church of Christ, which has ordained gays and lesbians since 1972 and supported marriage equality since 2005; and the LGBT-focused Metropolitan Community Church (MCC), founded in 1968, which now has fifty thousand members in three hundred congregations.[48]

There has even been movement within more conservative Christian denominations. American Baptist Churches, for example, tends toward traditional positions hostile to homosexuality,[49] and yet there are dozens of gay and lesbian pastors ministering to ABCUSA congregations, and the Association of Welcoming & Affirming Baptists has over seventy member congregations. African American churches have tended to preach strongly against homosexuality, but organizations such as Unity Fellowship and Refuge Ministries/Fellowship are growing, and there is considerable diversity within communities around the country, as well as important pro-LGBT voices such as those of Rev. Irene Monroe, William D. Hart, Juan Y. Reed, and many others. The Seventh-Day Adventist community, which tends to be quite conservative, nonetheless has an LGBT interest group, Kinship International, with over one thousand members.[50]

And contrary to generalizations about Pentecostal and evangelical Christians as being a uniform mass, there are numerous pro-gay evangelical churches and preachers, including Soulforce, founded by Rev. Mel White (formerly a speechwriter for Jerry Falwell), Evangelicals Concerned, the Gay Christian Network (gaychristian.net), and Rev. Jay Bakker (yes, the son of Jim and Tammy Bakker), whose new book, *Fall to Grace: A Revolution of God, Self and Society,* makes many of the same arguments explored in chapters 8 and 10.[51] Particularly in the "emerging church" and "Emergent church" communities, the evangelical world's historical obsession with homosexuality has come under criticism for being a distraction from more important issues.[52] There have even been reports that leading evangelical organizations in the Christian Right are rethinking their strategy of demonizing gays and lesbians.[53]

Within the Jewish world, all denominations except Orthodoxy (which represents between 15–20 percent of American Jews) have stated that most or all homosexual activity is permitted under Jewish law, and all ordain gay and lesbian rabbis. There has been movement within the Orthodox world for greater tolerance and inclusion, even as traditional interpretations of Jewish law remain in place.[54]

All of this diversity within religious communities shows that the old simplification "God versus Gay" not only oversimplifies Scripture but misstates the current geography of American religious communities. And, lest there be any confusion, the sum total of religion's interaction with homosexuality is not limited to questions of inclusion or validation. As we will see in chapter 17, LGBT people are already making unique, distinctive, and varied contributions to theology, ethics, and religious communal life. This book is about God *versus* Gay—but in fact, the more interesting, and inspiring, conversations begin when "God" and "Gay" come into dialogue with one another.

It is that conversation to which we now turn in part 3. If I have made my case so far, then I have shown that our shared religious values compel us to read narrowly the handful of ambiguous biblical verses that some use to condemn homosexuality. We do this not out of compromise, but out of affirmation: sexual diversity is part of the endless variety of nature, it is a path to love and companionship, and a means of expressing the sacred. Yes, the embrace of sexual diversity remains a contentious issue, one that threatens many deeply held beliefs held dear by many people. But, as with slavery and women's rights before it, it is also a debate that invokes the best in us: our capacity for empathy, for moral reasoning, and for love.

PART THREE

Why inclusion of sexual minorities is good, not bad, for religious values

CHAPTER 14

"You shall be holy, for I am holy"

*Equality for LGBT people is good for
families, marriage, and sexual ethics*

According to some people, accepting gays and lesbians into religious communities, giving us equal civil rights, and affirming the reality of sexual diversity as part of God's creation would lead to the end of civilization. According to Robert Knight of the Family Research Council, "[A]ll hell will break loose. We'll see a breakdown in social organizations, with more drug use, more disease, more unwanted pregnancies. You're mainstreaming dysfunction."[1]

Is that true? Is it really the case that affirming our gay and lesbian siblings, friends, and community members would weaken marriage, harm traditional values, and otherwise contribute to the decay of our society? Unlike many of my allies in the pro-gay movement, I take these concerns seriously, even if they are often expressed in hyperbolic ways. Many people across the country are sincerely concerned about the increasing vulgarization of our society, and link it to changes in our moral fabric. I am sympathetic to these concerns. But here's the point: there may be lines that distinguish wholesome values from unwholesome ones—but sexual orientation is not one of them.

Whatever your philosophy, you will find gay people, straight people, and any other kind of people who agree with you. Whether someone is gay or not—and whether that sexuality is affirmed or rejected by their community—does not determine one's moral character (however defined). Straight people and gay people may be honest or dishonest, conservative or liberal or radical, materialistic or spiritual, prudish or libertine—really, anything at all. There are straight people who lead very "alternative" lifestyles, some with multiple lovers and few emotional commitments, and there are gay people who lead very traditional lifestyles in monogamous marriages. However morality is defined, sexual orientation is just not a predictor for it.

To be clear, I'm not endorsing any particular view of what morality is. I know people (gay and straight) for whom traditional values are deeply nourishing and supportive, and I know people (gay and straight) for whom they are not. What I'm saying is that equality for, and acceptance of, LGBT people does not tip the balance one way or the other.

In this chapter and the chapters to come, I'm going to engage seriously with the claims that full acceptance of gay people would be bad for traditional religious values. In this chapter, we'll look at the family and questions of sexual ethics. In the next, we'll look at how the evolution from the traditional religious position on homosexuality represents a step forward for religious conscience. And in the final two chapters, we'll explore how increased diversity and the unique voices of LGBT people are transforming religious communities for the better. We've seen that our deepest religious values stress loving relationship, honesty, justice, compassion, and holiness. We've seen, in the light of those values, that the handful of texts that supposedly prohibit homosexuality actually don't prohibit it at all. So now we are inquiring into consequences.

Let's start with some of the facts. Our best studies of same-sex families find them not only as successful as opposite-sex ones, but, in terms of raising children, often *more* successful.[2] There is unanimity among two decades of scientific studies that the sexual orientation of parents does not influence the psychological health of the child.[3] It may be common folk wisdom that a child needs both male and female role models in the house, but that is not what the data shows, based on studies of countries with same-sex marriage and of the 2 to 6 million gay parents of 6 to 14 million children in America.[4] Children do better with two parents, but whether those two parents are of the same gender or not is not a determinative factor. (Except in cases of child abuse: children of lesbian parents report an astonishing zero percent of sexual abuse.)[5] Oh, and children of gay parents are no more likely to be gay than children of straight parents.[6] With respect to marriage, laws permitting same-sex marriage have been found to have no effect on marriage, divorce, abortion, or illegitimacy rates.[7]

Matthew 7:16–18 teaches: "You will know them by their fruits . . . A good tree cannot bring forth evil fruit, neither can a corrupt tree bring forth good fruit." This is a good way to think about gay and lesbian families. Yes, they are new, and different from the norm. But the fruits—love, steadfastness, children—are how we can know them.

I often advise folks who are sincerely troubled by the potential social ills of same-sex families to do two things. First, I suggest they seek out and meet same-sex families. As the data shows, and as popular films such as *The Kids Are All Right* have depicted, same-sex families are more like opposite-sex ones than they are different. Families are families, with most of the same joys and challenges. There is no substitute for firsthand knowledge. Media reports, sensationalistic accounts, and third- or fourth-hand reports are nothing compared to firsthand testimony. See for yourself. (If you can't do that, seek out books of testimony like Elizabeth A. Say and Mark R. Kowalewski's *Gays, Lesbians & Family Values,* which includes many interviews with gay and lesbian people in families, or memoirs such as Bishop Gene Robinson's *In the Eye of the Storm* and Mel White's *Stranger at the Gate.*)

Second, I suggest they read actual studies, and not rely on secondary sources. I've cited primary sources here; Judge Walker's opinion in *Perry v. Schwarzenegger,* the California Proposition 8 case, reviewed the evidence in detail and is an excellent introduction to this material.[8] Often, the same couple of sources are recycled over and over in anti-gay circles, giving the misleading interpretation that there is actually some dispute over the facts. For example, Dr. Paul Cameron's work is frequently cited in political and legal arguments, and often forms the backbone for anti-gay claims. Yet Dr. Cameron was expelled from the American Psychological Association for willfully misrepresenting research.[9] He also has, to put it mildly, some really weird ideas. For example:

> If you isolate sexuality as something solely for one's own personal amusement, and all you want is the most satisfying orgasm you can get—and that is what homosexuality seems to be—then homosexuality seems too powerful to resist. The evidence is that men do a better job on men and women on women, if all you are looking for is orgasm. . . . It's pure sexuality. It's almost like pure heroin. It's such a rush. . . . Marital

sex tends toward the boring end. Generally, it doesn't deliver the kind of sheer sexual pleasure that homosexual sex does.[10]

Really? I don't know about you, but my straight friends aren't tempted by that heroin-like rush of gay sex. Cameron's hysterical statement probably says more about his own repressed desires than about actual gay people. And yet, if you scratch beneath the surface of vague anti-gay statements citing the "many studies" showing that kids need both moms and dads to be healthy, at the end of the day they come back to Cameron, time and time again.

David Blankenhorn is another pseudoscholarly source for much of today's anti-gay (and, in particular, anti-same-sex-marriage) rhetoric. Yet as Judge Walker showed in devastating detail in *Perry*, Blankenhorn has no relevant academic credentials, has never published in a peer-reviewed academic journal, and bases most of his statements not on replicable scientific data but on "thought experiments" and personal opinion.[11] Once again, evaluate the evidence for yourself. Are the "experts" part of a community of similarly educated peers who critique one another's work and hold each other to objective standards? Or are they self-appointed experts who work at think tanks established for ideological reasons? None of this is to suggest that you need a PhD to have opinions. But if we are talking about facts, evidence, and data, then such qualifications do, indeed, count.

The anti-gay "science" of sexuality is just like the tobacco wars of a few years ago. First, the tobacco companies said smoking was good for you. Then they said we don't really know the facts. Eventually, when it became clear that they did know and actively suppressed the facts, they gave up on convincing people that smoking may not be bad for you and just argued that it's everyone's right to choose. Same thing here. First, homosexuality is a sin. Then homosexuality is somehow bad for civilization. Then, when that's shown not to be true—well, we'll see what folks come up with next.

Here's another example: pedophilia. How many times have we heard the claim that homosexuals are potential child molesters—even though, in reality, over 95 percent of child molestations are by heterosexual men?[12] This, too, isn't a fact—it's a lie, and a vicious one at that. Relatedly, every ex-gay and anti-gay book I've read talks about NAMBLA, the "North American Man-Boy Love Association." You'd get the sense, from these books, that they must be the leading sponsors of the gay pride parade. Well, here's my advice: anytime you hear someone talk about NAMBLA, you know that you're being conned. NAMBLA was a tiny fringe group of men in the 1970s who wanted to legitimize sexual activity between adults and adolescents. They were nearly universally condemned in the gay community from the very beginning, and the organization mostly exists today in the fevered imaginations of the scaremongers.

But let's be honest: most folks who are opposed to gay families and gay marriage are opposed to them for religious reasons, not factual ones. So instead of following these rabbit trails further, I'd prefer to have the values conversation head on: what would a world that affirmed sexual diversity look like? Would it be a world of moral anarchy—or, as I will suggest, moral improvement?

Let's begin with relatively conservative values, and then move to more liberal ones in the next section. In both cases, my point will be the same: whether your values are traditional or progressive, whether your view is that marriage and family are the bedrock of civilization, or that they are oppressive remnants of a patriarchal past—in short, whatever your sexual ethic, the line between heterosexual and homosexual does not separate amoral and moral.

First, does an acceptance of same-sex relationships undermine the institution of the family? Factually, we have already seen that the answer is no. However, as a matter of values, let's take the question seriously; sexuality may be powerful and delightful, but it can also lead to great abuse. And in part, traditional family structures exist to regulate it, control it, and connect it to stable social structures that promote the communal good. Conservatives are right to worry that any time we relax our standards, particularly traditional ones that have been with us a long time, we risk opening the floodgates to all kinds of dangerous and immoral behavior. Without agreeing or disagreeing with this point of view, we should at least be clear that it is coherent, sensible, and time honored. And for that reason, religious activists like myself have to take it seriously.[13]

At the same time, we cannot simply answer this question with recourse to the Bible alone. The Bible's "family values" include arranged marriages, sex with twelve-year-old girls, concubines, polygamy, and prostitution. Is this what we want for ourselves today? King Solomon, the Bible tells us, had seven hundred wives—what could marriage even *mean* in such a context? At the time of the New Testament, girls were married off as young as eight or nine years old, and Paul specifically mandates that women not have authority over their own bodies (1 Cor. 7:4). Obviously, we can and do use sacred texts as our guides, but if we simply xeroxed their sexual ethics, we would live in a bizarre, sexist, and often frightening world. Indeed, it is somewhat bizarre for politically minded preachers to have recourse to the Gospels for "family values" as construed in the modern way. As already noted in chapter 9, Jesus advised his followers to leave their families of origin, renounce domestic life, and commit themselves to a life of the spirit.[14] Paul said that it is best to "remain unmarried, as I am" (1 Cor. 7:8).[15] For the New Testament, the true family is not biological, and certainly not defined by procreation, but is spiritual: "Whoever does God's will is my brother and sister and mother" (Mark 3:34; Matt. 12:50). So we have to look elsewhere for guidance.

When we do so, we notice that while same-sex families do look like a marked departure from traditional, nuclear families, family and marriage have changed radically over time. We have moved from polygamy to monogamy, and from a labor-based model of marriage to a happiness-based one.[16] Arranged marriages were common throughout most of human history, with marriages often taking place when children reached adolescence. Interreligious and interracial marriages were completely banned, and not even regarded as marriages. For most of Jewish and Christian history, wives were regarded as the property of their husbands—this was the essence of marriage, which was the purchase of the bride by the groom. Consequently, for most of history, men were permitted to rape their wives—the very notion of "rape" was inapplicable in married contexts. As Christian ethicist Marvin Ellison writes, "elements of marriage once considered essential have been questioned and judged unjust, such as a husband's ownership of his wife's property and the legal impossibility of a husband's raping his spouse."[17] So what are we really changing?

Moreover, family constellations in Europe often included aunts and uncles and cousins, all sleeping in the same household—often the same room—with children being raised by the entire extended family, rather than by the mother and father alone. Prior to the modern period, families were seen primarily as economic units, not romantic ones.[18] And as unusual as two dads may seem, a working mom is even more so: this would have been unthinkable even a hundred years ago, let alone to the Church fathers who said that men should rule over their wives.

In short, what may seem like an always-and-forever ideal has actually only been with us for a short period of time. Traditions evolve, and that's why they endure. If the notion of the family were locked in place and we were committed to polygamy, primogeniture, and perhaps levirate marriage, then the family would become an archaic institution incapable of speaking to people's lives. On the other hand, if "family" simply means whatever we want it to mean, then it ceases to be meaningful as well. Thus, the determination of "what is good for the family" must be based on why families are valuable, and what values they promote. And in terms of promoting values such as commitment, love, care in times of need, and all the vows one typically hears at a wedding altar, same-sex families have been shown to be as effective as opposite-sex ones.[19]

Now, there are some who say that the real essence of a marriage, and by extension a family, is biologically producing children. This, they say, is what takes sexuality and relationship beyond pleasure, and what domesticates the sexual urge. Folks complain about married life, but precisely because it is less wild than the life of a rock star, it is more stable and less selfish. Having kids not only ensures the future of the species, but it binds people together in ways that are sacred.

This is an important point, but let's dismiss two unimportant side points right away. The first has to do with perpetuating the species. This is just a non-issue. Obviously, the great majority of human beings will continue to be predominantly heterosexual. The human race is not running out of babies, or of people interested in making them. The second point is made on the pro-gay side, and that has to do with infertile couples. If marriage is about having children, some gay advocates argue, then why do we allow infertile couples to marry? This claim, too, is a weak one. Maybe in some horrible, eugenic dystopia, society would invade the privacy of all individuals and determine their fitness to procreate. But fortunately we don't live in that world. A man and a woman are generally able to procreate, and that generality is good enough to also include some outlying cases. So this objection falls also.

These days, we know quite well that same-sex couples can raise (and even bear) children. True, adoption, in-vitro fertilization, and surrogacy are not as natural as procreative sex. But then again, neither is the Internet, or air-conditioning. And same-sex parenting *is* natural, found in dozens of animal species.[20] More importantly, and more personally, I have friends and relatives (both straight and gay) who have had children in these ways, and while it's not statistical proof, I can attest that their love is as natural, real, and powerful as anyone else's, and so are the bonds they have with their kids. Biology is part of parental bonding, but only a part—and, as all the studies have shown, a far less important part than years of parenting, love, and connection.

It's also just inaccurate to say that marriage has always been about procreation. It is also about fidelity, mutuality, accountability, identity, community, intimacy, and sex.[21] At a traditional Jewish wedding, the couple blesses God for creating love, joy, and sexual pleasure. And as we saw, Adam and Eve, the "first couple," were created for companionship, not breeding. Throughout most of Church history, marriage—following 1 Corinthians, chapter 7—was regarded not as an ideal, or some romantic union of complementary opposites, but as the best way to curb sexual lust, a kind of compromise with the material world.[22] For better or for worse, marriage has always been about more than producing and raising children.

The real problem here is the continued sexualization of homosexuality. As I noted earlier, it's quite telling that the same word "homosexuality" can refer to an identity and to a sexual act. If same-sex relationships are thought of as merely sexual, then it's easy to see why many traditionalists would be concerned by them. And if being gay were really the endless party that some people seem to imagine, then sure, it would be destructive of efforts to tame the animal instincts within us. Yet same-sex relationships are *not* merely sexual. They are just like opposite-sex relationships. They can be loving, or not; faithful, or not; nurturing, or not. They mix love and passion together.

Now, we've all been bombarded with media images of wild gay life: drag queens marching at pride parades, hedonistic gay dance parties. But that's just media. I've been to many pride parades over the years, in cities around the world. And I can tell you that for every ten drag queens, there are hundreds of boring gay and lesbian folks—chess teams, mountain biking clubs, religious organizations, the works. They're not as unusual, and so they're not reported. What gets people to watch TV are people in outlandish costumes, and so the myth of the endlessly sexual gay community is perpetuated.

But let's stay with those drag queens for a minute more. I have friends who are drag queens, and I totally support the way they choose to express their gender identity. More power to them! Drag queens are fun, and they are important, too; like the court jester who is able to speak truth to the king, the ways they poke fun at gender stereotypes call us to reexamine our assumptions about gender and how it is presented. They make us look at ourselves anew. Nor are they representative of anyone but themselves. The point of a pride parade isn't uniformity—it's diversity. It's not that everyone is secretly like the flamboyant drag queen in a pink feathered boa. It's that we want to create a community where people are allowed to be who they want to be. I know a lot of conservative gay guys who roll their eyes at the outrageously dressed (and undressed) participants in the parades. But the point of an inclusive community is to include the radical queers and the "good gays," the flamboyant performers and the strait-laced accountants and lawyers. And everyone in between.

Now, in addition to pride parades, I've also been to plenty of straight bars, festivals, and parties that are every bit as wild as gay ones. Numerically, more straight people are into "alternative sexualities" than gay people. And prostitution isn't the world's oldest profession because *gay* people are patronizing it. So if we're going to characterize gay people by the gay community's most outlandish fringe, we ought to do the same for straight people. What do you think—should we ban straight marriage because so many straight people like pornography and prostitution?

Obviously not. As we explored earlier, there is a spectrum of sexual expression from mild to wild. But whether that sexual expression is gay or straight does not determine where on the spectrum it falls. As gay congressman Barney Frank put it, "I've fought all my life to be boring." Homosexuality is no more like pornography, adultery, or whatever sexual practice one may wish to condemn than heterosexuality is.

Now, allow me to repeat: I'm not taking sides on which sexual expressions are to be celebrated in which religious contexts, because good people differ widely on that issue. Maybe you think "free love" is religiously ideal, or maybe you think it's the work of the devil. I don't know, and I don't want to convince you either way. The point I want to make is that whether a relationship is same-sex or opposite-sex is not a useful dividing line. There's just no correlation. If you want to affirm only monogamous, family-oriented sexual relation-ships, then fine: support gay and straight marriage, and work hard to reduce the sexualization and pornographication of our society. If you want to affirm a wide range of sexual and emotional bonds and behaviors, then fine: support free sexual expression in all its forms and oppose the privileging of some over others.[23] But the gay/straight axis is the wrong dividing line. It's like saying that only people with brown eyes can ride roller coasters. It's just the wrong characteristic to use.

Let me hone in on one of those last points: that if you want to encourage conservative values, you should support gay marriage.[24] I know this may seem counterintuitive. But it's not a new argument—Andrew Sullivan made it in his book *Virtually Normal* way back in 1996. The claim is that if you want to encourage conservative family values, then you should enable everyone to partake in them. Gays and lesbians, Sullivan argued, are amenable to being "tamed" by domestic family values just as much as straight people are. Give gays the op-tion to marry, and they will be less likely to find sexual expression in other, less stable ways. So if you want to build a society based upon the foundation of the family, enable everyone to have one.

Sullivan was ahead of his time fifteen years ago, and I think we still haven't yet caught up to him. But now we have the evidence to prove it. Where same-sex marriage has been legalized, there has indeed been a decrease in promiscuity among gay and lesbian people.[25] And, as we already noted, traditional heterosexual families have not been harmed by same-sex marriage in any of the states or countries that have it.[26] On the contrary, divorce rates have actually gone down—probably because so many long-term homosexual couples recently joined the wedding rolls. Has there been any measurable decline in respect for the institution of the family? Nope. It just hasn't happened. Lesbians and gays have raised children successfully, have joined the PTA and the Rotary Club, and have been every bit as conventional, law-abiding, and, yes, "boring" as straight families have. This is one reason why many radicals have opposed same-sex marriage from the left: it has worked all too well.[27]

Traditional notions of the family, and of sexual morality in general, are indeed under threat from many sides: hypersexualized teenage pop stars, increasingly casual sexual activity among teenagers, and a loss of respect for the marriage bond, to name a few. For folks who believe that the family unit is the fundamental building block of society, these are troubling times. But again—gays are not the source of this problem. It's easy to generalize and speculate that any change leads to decline overall. It's easy to make erroneous analogies to the Roman Empire or other supposed examples where liberalization of sexual mores led to societal decline. (Actually, Roman laws about homosexuality became *more* restrictive as the empire declined, not less. Likewise in Greece.) But this evidence is supported by neither facts nor values.

Really, though, none of the arguments I'm making here will be as persuasive as simply getting to know a lesbian or gay family. At times, the sexual revolution—of which the struggle for LGBT rights is a part—can seem truly revolutionary. And in many ways it is. But there is nothing so normal as two women standing under a Jewish wedding canopy, or two dads taking their daughter for a walk. Barney Frank was right: after all the fights and fireworks, at the end of the day, it's boring.

I want to conclude, though, by widening the sphere of consideration somewhat. We should not suppose that the only religious values that attach to sexuality are tied to marriage and family. Every sexual act is an opportunity for ethical choice, and even for spiritual transcendence. Is a sexual encounter loving, passionate, ethical, respectful, consensual, and safe? Does it celebrate the energies of the body, and invite in holiness, as you understand it? These are ethical, moral, and religious questions that present themselves in all sexual experiences, whether in traditional contexts or not. Yet there is only a small constituency interested in asking them. On the conservative side, there is a great deal of moral discourse but only a limited range of acceptance. On the liberal side, there is a wide range of acceptance but only a limited amount of moral, ethical, and spiritual discourse. This is a shame, because asking such questions can be empowering and liberating.

We need to have this conversation—not for gays or lesbians but for all of us. Perhaps coming to a more mature understanding of sexual diversity can help Christians and Jews heal the wounds that our traditions bear regarding sexuality in general. Christianity arose as an ascetic movement, with celibacy as its original ideal. Judaism's origins include deeply offensive notions about women's bodies. And both traditions bear their scars today. The vulgar, puerile sexuality that marks American public life is a direct consequence of religion's inability to talk seriously about sex. We urgently need a sexual conversation that recognizes that sex may be sacred as well as terrible, that values the erotic while cautioning against its misuse. Thinking about LGBT people can open the door to these wider considerations.

This is not a new theological topic. But it is one in which new theological reflection is desperately needed.[28] For example, theologian and ethicist James B. Nelson has devoted several books to creating an LGBT-inclusive, body-affirming, responsible Christian sexual ethic. In one volume, he frames the issue this way:

> The appropriate ethical question is this: What sexual behavior will serve and enhance, rather than inhibit and damage, the fuller realization of divinely intended humanity? The answer . . . is sexual behavior in accordance with love . . . commitment, trust, tenderness, respect for the other, and the desire for responsible communion. It means resisting cruelty, utterly impersonal sex, obsession with sexual gratification, and actions that display unwillingness to take responsibility for their personal and social consequences. This kind of ethic is equally appropriate to both heterosexual and homosexual.[29]

Likewise, the work of lesbian theologian Carter Heyward, discussed more fully in chapter 17, values the erotic—being in "right relation"—as essential to the human condition and our relationship with God. This does not mean that "anything goes"—quite the contrary, Heyward writes: "We need an ethical, or moral, apprehension of ourselves in relation that can inform our sexual behavior by helping us understand what is right or wrong for us."[30] Indeed, it is the failure of mainstream religion to create an ethic that appreciates the value and power of sexuality that has led to our present state in which "our collective body is badly abused and abusive, broken and violent."[31] "A sex-affirming ethic," she writes, "is morally imperative."[32]

We should not expect one single "gay sexual ethic" to emerge from the multitude of LGBT voices active today, some of which are relatively traditional, valuing monogamous relationships and opposing promiscuity,[33] while others are more radical, questioning our society's assumptions about eroticism and sexuality.[34] But one of the contributions that LGBT people may make to our ethical conversation is based on the affirmation of eros as a vital force of connection. Think about it: to be a self-accepting LGBT religious person, one must go through periods of rejection of sexuality, acceptance of sexuality, and at some point, an integration of sexuality and spirituality. The diverse ethical writings of the "queer theologians" we'll discuss in chapter 17 explore how this experience can be of value to all of us.

In my own experience, I have found, and felt personally, that sexuality can be ennobling or degrading. Sex has connected me to my deepest loves, desires, and values—and has caused me to feel deeply alienated as well. Contrary to what some might expect, most of my experience with the latter—most of the sexual encounters that, I felt, were betrayals of who I was and who I wanted to be—took place when I was still in the "closet." I felt that God hated what I was doing, and so I had to block God out. It's also much easier to be irresponsible, unsafe, and immoral when the only kind of sexual encounters you can imagine for yourself are transitory and anonymous. It's not like you're ever going to see the other person again anyway, and if you're already sinning against God and nature, who cares about consent and safety? Worrying about ethics is like rearranging the deck chairs on the *Titanic,* if you think that the entire sexual act is corrupted by sin. And since you're already an inveterate sinner who deserves to be punished, why worry about HIV or AIDS either? If you get it, you probably deserve it. I've experienced all of this firsthand.

Yet I also know firsthand that same-sex intimacy can be intimately connected with ethics, ecstasy, and the sacred. There are many inexplicable delights in this endlessly surprising and holy world, and sex is only one of them—but it certainly is a big one. When two become one, when you can feel the joys of being human and being embodied and having a few short decades to live and love on the Earth—isn't this part of what living is *for*? To know that, in this short span of life, it's possible to connect in this way, to feel and to move and to embrace and to hold? And even, sometimes, to join all of this with the possibility of love, with the ending of aloneness and the consummation of its opposite? Isn't this a big part of the point of being alive?

It is no coincidence that sexuality and mysticism share a common vocabulary, that St. Teresa writhes in her ecstasy the way that a lover contorts in hers. When by chance or design the energies of the moment are right, sexual union and mystical union are parallel motions of the soul. The boundaries of the ego recede, the illusions of self are smashed. And in their place emerges a joining with something larger, something greater.

If we are serious about the religious life, then what goes on in the bedroom is at least as significant as what goes on in the pews of a church. As we will see, I think there are good religious reasons why we might want the *government* to stay out of our bedrooms. But not spirituality. I want, I demand, and I have helped to bring about a spirituality that ennobles our bodies, our sexual selves, and the ways in which we can live more richly and more deliberately as emotional, physical beings. In large part because I was told that my sexuality was debased, I have worked, prayed, meditated, and learned to see that it is not. And in so doing I have seen how precisely those places cast in shadow can be receptive of the most light.

CHAPTER 15

"When I became a man, I put childish ways behind me"

The growth of religious values is good for individuals and religious communities

Iris Murdoch has written,

> The facts which will cure this prejudice belong to the ordinary talk of ordinary people, and should gradually become more accessible if those who know about homosexuality will refer to it sensibly, and as homosexuals gradually emerge from the demoralizing secrecy which is at present forced upon them. Doubtless homosexuals will always be a minority and doubtless they will always be with us. What is needed is not more science but just more humane and charitable recognition of our right to differ from one another.[1]

One reason the inclusion, acceptance, and affirmation of gays and lesbians can seem threatening to religiously minded people is it seems so *new*. Conservative religious rhetoric can be very persuasive: marriage has meant one man and one woman since the dawn of time, sodomy has been forbidden everywhere and always, and whenever homosexuality is sanctioned, it means the end of civilization. God's plan for humanity is clearly set forth in Genesis: one man and one woman, which leads to reproduction, stable families, and stable societies. And so on.

I've tried to show that each of these statements doesn't hold. In parts 1 and 2 of this book, I attempted to demonstrate that promoting spiritual and political equality for sexual minorities is not disobedi-

ence of God, but is actually in accord with God's fundamental commandments regarding love, integrity, dignity, justice, and partnership.
As fundamental as Adam and Eve are, their union is the solution to an
even more fundamental problem, the problem of aloneness, one that
must cause us to look for solutions for people who find themselves to
be gay or lesbian—solutions that are perfectly compatible with Scripture. And in part 3, so far, I've argued that the ethical aspects of society that religious people value will be improved, not hindered, by
equality for sexual minorities.

But even if everything I have argued is correct, I acknowledge that there is something to the *newness* of equality for gays and
lesbians that, itself, must give pause to a traditional believer. One reason so many religious people are conservative politically is that to be
conservative means to proceed, well, conservatively—to be skeptical
of social change, and of humanity's ability to achieve it, and move
slowly when considering changing existing institutions or principles.
This is why conservatives opposed civil rights for African Americans in the twentieth century: because liberals were proposing deep
changes in social order.

Then again, most conservatives today favor equality for people of
all races, right? We may disagree about the details of how that equality is to be achieved, but only a tiny fringe of conservatives believe
today what virtually all conservatives believed sixty years ago: that
God desires segregation of the races, and that Africans are cursed
to serve Europeans because of the sin of Ham. Conservatives and
traditionalists *do* eventually change their minds, individually and col-
lectively. Or to take another example, consider the role of women in
our society. Even conservatives who believe that women ought not to
pursue careers, and ought to focus only on the raising of children—
even this minority of conservatives still believe that women should be
educated and should have the right to vote. But 150 years ago, such a
view was considered radical. Conservatives today are far to the "left"
of conservatives of a century ago.

Surely this is a good thing. We now understand that centuries of
racism and prejudice clouded many of our moral judgments. Thus, we
should be deeply thankful that our religious communities have been
able to evolve on this point. Think about it for a moment. Most of
us today would say that racism is not only bad policy but is actually

immoral. It's *wrong* to have racist thoughts and support racist policies. This means that the social activism of the twentieth century, bitterly opposed as it was, was actually *good* for religious communities. At the time, many conservative preachers condemned Dr. King as a heretic, a fearmonger, and much, much worse. But from today's vantage point, he rescued the church from itself.

Now, as we've said before, gays are not the same as blacks, or women. And while we are united in the same overall struggle for liberation and equality, no one is arguing that sexual minorities are in the same social position as ethnic or racial minorities. But we can draw analogies between one struggle and another. As in these other areas, accepting sexual diversity is good for religious communities because it is precisely the flexibility of religious values that enables them to survive and adapt.[2] In stretching ourselves, we reflect on our values, refine our assumptions, and in so doing grow as religious individuals and communities.

The history of religion is marked by exactly this sort of progress— right from the very beginning. In Numbers 27:1–7, the daughters of Zelophehad come before Moses with a complaint: the law provides that a man's property passes to his eldest son, but Zelophehad had no son. Why, his daughters ask, should his property be lost? Give it to us instead. Moses turns to God, and God replies that the daughters of Zelophehad are right. The law, which God had set down only a few chapters earlier, changes when suppressed voices are heard and a cogent claim for justice is staked. This is how religion is meant to operate.

No doubt inspired by this example, the Talmudic rabbis ruled that Leviticus 24:19–20, which clearly requires punishment of an "eye for an eye," actually requires only monetary compensation.[3] They interpreted Deuteronomy 21:18–21, which required that a rebellious son be stoned to death, so narrowly that it could never be applied in practice.[4] It is not transgressive for religious people to preach against the status quo when the status quo is unjust; it is righteous to do so. As the saying goes, religion is meant to comfort the afflicted and afflict the comfortable.[5] This is why traditional Protestants like Walter Rauschenbush and Washington Gladden preached the "social gospel." It is why Dr. King's sermons resonated so deeply with the Judeo-Christian prophetic tradition. And surely it is why the Gospels tell stories of Jesus preaching against the hypocrisy of the Pharisees and the excesses of the rich.

Rethinking the place of sexual diversity in religious communities is an opportunity for both gay and straight people. For gay people, the challenge of sexual diversity "is a hidden blessing for LGBT believers. Because we are attacked for our faith, we are forced to examine it more closely."[6] And for straight people, it offers an opportunity to grow. Jack Rogers, a (heterosexual) Presbyterian theologian who served as Moderator of the 213th General Assembly of the Presbyterian Church (U.S.A.), described his journey this way:

> I opposed homosexuality reflexively—it was just what I thought Christians were supposed to do. However, studying this issue in depth for the first time brought me to a new understanding of the biblical texts and of God's will for our church. The process was both very serious and painful. I wasn't swayed by the culture or pressured by academic colleagues. I changed my mind initially by going back to the Bible and taking seriously its central message for our lives.[7]

I grew up in a midsize Southern city in the 1980s.[8] My teachers in religious school didn't teach us to be racist, but there was plenty of prejudice to go around. In my public high school, I remember that a black kid was beaten up because he was dating a white girl. This was pretty much accepted at the time. It wasn't official school policy—we had a black principal, for heaven's sake—but it was pretty well understood that some lines weren't meant to be crossed. Likewise, to call someone a fag in my public school was about the worst insult you could hurl. To not respond, either verbally or with violence, meant you really were a fag, which was even worse. There were one or two guys who, in retrospect, I think were probably gay. But even they never dared to actually admit that they were gay, or bring a boyfriend to the senior prom, or anything that public—at least nothing that I saw. To be gay in my high school was something to hide, to be ashamed of, and definitely something to lie about. Fortunately, in many places, times have changed. Religious communities shouldn't fear this kind of change; we should welcome it, because it is an invitation to reflection, to self-examination—and that is what the religious life is about.

Yet in many religious communities, we find the exact opposite. There are still preachers who support gay kids lying about who they are and being ashamed of their sexual identity. There are many who send them to bogus, abusive, and totally ineffective "reparative therapy" to learn how to crush and mutilate what God has created. There are even a few (not most) who say that gay kids who are subjected to violence—and according to FBI statistics, gay people are statistically the most likely to be targets of hate crimes[9]—get what's coming to them.[10] We need to own up to our religious communities' contribution to that kind of violence. We can't just blame the immediate perpetrators, when they've been egged on by leaders and elders. Of *course* it matters what preachers say in the pulpit—isn't that why they talk in the first place? So how could we imagine that their words would *not* have an effect when they are applied to gays and lesbians? Tell people that something is an abomination, and they'll work hard to remove it from their midst.

Things are coming to a head in our country. Just as the images of peaceful protesters being shot with water cannons awakened the nation's conscience fifty years ago, so too the images of gay teenagers killing themselves awaken us today. No, it's not the same struggle—but it is *one* struggle. It is the agency of conscience working against the soapstone of fear, which at first appears to be rock solid but soon proves itself amenable to transformation.

One of the reasons the movement for inclusion of gays and lesbians looks so new is the problem of invisibility, which we first explored in chapter 12. Sexual and gender minorities have been systematically written out of history, and so there's a sense sometimes that gays and lesbians simply didn't exist until the last few decades. Obviously, this is not so, but the sense that our existence is something radically new causes many people to feel uneasy about equality.

Let's remember, though, that if we determined who actually existed in the past solely on the basis of documentary evidence, we'd be forced to conclude that women, and many ethnic groups, never had any histories of their own either. As Virginia Woolf famously said, if Shakespeare had a sister, she would have been discouraged from ever taking up a pen. The potentially great women writers, poets, and artists of European history likely went uneducated and unsupported. So, as we try to reconstruct women's history, or guess what life might have been like for women, or what they might have thought about it, we are forced to read in the margins of conventional history, teasing out whatever hints and details we can. Likewise with sexual and gender minorities. We have existed in all places and all times. The terms "gay" and "homosexual," and the identities they convey, are social constructions, and originated only recently. But people we might today call gay, lesbian, bisexual, or transgender have indeed existed in all cultures around the world, and at all time periods. Sometimes they have been valued, sometimes devalued; sometimes honored, sometimes burned at the stake.

I want to give a few examples here, although to explore the subject fully would fill many books. Indeed, it already has, and some of them are listed in the bibliography: there are wonderful, lengthy studies of how gays and lesbians have been "hidden from history," and I have no new revelations to share here. My point here is simply to counter the myth that gay people are some new thing under the sun, or that the only way they were regarded in the past was as inveterate sinners, and thus that accepting gays and lesbians as full members of our religious and political communities would be some sort of radical revolution. Here, then, is a very short, very incomplete list of famous sexual and gender minorities in history:

- Alexander the Great: The greatest of ancient heroes not only had pederastic relationships with adolescents, but also a long-term love affair with a peer, Hephaestion.[11]
- Aristotle: The father of Western Democracy had young male lovers as well as female ones. So did Sophocles, Solon, Plato, and Euripides.[12]
- Sappho: Born in Lesbos, one of the first lyric poets in Western civilization wrote exquisite love poems to women.[13]
- Frederick the Great: The eighteenth-century king of Prussia was widely known to be homosexual in his time, and shared his homoerotic poetry with Voltaire, who "outed" him posthumously. Frederick surrounded himself with gay-themed art and had numerous male lovers. He also doubled the size of Prussia, setting the stage for a united Germany. Other European monarchs known to have had same-sex love affairs include Peter the Great, Richard Lionheart, and Henri III of France.[14]

- Queen Anne (1665–1714) had a twenty-five-year intimate friendship with Sarah Churchill, Duchess of Marlborough, despite the disapprobation of contemporaries. Most believe it to have included an erotic element (after the relationship soured, Sarah attempted to blackmail Queen Anne by exposing her letters).[15]
- Christina of Sweden (1626–1689) would probably today be recognized as transgender, or possibly intersex. Originally thought at birth to be a boy, Christina dressed as a man, refused to marry, and had passionate relationships with women, especially Ebba Sparre, a close companion.[16]
- Michelangelo: The painter of the Sistine Chapel and sculptor of *David* was known in his time to be attracted to men, especially Tommaso dei Cavalieri, to whom he dedicated over three hundred sonnets as well as a drawing of the iconic homoerotic myth of Ganymede (the youth seduced by Zeus). His sonnets were censored after his death.[17]
- Leonardo da Vinci: Arrested for sodomy when he was twenty-four, Leonardo never married, surrounded himself with beautiful young men, and made explicitly erotic drawings of men.[18]
- Christopher Marlowe: Shakespeare's rival wrote ceaselessly about same-sex love and was implicated in homosexual affairs.[19]
- Lord Byron: The nineteenth-century Romantic poet was a bisexual who had sexual relationships with men and women throughout his life. His masterpiece "Love and Death" dealt with an unrequited love for a Greek young man.[20]
- Hans Christian Andersen, whose "fairy tales" often had gay allegorical themes.[21]
- Walt Whitman: America's greatest poet composed erotic poems about men, praised "adhesiveness" (widely used as a term for what we now call homosexuality), had longtime male companions (the photograph of Whitman and Peter Doyle speaks volumes, though Whitman's diary entries about Doyle are even clearer), and never married. His same-sex-themed poems remain scandalous today, and are often edited out of editions of *Leaves of Grass*.[22]
- Pyotr Ilich Tchaikovsky: The *1812 Overture* composer's personal correspondence leaves no doubt that he was homosexual, and

the famous *Pathétique* symphony is dedicated to Tchaikovsky's nephew Bob, with whom he was in love.[23]

- James Hammond, one of the leading "great men" of the antebellum South, who articulated Southern defenses of slavery and conservative moralism, also wrote explicitly erotic letters to a male lover that reveal his broad sexual appetites to include both men and women.[24]
- George Washington Carver: The "wizard of Tuskegee" never married, was persistently rumored to be gay, and had many (apparently chaste) strong emotional attachments to certain male students, as well as to his personal assistant, Austin W. Curtis Jr.[25]

Not to mention prominent twentieth-century LGBT people including Eleanor Roosevelt, Marcel Proust, Gertrude Stein, Cole Porter, Grant Wood (the painter of *American Gothic*), Jasper Johns, Susan Sontag, Leonard Bernstein, Tennessee Williams, James Baldwin (and many other figures of the Harlem Renaissance and jazz age), E. M. Forster, Rudolf Nureyev, Errol Flynn, Florence Nightingale, James Dean, Rock Hudson, Montgomery Clift, and many, many more. This is the truth of the historical record: that even with the deliberate efforts at erasure, people we would today call gay, lesbian, bisexual, or transgender have existed at all historical time periods, in all cultures, everywhere.

Nor is it the case that homosexuality has been universally condemned throughout all history. In the nineteenth-century West, gay subcultures were often regarded with intrigue and curiosity; as historian George Chauncey writes, "[W]hile anti-gay discrimination is popularly thought to have ancient roots, in fact it is a unique and relatively short-lived product of the twentieth century."[26] John Boswell has brought forth provocative evidence that pairs of male and female saints in the first centuries of the Christian era were regarded as romantic couples, and may have been models for passionate vows of friendship and union.[27] Elsewhere, homosexuality is represented approvingly in seventeenth-century Indian manuscripts; twelfth-century Indian stone carvings (on a recent trip to India, I saw some myself); countless Greek myths (Zeus and Ganymede, Achilles and Patroclus, Narcissus and Echo, Apollo and Hyacinth); Greek vases; the legendary *1001 Nights* (sometimes called the *Arabian Nights*); the poetry of Rumi and Hafiz; and the Hebrew poetry of Judah Halevi.[28] Forms of homosexual behavior were part of Mamluk Egypt and throughout the Islamic world.[29] In early modern Japan, homosexuality was seen as a noble form of love and lionized in poetry, art, and philosophy:[30] One seventeenth-century collection of short stories on the varieties of love between men, *The Great Mirror of Male Love,* is among the most noted works of literature from the period, and the love of younger men was an essential part of the Samurai way of life.[31] Traditional Chinese society had several complimentary terms for homosexuality, each deriving from an ancient literary source: *longyang* comes from the tale of Longyang Jun and his lover (fourth century BCE); *fen tao zhi ai* (literally, "the love of the shared peach") comes from a story in the *Chronicles of the Warring States* (third century BCE) of a man sharing a peach with his male lover; and *duanxiu* (the "torn sleeve") comes from the first-century BCE story of an emperor whose lover was napping on his shoulder and who tore his sleeve rather than awaken his beloved.[32]

In fact, many cultures regard sexual diversity as sacred and assign to sexual minorities special roles, such as shamans and healers. We have already made mention of over one hundred Native American traditions that accorded special roles to gender-variant people.[33] People our culture might call gay, lesbian, or transgender were called *winkte* by the Lakota, *nadle* by the Navaho, *minquga* by the Omaha, and *hwame* by the Mohave, and served as shamans, healers, and warriors. Similar roles are played by the Polynesian *mahu* and Omani *xanith.* In India and Pakistan, the *hijra,* biological men whom we might call gay or transgender ("hijra" is often derogatory; *kinnar* and *khwaja saraa* are alternatives), live up until the present day in sacred intentional communities, dress as women, and venerate specific Divine figures. The *hijra*—and the *kothi,* who act similarly to the *hijra* but do not have particular religious roles—are part of a long-standing tradition that formed the basis of Nepal's recent recognition of "third gender" people,[34] and "third gender" people are mentioned in the Kama Sutra and Mahabharata. In the Ancient Near East, sexual and gender minorities had their own religious sects such as the Galli of ancient Rome.[35] There are Buddhist tales of women transformed into men, kabbalistic stories of women with male souls, Islamic poems in which the love of God is analogized to the love of one man for another.

The spectrum of perspectives on sexual minorities around the world is dazzling.

To repeat, it's not that all of these cultures venerated "gay" people. As theorists such as David Halperin and others have stressed, "homosexuality" is a socially constructed term that does not apply to every form of same-sex intimacy.[36] In China and Japan, for example, men still were required to fulfill familial and procreative roles, and the appropriate forms of male–male intimacy were carefully regulated. This does not mean that seventeenth-century Chinese people were "bisexual"; it means that our categories of intimacy do not apply to other cultures. Attitudes also varied over time; Chinese and Japanese societies were relatively approving of same-sex intimacy in the seventeenth century, disapproving in the eighteenth. But it is simply not the case, as some have alleged, that what we today call homosexuality simply didn't exist in history, or that where it did, it was always condemned. It just isn't so.

The consequences of our erasure from history, though, are severe. As Gerald Unks has written,

> Within the typical secondary school curriculum, homosexuals do not exist. They are "nonpersons" in the finest Stalinist sense. They have fought no battles, held no offices, explored nowhere, written no literature, built nothing, invented nothing and solved no equations. The lesson to the heterosexual student is abundantly clear: homosexuals do nothing of consequence. To the homosexual student, the message has even greater power: no one who has ever felt as you do has done anything worth mentioning.[37]

Sexual and gender minorities have always been with us. We just haven't always seen them.

All that being said, I want to be clear that I fully "get" the feeling of novelty and newness that makes religious people want to move slowly toward inclusion. I do not share the view that this concern is reducible to homophobia or bigotry. This is why the historical record is so important. Do your own research. Read the books out there on gay and lesbian history, and on the wide range of religious responses to homosexuality. Keep your mind and your heart open. Inclusion asks us to open our hearts to strangers to whom our hearts have often been hardened. We grow stronger each time we do.

We grow as religious people through an unlikely combination of courage and humility. It takes courage to question one's opinions, and humility to recognize that we may not be as right as we thought. Again, the example of the civil rights movement provides an important point of reference. The greatest courage was shown by those activists who stood in front of the water cannons, who risked everything—and who, in some cases, paid with their lives. But the great awakening of American conscience regarding civil rights also depended on millions of smaller, private acts of courage. When a white man in the South opened his heart to the suffering of others, when he questioned what he'd been taught in church and at home and in school—that took courage, and it took humility.

"When I was a child, I talked like a child, I thought like a child, I reasoned like a child. When I became a man, I put childish ways behind me." So says Paul of his own religious maturation process in 1 Corinthians 13:11. It may seem like strength to hold fast to unchanging religious beliefs, and there are times where steadfastness is an act of heroism. But it takes even more strength to heed the demands of our faith traditions to introspect, discern, and reflect on what we thought we knew. All of us who make religion or spirituality part of our lives are accustomed to this mandate. Whether we attend confession, or review our lives each Yom Kippur, or have heart-to-heart conversations with Christ, or enter periods of contemplation wherein we try to understand what course of action is the right one, or engage in any number of other procedures of self-examination and review, those of us serious about spiritual practice are invited, time and again, to look inward.

Yet even this process of introspection is not entirely interior in nature. Our minds are informed, saturated even, by the values we learn from our sacred traditions and the world around us. We all know this to be true, which is one reason so many believers choose to separate themselves from a world they perceive to be corrupt. But do we acknowledge the depth to which it is true? Even on a gut, instinctual level, we are shaped by assumptions and judgments that may be so familiar that they pass unnoticed. And these assumptions are culturally determined: show a picture of a dog to someone born into a Western society, and they may think "pet," and possibly feel affection. Show the same picture to someone born into some Asian societies, and they think "food," and feel hungry.

Notwithstanding all the commonsense advice to "trust your gut," I want to suggest that our guts are not trustworthy at all, and must instead be tempered by love. All animals have gut reactions, after all. Only humans (and perhaps a few others, in more limited ways) are able to reason beyond them. Our guts will always be primitive: lots of men will always want the biggest club to beat their enemies with, and the prettiest woman to have sex with. Many women want the biggest man. This is nature. But it's not the sum total of humanity. We are blessed with the ability to rise beyond our gut reactions—as some religious traditions put it, we have sparks of God within us. (Or, as some neuroscientists put it, we have prefrontal cortexes that can mediate the impulses of the amygdala.) And we all know from experience that you can feel something in your gut, and still be wrong. We've all trusted someone who turned out not to be trustworthy, and believed things "tradition" told us (e.g., whites are smarter than blacks, men are smarter than women) that turned out to be factually and morally wrong. The process of educating the moral conscience, of growing up religiously and ethically, is, in large part, the process of applying love and reason to what we think we already knew. Love teaches us how to think justly.

Really, what is this "gut" that is supposed to lie beneath our rational minds? Does it really exist? Of course not—it's just a word we use to describe a certain feeling. Some feelings *feel* deeper, others shallower. But there's no connection between those feelings and reality. So let's not dignify gut reactions with any kind of value.

This is how moral progress takes place, I think. We learn to stop trusting gut reactions that are based on falsehoods we've been taught. And it is one of the gifts that our national wrestling with the question of equality for LGBT people gives to each of us. This is an invitation to be uncomfortable, because discomfort is a sign of growth; it's a sign that you've reached your learning edge, where assumptions may be challenged and difficult lessons may be learned. If religion has taught us anything, it is that there is value in transcending our baser instincts—and that includes the snap judgments all of us make all the time. At first, and maybe for a while, these corrections along the course of moral conscience may not feel right. But they are the defining marks of our humanity. Love demands them.

Even our introspection must be subjected to introspection. For example, ex-gay guru Joe Dallas writes that when he was living a gay life and going to a gay church, he believed "what I wanted to believe instead of what I *truly* believed," which was that homosexuality was wrong. But how does he know the difference? Didn't he stop and wonder why one belief seemed "truer" than another? That the anti-gay myth seemed "truer" because it was drummed into him for twenty years? No, he just assumed that if something feels true, it is true. Well, if we all operated like that we'd still be riding segregated buses to separate and unequal schools. If Dallas were truly being introspective instead of rushing to judgment (no doubt based on fear), he would see that, actually, he's believing what he wants to believe after all. On some deep, psychological level, he *wants* to believe that his sexuality is sinful. I don't know why. Maybe sex scares him. Maybe he's actually bisexual. Or maybe the idea that homosexuality is wrong is just what he was taught for years, and it's more comforting for *that* to be okay than for his sexuality to be. Whatever the reason, he's not escaping from "what I wanted to believe"—he's indulging in it.

There is no substitute for a careful discernment process when it comes to questions like these. Personally, meditation is my primary way of doing so, as I've written about in my other books. Prayer is another way. So are the exercises of St. Ignatius of Loyola, or spiritual direction, or the process of spiritual discernment. I like to think of all of these as technologies—as tools, meant to help us see more clearly and act less rashly. At the very least, they will help wean us away from the notion that what feels right is right.

I have seen this process unfold hundreds of times. The organization PFLAG, for example—Parents and Friends of Lesbians And Gays—is largely made up of folks who have traveled this journey, from rejection to acceptance to embrace. These are ordinary people, not gay activists and not gay themselves, who once had anti-gay views, for whatever reason, but who were forced to reexamine those views when people they loved came out as gay or lesbian. This journey is a painful one, but it is also blessed. It is the unfolding of the moral conscience, and it is, in my opinion, religious consciousness at its very best.

But sometimes it comes too late. I urge you to read the book *Prayers for Bobby* by Leroy Aarons. This book (and TV movie) is the story of Mary Griffith, a devout, conservative Presbyterian who urged her son to "change" his sexual orientation. Bobby prayed and prayed, but could not change his sexuality. He eventually moved out of the house but was still tormented by his inability to feel accepted by his mother, or by God. Eventually, Bobby killed himself by jumping in front of a truck.

The story does not end there, however. Mary Griffith eventually begins to question her church's teachings about homosexuality, going over some of the same verses we read so closely in part 2. Her views about the nature of sexuality change, and she realizes that she had been asking her son to do the impossible: to change a trait which God gave him. Eventually, Griffith becomes an unlikely gay advocate, PFLAG member, and activist in her home community.

Griffith's story is tragic; her redemption comes too late to save her son. But it is a redemption nonetheless. It is exactly, I think, what the religious life is meant to be about: questioning our certainty, questioning what we thought we knew, and earnestly living in the light of God and conscience. People of faith are not called upon to be automatons. If our faith means anything, other than some meaningless badge of identity or piety, it means that we have taken up the challenge to live unlazily, according to our hopes and ideals. We wrestle with God, and in so doing wrestle with ourselves, our preconceptions, our notions of how we think the world is. Occasions for doing so—like the question of equality, dignity, and respect for sexual minorities—are not crises. They are invitations.

My most cherished tale of this kind of religious evolution is in Mark Twain's *Adventures of Huckleberry Finn*. For me, it perfectly epitomizes the kind of shift, motivated by conscience and experience, that is of so much religious value, and that is invited by the question of sexual diversity. I've taught it many times around the country, and almost every time someone has a tear in their eye. Often it's me. By the time this episode takes place, Huck has been floating down the Mississippi River with Jim, an escaped slave. They've had all sorts of colorful adventures and have spent long hours on the raft getting to know one another. Huck has already evolved a great deal over the course of the book, growing from a bratty, arrogant, and also racist kid into a young man; it is, after all, a coming-of-age story. Yet Huck is still troubled by his conscience, because he has been taught that if he helps an escaped slave, he will go to hell. One night, racked with guilt and indecision, he tries to decide what to do. Here's how we find him:

So I was full of trouble, full as I could be; and didn't know what to do. At last I had an idea; and I says, I'll go and write the letter—and then see if I can pray. Why, it was astonishing, the way I felt as light as a feather right straight off, and my troubles all gone. So I got a piece of paper and a pencil, all glad and excited, and set down and wrote:

Miss Watson, your runaway nigger Jim is down here two mile below Pikesville, and Mr. Phelps has got him and he will give him up for the reward if you send.

Huck Finn.

I felt good and all washed clean of sin for the first time I had ever felt so in my life, and I knowed I could pray now. But I didn't do it straight off, but laid the paper down and set there thinking—thinking how good it was all this happened so, and how near I come to being lost and going to hell. And went on thinking. And got to thinking over our trip down the river; and I see Jim before me all the time: in the day and in the night-time, sometimes moonlight, sometimes storms, and we a-floating along, talking and singing and laughing. But somehow I couldn't seem to strike no places to harden me against him, but only the other kind. I'd see him standing my watch on top of his'n, 'stead of calling me, so I could go on sleeping; and see him how glad he was when I come back out of the fog; and when I come to him again in the swamp, up there where the feud was; and suchlike times; and would always call me honey, and pet me, and do everything he could think of for me, and how good he always was; and at last I struck the time I saved him by telling the men we had small-pox aboard, and he was so grateful, and said I was the best friend old Jim ever had in the world, and the only one he's got now; and then I happened to look around and see that paper.

It was a close place. I took it up, and held it in my hand. I was a-trembling, because I'd got to decide, forever, betwixt two things, and I knowed it. I studied a minute, sort of holding my breath, and then says to myself:

"All right, then, I'll go to hell"—and tore it up.[38]

This is the invitation to which questions of conscience call us—and all of us would agree that Huck's decision to "go to hell" is in fact his most religious, most adult act. But notice how Huck's conscience evolves in this passage. At first, he is troubled and decides to turn Jim in. Initially, he feels relief, even redemption ("all washed clean of sin"), and reflects for a bit on how it is good how things have turned out in this way. But then there's that pivotal line: "And went on thinking." Huck doesn't stay with his initial response—he continues to contemplate. And what does he think about? Not dogma, but experience. He has been taught that Jim is less than human, but he has experienced that Jim *is* human: that he has helped Huck so many times, and loves him—and that Huck loves Jim back. Finally, Huck realizes that there is a choice to be made, and he makes it.

This process will be familiar to any of us who have been forced to examine a conflict between what we thought we knew and the deeper religious truths with which we have been confronted. Personally, I went through it in almost exactly the same way with regard to my own sexuality. There were times when the closeted life I was leading also made me feel "washed clean of sin." But then I went on thinking, and feeling, and wrestling with God. At one point, I remember saying to God in a prayer, "Look, I'm sorry, but this is how it is, and you're just going to have to deal with it. I've tried everything else, and I give up." Like Huck, I decided that I'd rather go to hell than betray the reality of love.

All of us have times when the old forms we've been taught are confronted by irreducible facts and unmistakable experiences. These are often called "crises of faith," and indeed they are crises of a simplistic faith, one that believes all the answers are clear, and all the paths are straightforward. But a mature faith, a spirituality worthy of its name, is not so naive. We may be childlike in our devotion, but we are adults in our contemplation. Does anyone believe that Huck would have been better off had he not had his crisis? Of course not. Huck isn't going to go to hell for his actions. Precisely by giving up on the stories he'd been told in church, he has a moment of religious salvation, of awakening. To go through this process does put one in "a close place." It can feel like the walls are caving in. And yet the only real walls are in the heart, and when the hardening of heart is let go, one is capable of being reborn.

CHAPTER 16

"Everyone whose spirit moved him brought an offering to God"

*Sexual diversity, like other forms of diversity,
enriches religious lives and communities*

Sexual diversity is good for religious communities because diversity in general is good for religious communities. All of us are enriched by having multiple perspectives on God, values, and how to live a meaningful life. Even when we share fundamental values, we learn from people who experience those values in different ways. This is how I have learned from my friends of other faiths: not by pretending that our differences do not exist, nor by supposing that they are so great that conversation between us is not possible, but by learning precisely from our differences that there are always multiple approaches to questions of value, and seemingly infinite permutations on the life well lived.

How dull it would be if all of us shared the same gender, the same ethnicity, or the same national background. Yet valuing diversity —the "gorgeous mosaic" of American ethnicities, nationalities, and religions—used to be taboo. Only a generation or two ago, it was considered unseemly for black and white folks to mix, or for people of different religious communities to associate with one another. Fortunately, today, as we recalled in the last chapter, even conservative religious communities welcome people of different nationalities and ethnic backgrounds.

Likewise with sexual orientation. Perhaps your church or synagogue now has some "out" gay people in it. Do you remember when they first appeared? At first, it might have seemed radical to have two women sit together as a couple. Maybe they were "the lesbians" at first. But eventually, chances are they just became Patty and Sue, and their lesbianism was no more and no less interesting than the Kaczynskis being Polish or the Aronsons being a multiracial family. Sexual and gender diversity is just another form of diversity in general.

Now, it's not that sexual orientation becomes invisible. I find it a little insulting when someone tells me it doesn't matter that I "happen to be gay." It does matter. It affects how I live, how I love, and how I relate to religion, style, politics, and culture, among other things. It's part of who I am, and I want to show up as my whole self with my religious community, not be told that part of me doesn't matter. The point is that it *does* matter, and that enriches my overall community.

By way of analogy, I often think about the contributions that women's and feminist theology have made to religious communities over the last several decades. I'm not a woman, but the ways I think about God, Torah, and Israel (three foundational values in Jewish philosophy) have been tremendously impacted by feminist theology. I use different liturgical language than I did growing up, because I internalized how relating to God only as male (e.g., "King," "Lord") is both insulting to many women, and a limiting way of thinking. My spiritual life has been enriched by being invited to think of God as Compassionate (which in Hebrew is related to the word for womb), multigendered, and within the world as much as beyond it. The way I understand Scripture has been shaped by the sudden effusion of women's Bible commentaries, legends, and myth making, all of which have appeared within the last half century. If women were still being told that their ideas weren't worth expressing, or weren't distinctive in any way, my own spiritual life would be much poorer.

So too, I am convinced, with the voices of sexual and gender minorities. What is being called "queer theology" has only just begun, but already it is shining new lights on Scripture and tradition. To take but one example, if masculinity is defined, as it often is, in terms of violence and aggression, isn't the injunction to love your enemy and turn the other cheek somewhat "queer"? Maybe these conventional boxes of masculine and feminine flatten *all* of our experiences, not just those of sexual minorities. Maybe the Bible is inviting all of us to be queer, again not construed narrowly in terms of sexual orientation, but understood broadly, in terms of defying conventional expectations of gender roles and taming precisely those instincts that might be understood as gendered in one way or another. If the Bible is asking males to curb our sexual appetites, curb our instincts to fight, and curb our desires to be as big and powerful as possible, maybe the insights of queer men can be of value to all of us who take these mandates seriously. Maybe the simple binaries of masculine/feminine don't capture the richness of who we are as human beings—and maybe their inadequacy points to the limitations of simple yes/no, black/white, permitted/forbidden, insider/outsider reasoning generally. As John McNeill writes, "the attempt to force humans into narrow heterosexist categories of 'masculinity' and 'femininity' can destroy the great richness and variety of God's creation."[1] Maybe the experiences of LGBT people remind all of us that our lives are more complex than dichotomies suggest.

This is but one small example. As with many topics I have touched upon, entire books have been written on these ideas, and we'll explore queer theology a bit more in the next chapter. The point here is that the different voices of sexual and gender minorities have only just begun to be heard and have the capacity to enrich all of our lives. Perhaps, as we will see in the next chapter, LGBT people may take on special roles within our religious communities, as they have in religious traditions around the world. Most likely, we do not yet even know what contributions they may make.

We all gain from this kind of diversity. Human fulfillment is achieved not by rigid categories and boxes of similar size, but by outgrowing such limitations on our way to wholeness.[2] For religious people, more diversity enables more appreciation of the many-patterned mosaic of our short lives here on Earth. The spectrum of sexual identity is so much more than genital activity and a few lines of Scripture. It impacts all kinds of life choices, values, and life experiences. And ironically, the more perspectives we are able to accommodate in our view of the world, the closer we are to the unity that underlies them.

There are multiple levels to this kind of diversity. Religious communities are strengthened on the inside by allowing diversity to flourish within, and they are strengthened from the outside by allowing diversity of religious opinion to flourish without. "One man considers one day more sacred than another; another man considers every day alike. Each one should be fully convinced in his own mind" (Rom.

14:5). We find ways to live together, even as we disagree, and we are enriched by the act of learning to do so. Nature abhors a monoculture, and so does civil society.

Take the highly contentious example of same-sex marriage. I want to suggest that one may take a very conservative religious position on same-sex marriage within one's religious community while at the same time supporting same-sex marriage politically. For example, Orthodox Jews believe that Jewish religious marriage must be performed, as the traditional liturgy has it, "according to the religion of Moses and Israel," requiring not only opposite-sex partners but the traditional purchase of the wife by the husband. Maintaining this view may be a religious obligation. But *politically* speaking, my claim is that the same Orthodox Jew, and his Catholic and Protestant counterparts, should nonetheless support civil marriage equality for everyone, for two sets of reasons. First, there are all the religious values we explored in part 1, which should compel all Christians and Jews to seek the most equality, justice, dignity, love, and human relationship for everyone, gays and lesbians included. Where religious traditions are constrained by their internal dynamics regarding particular questions, that is understandable. But where they have the opportunity to promote fundamental religious values by supporting liberty *outside* of their own traditions' constraints, then those values compel such a position. Where there is suffering, conscience calls us to alleviate it.

Second, and more to the point, there is the immense value of having the state not interfere in the church's domain, and the church not interfere in the state's. The most famous American formulation of this view originated with Roger Williams, in 1644. Williams advocated a "hedge or wall of separation between the garden of the church and the wilderness of the world."[3] Notice his language here: the "wall of separation" is not to preserve the state—but to preserve the *church*. Williams believed, and I think history has borne him out, that if religious denominations got too involved with American politics, they would be dirtied in the process, and that inevitably, the government would get too involved in religion. We seem to have forgotten this today—most of the loudest voices in favor of separation tend to be secular ones. But religious people have even more at stake. The last thing I, as a member of a religious minority, would want is different religious communities duking it out in public, to see who gets to set our nation's laws. Can you imagine the corruption of religious discourse that would ensue if religious truths were debated on the floor of the U.S. Congress?

This is precisely the corruption Williams feared—not the corruption of the secular by the involvement of the religious, but of the religious by involvement with the secular. It is one thing for religious values to impact our individual choices; that is what religion is all about. But for religion to dictate public laws means that religion itself is to be subjected to public debate, across denominational lines and with a deeply corrosive effect both on religious liberty and on the freedom of religious communities to decide matters for themselves. We religious people can't have it both ways, after all. Either Williams's garden wall is put into place, or the domains of politics and religion intermingle, with each having influence over the other.

This was also the view of John Locke, one of the most important philosophers for the Founders of the republic. Locke saw England driven apart by religious civil war between Catholics and Protestants, and he recognized that because religious truths were largely matters of faith, they could not really be debated. If I believe one thing on faith and you believe another, there are no objective criteria for evaluating which one of us is right. Thus, Locke reasoned, religious faith can never be a basis for a nation in which people have different religious views. Moreover, Locke observed, even when we think we have evidence for a view, that evidence may actually be quite limited due to the limits of human understanding. We just don't know all the things we think we know. Let's not be so sure of ourselves. And where there's no way to reconcile our disagreement, let's try not to fight about it so much.

Simple truths (and unfair reductions of Locke), but ones we tend not to pay enough attention to today. Are we *really* so sure of what the Bible says about sexuality, or slavery, or, for that matter, the age of the Earth and the meaning of life itself? And even if we feel sure for ourselves, do we really have public reasons—that is, reasons that all of us could see, debate, and discuss—for our views? Or would we be backing ourselves into precisely the corner that Locke is trying to avoid, in which it's just your faith against mine, with no possibility of dialogue?

When religion works right, it gets into our *kishkes,* into our guts. We may know some things by way of reason, but most of what matters religiously is transrational: it's emotional, spiritual, even embodied. Being moved by the Holy Spirit is not a "public reason"; it's a private experience, albeit one that may be shared by others in our community. Rest assured, the Catholic feels as certain of her faith as does the evangelical, as does the Muslim, as does the Jew. Religious experience feels authentic, wherever it happens. Which is why more pluralism is better for all of us.

We don't have to be relativists about religious values—but we oughtn't be so arrogant about them either. Precisely because we feel strongly and still disagree, the safest, most conservative policy for religious communities living together is to carefully distinguish between intrareligious matters and interreligious ones. And if we want to get along, we must learn to tolerate difference, even difference that offends our very core principles, because the alternative will eventually be bad for everyone. The political winds may favor a particular group at a particular time, but eventually those winds will shift.

When two women have their marriage recognized by the state, all religious people win, because in addition to sanctioning their union the state is sanctioning freedom. Yes, some religious people and some religious denominations may not support same-sex marriage within their churches. But their right not to support it is protected by the exact same liberty that the two women enjoy. Without a separation of church and state, the state would be entitled to coerce a particular church to perform not just gay weddings but interfaith weddings, weddings not in accord with particular religious rules, you name it. Mixing politics and religion is a two-way street. If we want religion to dictate political rules, then we must be prepared for politics to dictate religious ones.

Obviously, religious liberty does come at a cost. Many religious communities, after all, are interested not only in their internal affairs, but in creating a broader society that conforms to their vision of ethics and truth. This interest is, indeed, restricted by the principle of religious liberty. But the benefits more than justify this cost. In exchange for not being able to dictate terms to the wider society, religious communities gain the freedom to decide things for themselves.

I recognize that this view is not widely shared among religious conservatives. But it should be. The same principles of freedom that protect gays and lesbians also protect religious communities whose views differ from the majority. Mormons, Catholics, Jews, Muslims, Quakers, Buddhists, Presbyterians, Hindus, Methodists, evangelicals—all are minorities in America. And although we may have many shared religious values, each religious community also has values that set it apart, and that they ought to be able to decide for themselves. If we value our religious communities, we should value the constitutional principles that keep them separate from state interference.

Finally, Williams's metaphor of the garden of the church and the wilderness of the world was intended to teach us something about the corruption of power. If you map out the religiosity of majority-Christian countries against the presence of an official church, you see something really remarkable. Those countries with the strongest official churches also have the highest percentage of nonbelievers. Those countries with no official churches, like the United States, have the highest rates of religious affiliation. Now, shouldn't the opposite be the case? Shouldn't it be that if there is a powerful, established church, more people affiliate with it? Well, it turns out not to be so. Power corrupts. When a church becomes official, when it takes on political roles and has a political function, it inevitably becomes dirtied by politics.

This is true not only in Christian countries but also in Israel, where I lived for several years. There, the "chief rabbinate" is a body with political power, and it decides what weddings, funerals, conversions, and other life-cycle events have to look like, in order to be recognized by the state. The result? A polarization of the Israeli Jewish public, in which a majority of Israelis wants nothing whatsoever to do with the religious, and the religious minority grows ever more fundamentalist and extreme. It's tragic, really, but quite understandable. When my great-aunt died, she had lived as a proud secular Jew in Israel for over fifty years. She was a warm, loving human being who was beloved by her family, and who loved her secular Jewish identity. But her funeral, in accord with the law, was performed by an ultra-Orthodox rabbi the family had never met, who mumbled through the traditional funeral liturgy without any thought or feeling. It was nothing less than disgusting. And yet, it was nothing new for my Israeli relatives, who had endured such treatment from the "official rabbis" for their entire lives. There is nothing more destructive to religion than giving it political power.

To repeat, none of this means that our religious values shouldn't impact our political opinions. If ethical and spiritual teachings matter, they must have something to say about those political issues that have ethical or spiritual significance. But to say that, for example, because my church forbids same-sex marriage, then no one anywhere should have one—that is something entirely different. That is saying that my church's rules should be everyone's rules—and in the long run, that view is toxic to religion itself.

The ethical teachings of my religion have impacted my opinions on the environment, economics, and a dozen other issues. But I fear the day when my religion's particular views on particular questions become the law of the land. I have seen what that looks like in Israel, and it makes me both sad and sickened. Power corrupts, and political power corrupts in a particularly insidious way. It may seem like victory for a religious sect when its views are imposed on everyone in the country. In fact, it is a sign of its demise.

"And I have filled him with the spirit of God . . . to devise subtle works in gold, silver, and brass"

What is homosexuality for?

Throughout this book, I've tried to make the case that equality, dignity, and respect for sexual minorities are everybody's concern, and that the inclusion of sexual minorities is not only consonant with our shared religious values, but also for the benefit of religious communities. Religious people should care about inclusion not simply out of compassion for gay people, but because religious communities will benefit as a result. This is good for the church, good for the *sangha,* good for the *kehillah.*

Over the last few decades scholars and theologians have begun asking what specific contributions sexual minorities might make to religious communities, and how lesbian, gay, bisexual, and transgender people add to our collective understanding of ourselves and our religious lives. The answers to this question run the gamut from nothing to everything. For some religious traditions, LGBT people are marked by God for special religious roles. For others, they are simply no big deal. But if there is a religious case to be made for equality, it is unlikely to be based on the claim that it doesn't matter if someone "happens to be gay." Of course it matters, religiously speaking. It has to.

This is not an inquiry into why God has made people gay. Only the most naive believer would pretend to know the purpose of every quirk of creation—or perhaps the most arrogant. Perhaps there is deep Divine purpose to the myriad ways in which human beings and animals express their sexuality. For example, one rabbi told me that the reason there are so many "out" gay people these days is that the Earth needs more love, but fewer humans. We are overpopulating the globe, he told me, and homosexuality is the only way to maintain ecological equilibrium while affording the opportunity for sacred relationships between people. Certainly, this is a creative interpretation of sexual diversity, and one that regards homosexuality as a blessing, rather than a predicament. If it gives gay people a sense of meaning, that's a good thing. But from my perspective, I'm more interested in exploring the gifts of sexual diversity than guessing the reasons for it. Do I know *why* God made me gay, or six foot one, or good with words? No. But I know that all of those traits carry with them certain gifts, responsibilities, risks, and opportunities. This, to me, seems the more fertile line of inquiry.

And it has already begun to bear fruit. Do LGBT people, as Jung said, have a special "spiritual receptivity"?[1] Do gay people experience (or transcend) the balance between masculine and feminine, at the heart of so many mystical and religious traditions, in different ways that may enrich all our experiences of gender? Are there special perspectives on the key questions of religion that are afforded to sexual and gender minorities? Already, scholars in the discipline known as "queer theology" have begun opening exciting lines of investigation in religious thought,[2] while outside traditional structures the "gay spirituality" and women's spirituality movements have explored similar avenues. Some of the key names in queer theology have already been mentioned: Donald Boisvert, James B. Nelson, Elizabeth Stuart, Audre Lorde, Carter Heyward, Robert Goss, Gary Comstock, Patrick Cheng, Rebecca T. Alpert, Irene Monroe, George Edwards, Virginia Ramey Mollenkott, Marcella Althaus-Reid, Gerald Loughlin, Justin Tanis, Michael Kelly, Nancy Wilson, and, on the (somewhat) more traditional side, John McNeill, Rev. Candace Chellew-Hodge, J. Michael Clark, Michael S. Piazza, Chris Glaser, and Malcolm Boyd. Key queer biblical scholars include Ken Stone, Theodore Jennings, and Stephen D. Moore, as well as many of the theologians listed above. And key writers in gay spirituality include Toby Johnson, Mark Thompson, Christian de la Huerta, Randy Conner, Joe Perez, and Andrew Ramer. Obviously, these fields are much too large to treat properly here, so I will instead focus on a handful of examples.

Episcopal lesbian theologian Carter Heyward, whose work we briefly noted in part 1, has described her project this way: "I am attempting to give voice to an embodied—sensual—relational movement among women and men who experience our sexualities as a liberating resource and who, at least in part through this experience, have been strengthened in the struggle for justice for all."[3] Heyward and others, such as Michael Kelly, James B. Nelson, Robert Goss, Virginia Ramey Mollenkott, Donald Boisvert, and Marcella Althaus-Reid, are attempting nothing less than a recovery of the physical, embodied, and erotic within Christian traditions that have traditionally suppressed them.[4] Building a theology of relationality that is reminiscent of the work of Jewish philosophers Martin Buber and Emmanuel Levinas, Heyward has proposed a spiritual valuation of eros—which she defines as "our embodied yearning for mutuality."[5] Openness to embodied love opens us to other people, the biological processes of the universe, and to God. Thus, Heyward writes, "my eroticism is my participation in the universe" and "we are the womb in which God is born."[6]

LGBT people, Heyward says, are uniquely able to actualize this Divine process. Coming out, for example, is a process of coming to accept the reality of one's own love, one's own erotic soul. Thus, "coming out, we well may be drawn into our power in right relation."[7] Everyone *ought* to do this, but LGBT people, if they are honest, must. Heyward's understanding of the erotic as "our most fully embodied experience of the love of God"[8] may be challenging to some, profoundly liberating for others. Personally, I find it profound—and, as a theologian, Heyward is quite precise in her criticism of previous thinkers ("Augustine was confused, spiritually and sexually. . . . Rather than embracing sexuality as a dimension of sacred passion, Augustine targeted it as its opposite.").[9] She is also clear about the potential radicalism of her own approach ("No person, religion, tradition, profession, rule, or resource should be inherently authoritative for us. We should always ask this question: Does it help us realize more fundamentally our connectedness to one another and hence the shape of our own identities as persons-in-relation?").[10] Hers is one queer theological voice that invites, and demands, careful listening.

A more traditional queer theologian is ordained Catholic priest John McNeill, whose work on the Bible and homosexuality—some of the first of its kind—we have encountered already. Like Heyward, McNeill believes that gay and lesbian people possess "special gifts and qualities and a very positive contribution to make to the development of society [and that] there is a special providence in the emergence of visible gay and lesbian communities within the Church at this point in history."[11] In his pioneering pastoral work—for which he was expelled from the Jesuits in 1987—McNeill has explored how the Church can meet the emotional and spiritual needs of gay and lesbian people, and he helped found Dignity, the leading organization of LGBT Catholics.[12] In his theological writing, he has explored the "unique gay and lesbian experience of God," and its many consequences, such as how gay men may have a special connection to the devotion to Mary as embodiment of the Divine Feminine, or how LGBT people may help all of us move to a mature ethic of relationality rather than the emphasis on procreation which, he says, has become "positively harmful."[13] Above all, McNeill has been a leading Catholic voice for the dignity and self-worth of all people, including sexual minorities, in the face of an increasingly hostile Church hierarchy. He is a hero who has paid the price for his courage.

These are just a couple of examples; there are dozens more. MCC pastor Nancy Wilson identifies five distinct gifts that LGBT people bring to the wider religious community: the narrative of coming out, "subject–subject" spirituality, a camp/trickster sensibility, creativity as expressed in art and theater, and new aspects of what it is to be in the image of God.[14] Writer Peter Sweasey lists nine specifically LGBT religious journeys: questioning ourselves, not fitting in, coming out, self-examination, truth-telling, valuing our personal experience, questioning orthodoxies, testing faith, and embracing paradox and humor.[15] Reverend Irene Monroe has written over one hundred articles on the intersections of African American, queer, and religious issues.[16] Daniel Spencer has related queer theology to questions of ecological sustainability.[17] Rebecca T. Alpert has explored distinctive ways in which lesbians reinterpret Torah, gain visibility in religious communities, and have historically led campaigns for justice within the Jewish community.[18] And many theologians have reflected on how the tragedy of the AIDS crisis caused LGBT people to develop compassion and activism for the most vulnerable, to assert themselves more boldly in the face of injustice, and to rethink the activist message of Jesus in a time of crisis.[19] (Of course, the AIDS plague also brought out the worst in many religious leaders, who quickly ascribed it to Divine punishment for homosexuality. It is interesting to note that today, while many Christian organizations have taken a leading role in fighting AIDS in Africa, and no one today thinks that AIDS is a "gay disease," I am not aware of a single organization that has apologized for the genocidal rants of so-called religious leaders before we as a society knew better.)

Finally, we have only begun to learn from transgender biblical scholars and theologians. Consider the work of Virginia Ramey Mollenkott, author of the pioneering *Is the Homosexual My Neighbor?* (1978) and, more recently, such books as *Sensuous Spirituality* (2008) and *Omnigender: A Trans-religious Approach* (2007). Mollenkott's work has evolved from the relatively traditional to the radical, offering within one career a spectrum of options for queer theological thinking. Often, Mollenkott's work corrects blind spots within queer theological discourse itself: for example, Mollenkott is critical of male-centered experiences such as coming out, and reminds us that tricksters and schemers are often the ablest responders to oppression, as in the cases of Rebecca, the Egyptian midwives, and Miriam, all biblical women who empower themselves (and propel biblical history) through subversion and subterfuge rather than bold declaration.[20] In *Omnigender,* Mollenkott offers gender-inclusive readings of the Creation story, virgin birth, and many other biblical tales and figures.[21] Others, including Marcella Althaus-Reid, Lisa Isherwood, Justin Tanis, and Noach Dzmura, have also made powerful contributions to our understanding of transgender and religion.[22]

Outside the Jewish and Christian religious traditions, there have been many interesting efforts to discern particular spiritual roles for LGBT people. For example, in many cultures, sexual and gender minorities are seen as "in-between," sometimes referred to as "third-gendered," or as possessing both masculine and feminine genders within them. And indeed, in many cultures, this is for the better, as we have already explored with reference to indigenous peoples around the world. From the gender-variant *berdaches* or *winktes* in Native American traditions to the shamans of Siberia, the *basir* of Borneo to the *isangoma* of the Zulu, people we might call gays and lesbians act as sacred priests of the liminal, the in-between.[23] Sexual minorities, in transcending dichotomy, enter the zone of the sacred. (As we saw in part 2, boundary crossing is usually taboo for biblical religion, but in these traditions, it is holy.) In a sense, these cultures' regard for people we would identify as LGBT is not dissimilar from the scientific view that "queer" people fill important communal roles precisely because they are less likely to have children. It may seem strange to say so, but perhaps the overwhelming predominance of gays and lesbians in arts and culture is part of the same basic phenomenon as "gay" animals helping to take care of their communities.

Building on these traditions, the growing gay spirituality movement has sought to articulate distinctive roles for gay men as healers, bridge builders, and, in general, people able to integrate masculine and feminine in ways that are of value to everyone.[24] Christian de la Huerta, for example, has proposed ten archetypes of LGBT spirituality, drawing on diverse world traditions.[25] Toby Johnson has proposed that gay men offer new models of masculinity that are based upon cooperation rather than competition.[26] And spiritual radical Harry Hay argued that "third gender people were and are those who were assigned responsibilities for discovering, developing, and managing the frontiers between the seen and the unseen, between the known and the unknown."[27] The gay spirituality movement has helped countless men find ways to express their spirituality, and to celebrate rather than hide their difference from the norm. Once again, gay spirituality folks aren't trying to explain *why* they are gay. Rather, like anyone who wants to celebrate the gifts of who they are, they are exploring the possibilities enabled by their sexual identities.

This is, of course, a wide range—from "a born again, conservative, Bible believing, evangelical, gay Christian"[28] to "third gender" gay spirituality radicals. There is, and will be, no single queer theology, just as there can be no single religious case for equality. Yet for all these theologians, as for myself and millions of other religious LGBT people, being gay and religious isn't a predicament—it's a gift. As Donald Boisvert has written, "[S]exuality is a gift from God, and it is a gift because of its varied manifestations. Being gay is therefore a blessing."[29] And as Michael Kelly has written, "[W]e are a gift to the church."[30]

Ultimately, love is more complex than our estimations can guess. Do gays and lesbians have special roles to play in the unfolding of the

Divine will? Undoubtedly we do, just as do people of different ethnic groups, religions, genders, and nationalities. Do I know exactly what those roles are? No, and nor do I want to. I find myself most affirmed not in formulas that spell out what my role is supposed to be, but in appreciating the vast multiplicity of those potentials. Some cultures have regarded people like me as magicians; others as warriors, musicians, shamans, and priests. Precisely because there is no firm agreement among religious and cultural traditions, I find there is no limit to the complexity of human affection. If love is indeed as holy as Scripture says it is, surely this is how it should be.

CHAPTER 18

"For nothing in creation can separate you from the love of God"

Postscript

At this moment, there are people who are contemplating ending their lives because they believe their sexuality to be a sin, a flaw in the fabric of their soul, or perhaps a curse from God. Misled by a cruel misreading of a handful of biblical verses, they miss the much more important messages of many others: that love is sacred, that God does not want us to be alone. That justice and compassion are Divine mandates. That every human being is created in the image of God, and that the way we love is one of the paramount expressions of that likeness.

While you come to the last pages of this book, they may be coming to the last hours of their lives. This is why, if we are religious, we cannot consider the words of a sacred text dispassionately, or fall back on familiar teachings we've heard. There is death around us, and even when there is not physical death, there is unconscionable spiritual suffering. It is present in your church pews, when a friend of yours feels excluded or marginalized. It is at your family table, in the hearts of the uncle who never married, or the girl who prefers boys' clothes to dresses.

The irony of "God versus Gay" is that, actually, Gay and God go together. Opening to one leads to opening to the other. If we really open to grace in our lives, then we, like Huck Finn on the raft, are called upon to hear the voices of our conscience as well. We have to "go on thinking," just like he did, about our friends and neighbors whom we were taught to dehumanize. Hopefully they will go on thinking too.

I have spent many months on meditation retreat, many long and late hours at prayer, and many years reflecting on these questions of spirituality and sexuality. So I want to close with the following invitation. Reflect, for a moment, on a time when the presence of what some of us call God was as real for you as the presence of these words are right now. It doesn't matter if your God is traditional, or nontraditional, or even nonexistent. Just invite in the experience. Maybe it was when a child was born, or a parent died, or when you watched the sun set or rise. Or maybe it was an ordinary moment, suddenly transfigured by your own attentiveness to the realm of the miraculous. Sit with this memory until, if you are fortunate, you can feel anew the wonder and love you may have felt before.

In this moment, in this presence, conceive of a love that does not depend upon conditions—a love that is unconditional and unwavering, that is inherent in the simple fact that we are here, blessed, for a brief instant of time. Entertain the possibility that this love is true, and that all our verses and traditions are trying to return us to it, and to guide us to live justly in its light. Consider that this love, present in moments of Divine communion and also of human affection, is present in an infinite variety of forms, far greater than what we think we know.

Even our most revered teachers have gotten things wrong in the past. They were wrong about racism, wrong about geography, wrong about astronomy, wrong about time. They were also wrong about sexual orientation. But we revere them still because they were right about something greater. Across time and space and language and culture, through all the fogs of desire and confusion, they glimpsed something that was real, and were profoundly correct about what it was. That reality is far stronger than any language we use to name it, or any momentary struggle about this or that political issue. It survived Copernicus, and it will survive the sexual revolution. Not only that—it thrives because of both of them. Whatever fears we may have about change or transformation, they are but ripples on the ocean of truth. Or of love. Or of God.

Acknowledgments

Many thanks to Gayatri Patnaik, Michael Bronski, Tom Hallock, Alyssa Hassan, Sarah Laxton, Pam MacColl, Rachael Marks, and Reshma Melwani at Beacon; to Jill Marr, Rabbi Michael Lerner, Andrew Novak, Paul Dakin, and Margaret Vetare for helping to put it all together; to theologians Rebecca T. Alpert, Patrick Cheng, Michael Kelly, Malachi Kosanovich, John Stasio, and Ken Stone for ensuring this nice Jewish boy didn't get it all wrong; to fellow activists Ann Craig, Gregg Drinkwater, Sharon Groves, Idit Klein, Harry Knox, Ross Murray, and Rebecca Voelkel, for helping to ensure this book is of use in their holy work; teachers Daniel Boyarin, Michael Cohen, Rabbi David Cooper, Rachel Elior, Kenneth Folk, Rabbi Steven Greenberg, Rabbi Jill Hammer, Toby Johnson, Joseph Kramer, Rabbi Michael Paley, Andrew Ramer, Rabbi Zalman Schachter-Shalomi, and Ven. Vivekananda; to the editors and staff of the *Forward, Tikkun, Religion Dispatches, Zeek, Reality Sandwich,* the CNN *Belief Blog, Huffington Post,* and *White Crane* for publishing earlier versions of parts of this work, and for putting out quality writing about religion and spirituality at a time when we need it dearly; and to my LGBT spiritual communities at Nehirim, Easton Mountain, Short Mountain, Pride in the Pulpit, the National Religious Leadership Roundtable, and elsewhere for nourishing mind, body, and spirit. This book is dedicated to my husband, Paul, who makes the religious case for love.

Table of Scriptural Authorities

Lamentations 4:6
Ezra 9:1, 9:11, 9:14
2 Chronicles 28:3, 33:2, 34:33, 36:8, 36:14

NEW TESTAMENT

Matthew 5:28, 5:32–33, 5:39, 6:2, 6:25, 7:1, 7:16–18, 8:5–13, 10:15,
    11:23–24, 12:50, 17:22, 19:12, 19:24, 20:18–19, 22:37–39, 24:15, 26:2,
    26:45, 27:26
Mark 1:41, 3:34, 7:1–22, 13:14
Luke 7:1–10, 7:44–46, 10:12, 13:10–17, 14:16, 16:15, 17:29
John 3:16, 4:27, 8:1–11, 8:32
Acts 8:26–40
Romans 1:18–29, 2:12, 2:22, 8:38–39, 9:29, 12:13, 13:10, 14:5, 16:12
1 Corinthians 6:1–20, 7:4, 7:8, 13:4–8, 13:11
Galatians 5:14, 5:22
Philippians 4:1
1 Timothy 1:8–10, 3:2
Titus 1:8
Hebrews 13:2
James 3:17
2 Peter 2:6
1 John 4:8, 4:16, 4:19–20
Jude 1:7
Revelation 17:4–5, 21:27

OTHER RELIGIOUS SOURCES

Shir Hashirim Rabbah 1:9
Wisdom of Solomon 12:23, 16:4
Mishna Avot 5:1
Mishna Makkot 1:10
BT Bava Kamma 83b
BT Eruvin 49a
BT Ketubot 32b, 103a
BT Sanhedrin 71a, 109a
BT Yevamot 79a–80b
Philo Judaeus, *On Abraham* §135
Clement of Alexandria, *Stromata* III.1
Augustine, *Confessions,* book 4, chapters 4 and 6
Thomas Aquinas, *Summa Theologica* II:ii, 154:11–12

For Further Reading

Here are a few suggestions for further reading on some of the key issues raised in this book. Full publication information is provided in the bibliography.

GENERAL INTRODUCTORY BOOKS

Donald Boisvert, *Out on Holy Ground: Meditations on Gay Men's Spirituality*
Carter Heyward, *Touching Our Strength: The Erotic as Power and the Love of God*
John McNeill, *The Church and the Homosexual*
Virginia Ramey Mollenkott and Letha Scanzoni, *Is the Homosexual My Neighbor? Another Christian View*
Andrew Sullivan, *Virtually Normal: An Argument about Homosexuality*

CHRISTIAN PRO-GAY READINGS OF THE BIBLE

Rick Brentlinger, *Gay Christian 101: Spiritual Self-Defense for Gay Christians*
Daniel Helminiak, *What the Bible Really Says About Homosexuality*
Rev. Jeff Miner and John Tyler Connoley, *The Children Are Free: Reexamining the Biblical Evidence on Same-Sex Relationships*
Linda J. Patterson, *Hate Thy Neighbor: How the Bible Is Misused to Condemn Homosexuality*
Mel White, *Stranger at the Gate: To Be Gay and Christian in America*

TESTIMONIES AND AUTOBIOGRAPHIES
OF FAITHFUL GAY CHRISTIANS

Leroy Aarons, *Prayers for Bobby: A Mother's Coming to Terms with the Suicide of Her Gay Son*
Malcolm Boyd, *Take Off the Masks*
Chris Glaser, *Uncommon Calling: A Gay Christian's Struggle to Serve the Church*

Raymond C. Holtz, *Listen to the Stories: Gay and Lesbian Catholics Talk About Their Lives and the Church*

Michael Maher Jr., *Being Gay and Lesbian in a Catholic High School: Beyond the Uniform*

Troy Perry, *The Lord Is My Shepherd and He Knows I'm Gay*

David Shallenberger, *Reclaiming the Spirit: Gay Men and Lesbians Come to Terms with Their Religions*

CATHOLIC

James Alison, *Faith beyond Resentment: Fragments Catholic and Gay*

Richard Cleaver, *Know My Name: A Gay Liberation Theology*

Margaret Farley, *Just Love: A Framework for Christian Sexual Ethics*

Mark Jordan, *The Silence of Sodom: Homosexuality in Modern Catholicism*

Patricia Beattie Jung, ed., *Sexual Diversity and Catholicism: Toward the Development of Moral Theology*

John McNeill, *The Church and the Homosexual; Freedom, Glorious Freedom: The Spiritual Journey to the Fullness of Life for Gays, Lesbians, and Everybody Else;* and *Taking a Chance on God: Liberating Theology for Gays, Lesbians, and Their Lovers, Families, and Friends*

Gareth Moore, *A Question of Truth: Christianity and Homosexuality*

JEWISH

Rebecca Alpert, *Like Bread on the Seder Plate: Jewish Lesbians and the Transformation of Tradition*

Christie Balka and Andy Rose, eds., *Twice Blessed: On Being Lesbian or Gay and Jewish*

Gregg Drinkwater, Joshua Lesser, and David Shneer, eds., *Torah Queeries: Weekly Commentary on the Hebrew Bible*

Steven Greenberg, *Wrestling with God and Men: Homosexuality in the Jewish Tradition*

PROTESTANT

Malcolm Boyd, *Are You Running with Me, Jesus?*

Jack Rogers, *Jesus, the Bible, and Homosexuality: Explode the Myths, Heal the Church*

Elizabeth Stuart, *Religion Is a Queer Thing: A Guide to the Christian Faith for Lesbian, Gay, Bisexual, and Transgendered People*

LESBIAN

Rebecca T. Alpert, *Like Bread on the Seder Plate: Jewish Lesbians and the Transformation of Tradition*

Judith Brown, *Immodest Acts: The Life of a Lesbian Nun in Renaissance Italy*

Elizabeth Stuart, *Just Good Friends: Towards a Lesbian and Gay Theology of Relationships*

TRANSGENDER

Noach Dzmura, *Balancing on the Mechitza: Transgender in the Jewish Community*

Virginia Ramey Mollenkott, *Omnigender: A Trans-Religious Approach*

Justin Tanis, *Trans-Gendered: Theology, Ministry, and Communities of Faith*

Leanne McCall Tigert and Maren C. Tirabassi, eds., *Transgendering Faith: Identity, Sexuality, and Spirituality*

QUEER THEOLOGY AND ETHICS

Patrick Cheng, *Radical Love: An Introduction to Queer Theology*

Gary David Comstock, *Gay Theology Without Apology* and (with Susan Henking) *Que(e)rying Religion: A Critical Anthology*

Robert Goss, *Jesus Acted Up: A Gay and Lesbian Manifesto* and *Queering Christ: Beyond Jesus Acted Up*

James B. Nelson, *Between Two Gardens: Reflections on Sexuality and Religious Experience*

Kenneth Stone, *Practicing Safer Texts: Food, Sex, and Bible in Queer Perspective*

Elizabeth Stuart, *Gay and Lesbian Theologies: Repetitions with Critical Difference*

Nancy Wilson, *Our Tribe: Queer Folks, God, Jesus, and the Bible*

GAY SPIRITUALITY

Robert Barzan, *Sex and Spirit: Exploring Gay Men's Spirituality*

Randy P. Conner, *Blossom of Bone: Reclaiming the Connections between Homoeroticism and the Sacred*

Toby Johnson, *Gay Spirituality: Gay Identity and the Transformation of Human Consciousness*

Rollan McCleary, *A Special Illumination: Authority, Inspiration, and Heresy in Gay Spirituality*

Mark Thompson, *Gay Spirit: Myth and Meaning*

SCIENCE OF SEXUAL ORIENTATION

Bruce Bagemihl, *Biological Exuberance: Animal Homosexuality and Natural Diversity*

Simon LeVay, *Gay, Straight, and the Reason Why: The Science of Sexual Orientation*

Joan Roughgarden, *Evolution's Rainbow: Diversity, Gender, and Sexuality in Nature and People*

Volker Sommer and Paul L. Vasey, eds., *Homosexual Behaviour in Animals: An Evolutionary Perspective*

HISTORY

Martin Duberman et al., *Hidden from History: Reclaiming the Gay and Lesbian Past*

David F. Greenberg, *The Construction of Homosexuality*

Neil Miller, *Out of the Past: Gay and Lesbian History from 1869 to the Present*

WORLD RELIGIONS AND CULTURES

Gilbert Herdt, *Same Sex, Different Cultures: Exploring Gay and Lesbian Lives*

Scott Kugle, *Homosexuality in Islam: Islamic Reflection on Gay, Lesbian, and Transgender Muslims*

Stephen O. Murray, *Homosexualities*

Stephen O. Murray and Will Roscoe, eds., *Boy-Wives and Female Husbands: Studies in African Homosexualities*

Serena Nanda, *Neither Man nor Woman: The Hijras of India*

Arlene Swidler, ed., *Homosexuality and World Religions*

Walter Williams, *The Spirit and the Flesh: Sexual Diversity in American Indian Culture*

LGBT RELIGIOUS WEBSITES

Gay Christian Network, www.gaychristian.net

Gay Wisdom, www.gaywisdom.org

LGBT Religious Archives Network, www.lgbtran.org

Other Sheep, www.othersheep.org/

Queering the Church, queering-the-church.com/blog/

Whosoever: An Online Magazine for Gay, Lesbian, Bisexual, and Transgender Christians, www.whosoever.org

EX-EX-GAY RESOURCES

Beyond Ex-Gay, www.beyondexgay.com

Ex-Gay Watch, www.exgaywatch.com

Truth Wins Out, www.truthwinsout.org

LGBT Religious Organizations

Affirmation (Mormon)
Affirmation (United Methodist)
Affirm United (United Church of Canada)
Al-Fatiha (Islam)
Association of Welcoming and Affirming Baptists
Axios (Eastern Orthodox)
Beyond Inclusion (Episcopal)
Brethren (Mennonite)
A Common Bond (Jehovah's Witness)
Dignity (Catholic)
Emergence International (Christian Scientists)
Eshel (Orthodox Jewish)
Evangelicals Concerned
Friends for LGBT (Quaker)
Gay, Lesbian, and Affirming Disciples of Christ (Disciples of Christ)
Integrity (Episcopal)
Interfaith Coalition for Transgender Equality (Multifaith)
Institute for Welcoming Resources (Multifaith)
Interweave (Unitarian Universalist)
Keshet (Jewish)
Kinship International (Seventh-Day Adventist)
Lutherans Concerned
Metropolitan Community Church
More Light Presbyterians
Nehirim (Jewish)
Rainbow Baptists
Reconciling Ministries (United Methodist)
Reconciling Pentecostals
Room for All (Reformed Church in America)

TransFaith Online (Multifaith)
Unitarian Universalist Association LGBT Ministries
United Church of Christ Coalition for LGBT Concerns
World Congress of GLBT Jews

Notes

1. On the Hamite myth and Christian justifications of slavery, see Haynes, *Noah's Curse;* Gomes, *The Good Book,* 84–101. On similarities to the case of sexual minorities, see Rogers, *Jesus, the Bible, and Homosexuality,* 18–25.

2. Not all religious people agree with this view. See, e.g., Plaskow, "Sexual Orientation and Human Rights," 29–34.

3. Chellew-Hodge, *Bulletproof Faith,* 73.

CHAPTER 1: "IT IS NOT GOOD FOR A PERSON TO BE ALONE"

Title. Gen. 2:18.

1. D'Augelli et al., "Suicidality Patterns and Sexual Orientation-Related Factors among Lesbian, Gay, and Bisexual Youths," 250; Garofalo et al., "Sexual Orientation and Risk of Suicide Attempts," 487; Rotheram-Borus et al., "Suicidal Behavior and Gay-Related Stress," 498. Silenzio et al. reported a lower rate of suicidal ideation but a similar ratio of gay to straight (17 percent among LGB youth; 6.3 percent among straight): Silenzio et al., "Sexual Orientation and Risk Factors for Suicidal Ideation," 2017. Readers will notice that, throughout this book, I try to refer to the original source material, rather than secondary sources. Many anti-gay and ex-gay books refer to the same discredited sources—books by Joseph Nicolosi or Charles Socarides, for example—again and again. If this all seems like a game of "he said/she said," I encourage you to read the original studies yourself and make up your own mind. Look for sound sociological evidence, peer-reviewed journals, and data from reliable studies, not secondary sources.

2. See Greenberg, *Wrestling with God and Men,* 50–52; Mollenkott and Scanzoni, *Is the Homosexual My Neighbor?,* 129–32. For an evangelical leader's personal story of the loneliness of the closet, see White, *Stranger at the Gate,* 28–62.

3. Vaid, *Virtual Equality,* 374.

4. Shakespeare, *Merchant of Venice,* act I, scene 3.

5. See Sullivan, *Virtually Normal,* 16–17: "The homosexual experience may be deemed an illness, a disorder, a privilege, or a curse; it may be deemed worthy of a 'cure,' rectified, embraced, or endured. *But it exists.*"

6. This is John Wesley's "four-legged stool" of theology. See Chellew-Hodge, *Bulletproof Faith,* 56.

7. See Sullivan, *Love Undetectable,* 48–49.

8. Nelson, *Between Two Gardens,* 6.

9. LeVay, *Gay, Straight, and the Reason Why,* 16–17. See Plaskow, "Sexual Orientation and Human Rights," 30–34; Sullivan, *Virtually Normal,* 16–17, 170–71.

10. Rich, "Compulsory Heterosexuality and Lesbian Existence," 631; reprinted in Rich, *Blood, Bread, and Poetry.*

11. Faderman, *Surpassing the Love of Men,* 15–20. On the "Boston marriage," in which two women would live together, see 190–203.

12. See Halperin, *One Hundred Years of Homosexuality,* 15–53; Katz, *The Invention of Heterosexuality;* Warner, *The Trouble with Normal,* 9–10; Boswell, "Concepts, Experience, and Sexuality," 116–29. Much of this debate has subsided. It is clear that "homosexuality" is a recent construction, but also that there have been people erotically interested in the same sex for millennia. I will return to this point several times in the text. See Greenberg, *Construction of Homosexuality;* Jordan, *Silence of Sodom,* 228–35.

13. See Newman, "Constructing a Jewish Sexual Ethic," 46–48.

14. See Jordan, *Silence of Sodom,* 60–62.

15. Nygren, *Eros et Agape;* Black, "Broken Wings of Eros," 106; Grant, "For the Love of God," 3.

16. Grant, "For the Love of God," 3–7.

17. Black, "Broken Wings of Eros," 108.

18. See, e.g., Nelson, *Between Two Gardens,* 31; Heyward, *Touching Our Strength;* Avis, *Eros and the Sacred;* Boswell, *Same-Sex Unions in Premodern Europe,* 6–8. The distinction may not even be present in the sources—the Church father Origen says that eros and agape are really the same thing. Black, "Broken Wings of Eros," 110.

19. Heyward, *Touching Our Strength;* Lorde, "The Use of the Erotic," 73. I discuss Heyward and Lorde in chapter 17.

CHAPTER 2: "I AM ASLEEP BUT MY HEART IS AWAKE: THE VOICE OF MY BELOVED KNOCKS"

Title. Song of Songs 5:2.

1. Hume, *Mystery of Love,* 20.

2. Moore, *A Question of Truth,* 9.

3. See Ostriker, *For the Love of God,* 9–33; Carr, *Erotic Word,* 109–51.

4. Carr, *Erotic Word,* 117.

5. See King, "A Love as Fierce as Death," 126; Comstock, *Gay Theology without Apology,* 27–48.

6. Chellew-Hodge, *Bulletproof Faith,* 11.

CHAPTER 3: "LOVE YOUR NEIGHBOR AS YOURSELF"

Title. Lev. 19:18.

1. See Moore, *Question of Truth,* 40.

2. Mishnah Makkot 1:10.

3. Miner and Connoley, *Children Are Free,* 69. See also Johnston, *Gays Under Grace*; Brentlinger, *Gay Christian 101.*

4. Miner and Connoley, *Children Are Free,* 22.

5. Martin, "Arsenokoites and Malakos," 117, 130–31.

CHAPTER 4: "BY THE WORD OF GOD WERE THE HEAVENS MADE"

Title. Psalm 33:6.

1. Roughgarden, *Evolution's Rainbow,* 137

2. Laumann et al., *Social Organization of Sexuality.*

3. LeVay, *Gay, Straight, and the Reason Why,* 195–201

4. Ibid., 46–48; Roughgarden, *Evolution's Rainbow,* 245–61.

5. LeVay, *Gay, Straight, and the Reason Why,* 274.

6. Ibid., 46–71. Birth order may actually be a subcategory of hormonal level, as later children are exposed to different hormones.

7. Roughgarden, *Evolution's Rainbow,* 238–44.

8. LeVay, *Gay, Straight, and the Reason Why.*

9. Ibid., 85. LeVay cites several studies reaching the same conclusion. Ibid., 84–93.

10. Roughgarden, *Evolution's Rainbow,* 127–58; , Bagemihl, *Biological Exuberance,* 299ff. Bagemihl's book includes a veritable bestiary, going species by species through some of the most notable instances of "homosexuality" and gender diversity.

11. Vasey, "The Pursuit of Pleasure," 191–219.

12. Some may remember that, back in the 1970s, anti-gay activist Anita Bryant claimed that "even barnyard animals" don't engage in homosexual behavior. The irony was that shepherds and farmers have known about homosexuality among sheep for thousands of years. Even Aristotle was aware of animal homosexuality. Brooten, *Love Between Women,* 272–80.

13. LeVay, *Gay, Straight, and the Reason Why,* 69–71. See also Roughgarden, *Evolution's Rainbow,* 137–42.

14. See Lancaster, *The Trouble with Nature* (documenting religious and political uses of "nature" and arguing against simplifications such as a "gay gene"); Mooallem, "Can Animals Be Gay?"

15. LeVay, *Gay, Straight, and the Reason Why,* 66–68; Kotrschal et al., "Making the Best of a Bad Situation," 45–76.

16. That being said, Bagemihl notes that we use equally inappropriate human terms like "courtship" to apply to animal behavior. Bagemihl, *Biological Exuberance,* 3.

17. See Wilson, *Sociobiology,* 117–22; Bagemihl, *Biological Exuberance,* 168–70.

18. Roughgarden, *Evolution's Rainbow,* 329–51; Roscoe, *Changing Ones,* 222–47; Williams, *Spirit and the Flesh,* 17–109; Murray, *Homosexualities,* 314–22, 348–53; Bronski, *Queer History of the United States,* 3–5; Harvey, *Essential Gay Mystics,* 52–61.

19. See Bagemihl, *Biological Exuberance,* 215–41.

20. LeVay, *Gay, Straight, and the Reason Why,* 185.

21. Roughgarden, *Evolution's Rainbow,* 159–81.

22. LeVay, *Gay, Straight, and the Reason Why,* 68–69; Fruth and Hohmann, "Social Grease for Females?" 294–315; Roughgarden, *Evolution's Rainbow,* 142–53.

23. Quoted in Dreyfuss, "The Holy War on Gays."

24. See, e.g., Spencer, *Gay and Gaia,* 27–29.

25. UNAIDS, *2007 Epidemic Update,* 1.

26. Perez, *Soulfully Gay,* 73.

27. See Vaid, *Virtual Equality,* 374–76, comparing gay pride parades to "carnival mirror" portrayals of gay people.

28. On queerness and queer theology, see Loughlin, *Queer Theology;* Boisvert, *Out on Holy Ground,* 4–5; Cheng, *Radical Love.*

29. The first ex-gay conference was held in 1976. The movement is a very recent one. Efforts to "repair" homosexuality go back much further, with therapies including electroshock therapy, castration, female genital mutilation, and even eating graham crackers. The results have been uniformly unsuccessful. In 1961, for example, Irving Bieber, a "reparative" therapist of his day, claimed many successes but couldn't offer a single one for an interview by Alfred Kinsey's research team. See Johnston, *Gays Under Grace,* 20–21. Ex-ex-gay resources are listed in the bibliography.

30. See Associated Press, "Psychologists Reject Gay 'Therapy,'" citing 125–4 vote by American Psychological Association; Sullivan, *Love Undetectable,* 108–28.

31. "The Creation of Exodus International," www.youtube.com/watch ?v=zraXAiOtdFw.

32. "Former Ex-Gay Leaders Apologize," www.youtube.com/watch ?v=aDiYeJ_bsQo.

33. See, e.g., Chapman, *Thou Shalt Not Love*, 7–9; Cervantes, "My Ex-Gay Experience Part 2," www.youtube.com/watch?v=vY6vXQooPzM; "Ex-Gay Survivors on Tyra," www.youtube.com/watch?v=S-J5T6wsnEQ.

34. Piazza, *Gay by God*, 11. For theological examinations of the ex-gay movement generally, see 14–17; McNeill, *Taking a Chance on God*, 19–20.

35. See LeVay, *Gay, Straight, and the Reason Why*, 28–33.

36. See Robb, *Strangers*, 68–79.

37. See Edwards, *Gay/Lesbian Liberation*, 13–22; Rogers, *Jesus, the Bible, and Homosexuality*, 53–65.

38. See Gudorf, "The Bible and Science on Sexuality"; Moore, *Question of Truth*, 25–27.

39. Roughgarden, *Evolution's Rainbow*, 13–15.

40. Ibid., 30–42, 76–105.

CHAPTER 5: "THOU SHALT NOT BEAR FALSE WITNESS"

Title. Exod. 20:13.

1. See, e.g., Glaser, *Coming Out as Sacrament*; Glaser, *Coming Out to God*; Hannant, *God Comes Out*; Heyward, *Our Passion for Justice*, 82; Clark, "Coming Out," 191–208.

2. Hannant, *God Comes Out*, 18.

3. Glaser, *Coming Out to God*, 9.

4. The comments, which appeared on Andrew Sullivan's *Daily Dish* blog on November 5, 2006, were quoted in Edberg, "Bearing False Witness."

5. Family Research Council, "Washington Update."

6. Quoted in Hume, *Mystery of Love*, i.

CHAPTER 6: "JUSTICE—JUSTICE SHALL YOU PURSUE"

Title. Deut. 16:20.

1. For an application of this teaching to gay ethics, see Alpert, "Do Justice, Love Mercy, Walk Humbly," 170–78.

2. Frank, "Rep. Barney Frank on the Radical Homosexual Agenda"; "Barney Frank Reveals Gay Agenda," *Advocate*, December 22, 2010.

3. See Wade, "Depth of the Kindness Hormone Appears to Know Some Bounds."

4. See, e.g., Dallas, *Gay Gospel*, 37.

5. See Goss, *Jesus Acted Up*, 72–77; Heyward, *Touching Our Strength*, 84–85.

CHAPTER 7: LEVITICUS

1. Gomes, *Good Book,* 82.

2. Miner and Connoley, *Children Are Free,* 9.

3. Helminiak, *What the Bible Really Says,* 31.

4. See Greenberg, *Wrestling with God and Men,* 192–214. Rabbi Greenberg offers several possible rationales for the Levitical prohibition, including concerns about reproduction and category confusion (147–52, 175–91).

5. See Alpert, *Like Bread on the Seder Plate,* 29–35; Greenberg, *Wrestling with God and Men,* 86–95. The original source of the prohibition is the Sifra's commentary on Leviticus 18:3, which says that in Egypt, men would marry men and women would marry women. Interestingly, this may have been true historically at the time the Sifra was compiled. See Brooten, *Love Between Women,* 65–66.

6. Olyan, "And with a Man You Shall Not Lie the Lying Down of a Woman," 400–401. In Numbers 31:17–18, the term *mishkav zachar* is used in connection with whether a woman is a virgin or not. If she has known *mishkav zachar,* she is not.

7. Bell, "Homosexual Men and Women," 452–55.

8. Some religious leaders have the same opinion of gays. See Alpert, *Like Bread on the Seder Plate,* 28 (quoting Orthodox rabbi Norman Lamm).

9. See Olyan, "And with a Man," 398–414. Olyan calls *toevah* a "socially constructed boundary" (399). But his view is that the purpose of the prohibition is not to guard against idolatry, but to prevent defiling emissions from mixing with one another (408–13).

10. Deut. 12:31, 13:14, 17:4, 20:18, 27:15, 32:16.

11. 1 Kings 14:24 (general); 2 Kings 16:3 (child sacrifice); 2 Kings 21:2 and 21:11 (idolatry); 2 Chron. 28:3 (child sacrifice); 2 Chron. 33:2 (idolatry); 2 Chron. 34:33, 36:8, and 36:14 (general).

12. Jer. 2:7, 7:10, 32:35; Jer. 6:15, 8:12, 44:22.

13. Idolatry: Ezek. 5:11, 6:9, 6:11, 7:20, 14:6, 20:7–8, 22:2, 44:6–7, 44:13; usury: Ezek. 18:13; haughtiness and pride: Ezek. 16:47–50; heterosexual adultery: Ezek. 22:11, 33:26; violence: Ezek. 33:26; foreign acts or transgression: Ezek. 5:9, 7:3–4, 7:8–9, 9:4, 11:18, 11:21, 12:16, 16:2, 16:43, 16:51, 18:24, 20:4, 33:29, 36:31.

14. Ezek. 16:22, 16:36, 16:58, 23:26, 43:8.

15. Isa. 1:13, 44:19, 41:14, 66:3.

16. The wicked: Prov. 3:32, 13:19, 15:8–9, 15:26, 16:12, 21:27, 28:9, 29:27; pride: Prov. 6:16, 16:5; evil speech: Prov. 8:7; false weights: Prov. 11:1, 20:10, 20:23; deviousness: Prov. 11:20; lying: Prov. 12:22, 26:25; scoffing: Prov. 24:9; justify the wicked and defaming the righteous: Prov. 17:15.

17. Matt. 24:15, Mark 13:14, Luke 16:15, Rev. 17:4–5, 21:27.

18. Olyan denies significance to this juxtaposition, since he believes the Levitical text may have been redacted. Olyan, "And with a Man," 408.

19. Olyan adds that other prohibitions, such as those against adultery and incest, are found in numerous places in the Bible, but the ban on male anal sex is found only in these two Levitical passages. "There is no reason to assume any necessary association between the prohibitions of male couplings . . . and the various incest, adultery, and bestiality interdictions." Olyan, "And with a Man," 399.

20. 1 Kings 15:12, 2 Kings 23:7.

21. Herodotus, *Histories*, 58.

22. See Greenberg, *Construction of Homosexuality*, 94–100; Edwards, *Gay/Lesbian Liberation*, 51–64.

23. See Stone, *Practicing Safer Texts*, 46–67; Brooten, 298; Michaelson, "Chaos, Law, and God," 41; Davis, "Religious Boundaries and Sexual Morality," 39–60. I return to the question of boundary in chapter 17.

24. See Michaelson, "It's the Purity, Stupid," 145–50; Helminiak, *What the Bible Really Says*, 51–67.

CHAPTER 8: SODOM

1. Comments made by Savage (Michael Alan Weiner) on his radio show, July 5, 2003. The partial transcript is available at "MSNBC Fires Shock Host Michael Savage," on the Democracy Now website.

2. For excellent treatments of the Sodom story and its misinterpretation, see Carden, *Sodomy*; Jordan, *Invention of Sodomy in Christian Theology*; Noort and Tigchelaar, *Sodom's Sin*.

3. Some scholars maintain that to "know" does not necessarily have a sexual connotation. See, e.g., Morchauser, "'Hospitality,' Hostiles, and Hostages," 461–85.

4. Christian readings of the Sodom story that focus on these elements include McNeill, *Church and the Homosexual*, 42–50; Brentlinger, *Gay Christian 101*, 33–40; Piazza, *Gay by God*, 38–41; Helminiak, *What the Bible Really Says*, 43–50; Edwards, *Gay/Lesbian Liberation*, 24–50; White, *Stranger at the Gate*, 37–40. McNeill notes that there are similar ancient Near Eastern stories, all of which are about hospitality and the abuse of strangers. McNeill, *Church and the Homosexual*, 44. See also Matthews, "Hospitality and Hostility in Genesis 19 and Judges 19," 3–11.

5. For parallel readings of this story with that of Sodom, see Carden, *Sodomy*, 14–41; Rogers, *Jesus, the Bible, and Homosexuality*, 67–68; Dwyer, *Those 7 References*, 12–20; McNeill, *Church and the Homosexual*, 47–48; De Hoop, "Saul the Sodomite," 17–28.

6. This analogy was suggested by Miner and Connoley, *Children Are Free,* 4. Even anti-gay writer Gagnon has said that the story of Sodom is "not ideal" because it is about nonconsensual activity. Gagnon, *Bible and Homosexual Practice,* 71.

7. See Carden, *Sodomy,* 44–48.

8. Deut. 32:16–32.

9. Isa. 1:9–10 [quoted in Rom. 9:29], Isa. 3:9, 2 Pet. 2:6.

10. Isa. 13:19, Jer. 49:18, Jer. 50:40, Lam. 4:6, Amos 4:11, Zeph. 2:9, Matt. 10:15, Matt. 11:23–24, Luke 10:12.

11. See Miner and Connoley, *Children are Free,* 6.

12. Carden, *Sodomy,* 116–28.

13. Greenberg, *Wrestling with God and Men,* 64–69. Rabbinical sources include Genesis Rabbah 42, 49, Leviticus Rabbah 5, and Numbers Rabbah 9.

14. Carden, *Sodomy,* 61–62; Crompton, *Homosexuality and Civilization,* 136–37. "Philo is the inventor of the homophobic reading of Genesis," Carden says (61).

15. Carden, *Sodomy,* 130–33.

16. Ibid. at 141–45. See, generally, McNeill, *Church and the Homosexual,* 68–76 (tracing reception of the Sodom story among various church authorities).

17. Jordan, *Invention of Sodomy,* 57–60, 160–63; Carden, *Sodomy,* 174–80. Jordan says that Peter Damian "pretends to speak a lesson form Genesis 19. In fact, it misreads that chapter allegorically and then illicitly generalizes from allegory to lawlike definition and prescription" (163). For a fascinating insight into Peter Damian's own troubled childhood and psychological makeup, see Vandermeersch, "Sodomites, Gays, and Biblical Scholars," 149–72, 162–67.

18. By the strict definition, the majority of Christians practice sodomy. Jordan, *Invention of Sodomy,* 12.

CHAPTER 9: THE GOSPELS

1. See Rogers, *Jesus, the Bible, and Homosexuality,* 68–69.

2. Readings similar to the ones I provide here include Robinson, "Jesus, the Centurion, and His Lover"; Jennings, *Man Jesus Loved,* 131–44; Brentlinger, *Gay Christian 101,* 193–221; Miner and Connoley, *Children Are Free,* 46–51.

3. On the sexual connotations of *pais,* see Cantarella, *Bisexuality in the Ancient World,* 29–31.

4. See Jennings, *Man Jesus Loved,* 145–69. On same-sex desire and the "beloved disciple," see 13–54.

5. On other possible same-sex stories in the Gospels, see Jennings, *Man Jesus Loved,* 105–30.

6. The Talmud, in Yevamot 79a–80b, also distinguishes between a eunuch by nature (*saris chamah*) and a man-made eunuch (*saris adam*). The *saris chamah* is distinguished by physical characteristics. However, these characteristics are strikingly similar to ancient images of "effeminates," i.e., homosexuals: absence of pubic hair at the age of twenty, absence of froth in urine, watery semen, urine that does not ferment, absence of steam from the body after a winter bath, and finally a voice that is so abnormal that one cannot distinguish whether it is that of a man or a woman. Many of these characteristics indicate a "coolness" in the eunuch's body, which according to ancient medicine was a sign of femininity. See Malik, "The Ancient Roman and Talmudic Definition of Natural Eunuchs."

7. Contemporary iterations of this theory include McNeill, *Church and the Homosexual,* 65; Johnston, *Gays Under Grace,* 123–25.

8. Clement of Alexandria, Stromata III, chapter 1, cited in Brentlinger, *Gay Christian 101,* 242.

CHAPTER 10: ROMANS

1. See Rogers, *Jesus, The Bible, and Homosexuality,* 73–74.

2. Brooten, *Love Between Women,* 144–59; Cantarella, *Bisexuality,* 164–72. For Brooten's response to constructionist critics, see Brooten, *Love Between Women,* 17, 26–29, 161–62. Brooten notes that, contrary to Foucault's theory that the medicalization of homosexuality arose only in the modern period, lesbianism was medicalized in the ancient world (149–59) and that Ptolemy even ascribed an erotic orientation to astrology (124–28, 115). Brooten argues that Romans 1:26 does indeed refer to lesbianism (249–51). See also Alpert, *Like Bread on the Seder Plate,* 29–30.

3. See Brooten, *Love Between Women,* 353; Boswell, *Christianity, Social Tolerance, and Homosexuality,* 161. Augustine did condemn homosexuality, but on the grounds of natural law, not the Pauline texts (Boswell, *Christianity,* 349). Ambrose, Chrysostom, and Anselm interpret the verse as applying to lesbianism. Brown, "Lesbian Sexuality in Medieval and Modern Europe," 68.

4. On natural law and sexuality in Paul, see Brooten, *Love Between Women,* 222–28, 266–71.

5. This is where the image of "carnal Israel" comes from: the notion that Israelite law is excessively involved with the body (dietary laws, circumcision) and not concerned with matters of the spirit (faith, belief, feelings in the heart). See Boyarin, *Carnal Israel,* 30–33, 230–35; Michaelson, "Anti-Legalism and Anti-Judaism."

6. See Miller, "The Practices of Romans 1:26: Homosexual or Hetero-sexual?"

7. Brooten, *Love Between Women,* 2. See also Heyward, *Touching Our Strength,* 62.

8. Philo Judaeus, *On Abraham,* section 135, cited in Carden, *Sodomy,* 62.

9. See Murray, *Homosexualities,* 255–57; Crompton, *Homosexuality and Civilization,* 79–82.

10. Brooten, *Love Between Women,* 241. See also Murray, *Homosexualities,* 112–28.

11. Of course, many other religious sources teach that women must be sexually as well as socially subservient to men. For example, the nineteenth-century Jewish legal compendium Kitzur Shulchan Aruch says that women being "on top" during the sex act is "perversion." Kitzur Shulchan Aruch, 150a.

12. See Scroggs, *New Testament and Homosexuality,* 116ff.

13. St. Thomas Aquinas, *Summa Theologica.* Boswell uses this quote as one of the epigraphs of his book.

14. Boswell, *Christianity,* 108–9. See also Edwards, *Gay/Lesbian Liberation,* 85–100. Richard Hays offers a strong rejoinder to Boswell's view, arguing that Paul is speaking in terms of groups, not individuals (see Hays, "Relations Natural and Unnatural," 184–215). Yet Hays goes onto claim that Paul's "nature" is somehow referring back to Genesis, which it does not cite and does not parallel in any way, weakening his case.

15. Piazza, *Gay by God,* 46.

16. See Rogers, *Jesus, the Bible, and Homosexuality,* 74.

17. See, e.g., Matt. 20:18–19, 26:2, 26:45, 27:26. The word occurs 117 times in the New Testament. See Dwyer, *Those 7 References,* 46–49.

18. Countryman, *Dirt, Greed, and Sex,* 109–23, arrives at the same end-point but suggests that Paul's agenda is one of purity, not gender confusion. I agree that Paul's concern is largely about boundary, but that concern is expressed in terms of gender boundaries and national boundaries, rather than impurity per se.

CHAPTER 11: CORINTHIANS AND TIMOTHY

1. See Helminiak, *What the Bible Really Says,* 105–15.

2. Scroggs, *New Testament,* 106–7; Helminiak, *What the Bible Really Says,* 105–10 (discussing "wide variation in translations" of the terms); Boswell, *Christianity,* 345–46.

3. Scroggs, *New Testament,* 106.

4. Cantarella, *Bisexuality,* 192.

5. Boswell, *Christianity,* 107.

6. Ibid., 348.

7. Ibid., 109.

8. Ibid. But see Wold, *Out of Order,* 188–98 (disputing such readings).

9. Boswell, *Christianity,* 345. Boswell calls Scroggs's theory "fanciful and unsubstantiated by lexicographical evidence" (341). But see Wright, "Homosexuals or Prostitutes?," 125, 144 (challenging Boswell).

10. See Petersen, "Can ΑΡΣΕΝΟΚΟΙΤΑΙ Be Translated by 'Homosexuals'?" 187, 189 ("Homosexual fails as a translation for it violates historical and linguistic fact by attempting to read a modern concept back into antiquity, where no equivalent concepts existed.").

11. Nissinen, *Homoeroticism in the Biblical World,* 118.

12. Many scholars believe that 1 Timothy was not actually written by Paul. For our purposes, this controversy is irrelevant, as the same issues that arose in 1 Corinthians arise here as well.

CHAPTER 12: DAVID AND JONATHAN

1. See Horner, *Jonathan Loved David,* 40–46; Jennings, *Jacob's Wound,* 227–34; Piazza, *Gay by God,* 54–62.

2. Rich, "Compulsory Heterosexuality and Lesbian Existence," 631–60.

3. Hunt, "Lovingly Lesbian," 172–78; Faderman, "Surpassing the Love of Men," 179–81; D'Angelo, "Women Partners in the New Testament," 65. Other applications of Rich's "lesbian continuum" include di Leonardo, "Warrior Virgins and Boston Marriages," 138–55.

4. Miner and Connoley, *Children Are Free,* 33. See also Duncan, "Book of Ruth," 92–102.

5. See Brentlinger, *Gay Christian 101,* 132–34.

6. Scholarly studies that locate the David and Jonathan story within the warrior love convention include Ackerman, *When Heroes Love;* Jennings, *Jacob's Wound,* 3–80; Halperin, *One Hundred Years,* 75–87; Nardelli, *Homosexuality and Liminality;* Nissinen, *Homoeroticism;* and Horner, *Jonathan Loved David.* My analysis here is indebted to these sources. Horner's book was a pioneering one in this genre, and he has a down-to-earth style that makes the book an easy read for laypeople. Ackerman and Jennings are more academic. See also Dover, "Greek Homosexuality and Initiation," 20–33.

7. See Crompton, *Homosexuality and Civilization,* 262–69; Boswell, *Same-Sex Unions,* 137–45; Horner, *Jonathan Loved David,* 27.

8. Roden, "What a Friend We Have in Jesus," 118–21.

9. Nissinen, 53–56. See Horner, *Jonathan Loved David,* 26–39; Greenberg, *Wrestling with God and Men,* 99–105; Brentlinger, *Gay Christian 101,* 140–91 (providing a thorough linguistic analysis).

10. Horner, *Jonathan Loved David,* 27–28.

11. Jennings, *Jacob's Wound,* 37–76.

12. Comstock, *Gay Theology without Apology,* 79–90.

CHAPTER 13: SEXUAL DIVERSITY IN CHRISTIAN THEOLOGY

1. McNeill, *Church and the Homosexual,* 82.

2. See Laeuchli, *Power and Sexuality;* Heyward, *Touching Our Strength,* 42–45.

3. McNeill, *Church and the Homosexual,* 91–98; DeSilva, "Paul and the Stoa," 549–64.

4. Crompton, *Homosexuality and Civilization,* 130–42; Boswell, *Christianity,* 131; McNeill, *Church and the Homosexual,* 74.

5. See Augustine, *Confessions,* book 4, chapters 4 and 6. See Crompton, *Homosexuality and Civilization,* 137.

6. See Heyward, *Touching Our Strength,* 89–90; Boswell, *Christianity,* 164.

7. Boswell, *Christianity,* 149.

8. For example, the Council of Toledo (693), canon 3; Council of Paris (829), canons 34 and 69; and the Council of Trosly (909), canon 15. See Crompton, *Homosexuality and Civilization,* 131–36 (noting fourth-century councils).

9. Boswell, *Christianity,* 135.

10. Ibid., 170

11. Ibid., 128–29.

12. Ibid., 131.

13. Brooten, *Love Between Women,* 11–12.

14. See Crompton, *Homosexuality and Civilization,* 130–36.

15. Boswell, *Christianity,* 165.

16. Jordan, *Invention of Sodomy,* 165; Jordan, *Silence of Sodom,* 114–17; Carden, *Sodomy,* 174–78. Damian was also interested in eliminating simony and clerical marriage (Greenberg, *Construction of Homosexuality,* 287–90).

17. See Carden, *Sodomy,* 169–74.

18. Boswell, *Christianity,* 185–94, 220–21, 214–15.

19. Ibid., 213–15.

20. Ibid., 218–21.

21. Ibid., 220–21.

22. See McGuire, *Brother and Lover;* Boswell, *Christianity,* 221–26; Jordan, *Silence of Sodom,* 193–94; McCleary, *Special Illumination,* 240–44; Quero, "Friendship with Benefits," 26–46.

23. This attitude was quite different from the predominant view that particular friendships among monks disrupt communal life. See McGuire,

Brother and Lover, 106. Aelred even states that carnal friendship among men is worthy, since it may lead to higher forms.

24. See Jennings, *Man Jesus Loved,* 74–79.

25. Crompton, *Homosexuality and Civilization,* 161–72.

26. Ibid., 195–97, 277–95; Greenberg, *Construction of Heterosexuality,* 268–82.

27. Crompton, *Homosexuality and Civilization,* 295.

28. See Moore, *Question of Truth,* 56.

29. Jordan, *Silence of Sodom,* 60–62. See Boswell, *Christianity,* 319–31.

30. Thomas Aquinas, *Summa Theologica* II:ii, 154: 11–12.

31. Boswell, *Christianity,* 331.

32. Brown, "Lesbian Sexuality in Medieval and Modern Europe," 67–75, 71.

33. Brooten, *Love Between Women,* 26–29, 305–14.

34. See Greenberg, *Construction of Homosexuality,* 303–6.

35. See, e.g., Robb, *Strangers,* 19–36; Duberman, *Hidden from History;* Greenberg, *Construction of Homosexuality,* 301–46.

36. Robb, *Strangers,* 4.

37. Ibid., 3.

38. Paragraphs 2357–2359. These teachings are based on the 1975 "Declaration on Certain Questions Concerning Sexual Ethics" and the 1986 "Letter to the Bishops of the Catholic Church on the Pastoral Care of Homosexual Persons." For the sake of brevity, I will focus on the teaching as codified in the catechism. Scholarly and theological treatments of the church teachings are listed below. Earlier twentieth-century Church documents are collected in Gallagher, *Homosexuality and the Magisterium.*

39. "Declaration on Certain Questions Concerning Sexual Ethics," section 8, Congregation for the Doctrine of the Faith, Persona Humana.

40. See Gramick and Furey, *Vatican and Homosexuality;* Gramick and Nugent, *Voices of Hope;* Moore, *A Question of Truth;* McNeill, *Church and the Homosexual;* Jordan, *Silence of Sodom;* Liuzzi, *With Listening Hearts;* Kelly, *Seduced by Grace.*

41. Liuzzi, *With Listening Hearts,* 39, citing John Paul II, *The Splendor of Truth* encyclical.

42. Jordan, *Silence of Sodom,* 101–2, citing studies by sociologists James Wolf and Sheila Murphy. On the lives of secretly gay priests, see Kelly, *Seduced by Grace,* 126–35; Wolf, *Gay Priests.*

43. See Wilson, *Our Tribe,* 50; U.S. Department of Justice, *Sexually Assaulted Children.*

44. Jordan, *Silence of Sodom,* 260. Jordan argues forcefully that attempts to read the biblical verses in a less condemning way (such as my own) are futile until we have "an adequate descriptive language for homoerotic lives in the church" and can "reveal how divine grace works within same sex relations," i.e., until LGBT people can "come out' in the pews and in the hierarchy (77). As a non-Catholic, I cannot comment on Jordan's argument. Certainly, he is correct that the many Catholic attempts to internally critique church teaching have been ineffectual. For another perspective on "us versus us" in the Catholic Church, see Moore, *Question of Truth,* 5–7.

45. Goodstein, "Presbyterians Approve Ordination."

46. See Rogers, *Jesus, the Bible, and Homosexuality,* 9–15.

47. Ibid., 140.

48. See Boisvert, *Out on Holy Ground,* 21. One outstanding reading of the Bible by an MCC minister is in Wilson, *Our Tribe.* For a sympathetic critique of MCC theology, see Jordan, *Silence of Sodom,* 253–56.

49. See Ellison, "Homosexuality and Protestantism," 151 (discussing 1988 Southern Baptist convention).

50. See Ferguson, *Christianity and Homosexuality.*

51. See Evangelicals Concerned; Brentlinger, *Gay Christian 101;* Bakker, *Fall to Grace;* DiNovo, *Que(e)rying Evangelism;* Rogers, *Jesus, the Bible, and Homosexuality,* 7–8; Banerjee, "Gay and Evangelical."

52. Falsani, "Is Evangelical Christianity Having a Great Gay Awakening?"

53. Stone, "Dobson's Successor Gives Mega-Ministry New Focus."

54. Greenberg, *Wrestling with God and Men,* 215–61; *Statement of Principles on the Place of Jews with a Homosexual Orientation in Our Community.*

CHAPTER 14: "YOU SHALL BE HOLY, FOR I AM HOLY"

1. Quoted in Dreyfuss, "The Holy War on Gays," 40.

2. See evidence collected in American Psychological Association, *Lesbian and Gay Parenting;* Eskridge, *Gay Marriage.*

3. Patterson, "Children of Lesbian and Gay Parents," 241. Patterson's article cites dozens of studies. See also Fitzgerald, "Children of Lesbian and Gay Parents," 57–75. No sociological study has ever shown that children do better with a mother and a father than with two fathers or two mothers.

4. Fitzgerald, "Children of Lesbian and Gay Parents."

5. Gartrell, "Adolescents of the U.S. National Longitudinal Lesbian Family Study."

6. Bos, "Children's Gender Identity," 114–12. The reported rate of exclusive homosexuality among these children is about 2.8 percent.

7. Langbein, "Same-Sex Marriage and Negative Externalities," 2; Badgett, *When Gay People Get Married*, 64–85.

8. *Perry v. Schwarzenegger.*

9. See Herek, *Stigma and Sexual Orientation.*

10. Quoted in Dreyfuss, "The Holy War on Gays," 40. The original copy of this statement has been removed from the FRC's website. See also Stacey, "Cruising to Familyland," 181–97.

11. *Perry v. Schwarzenegger*, 945–50.

12. See Wilson, *Our Tribe*, 50; U.S. Department of Justice, *Sexually Assaulted Children.*

13. Works by conservative pro-gay, pro-family Christian writers include Piazza, *Gay by God*, 157–69; Rogers, *Jesus, the Bible, and Homosexuality*, 88–105; Johnston, *Gays Under Grace*, 133–82.

14. See Jennings, *Man Jesus Loved*, 174–93; Glaser, *Coming Out as Sacrament*, 69.

15. See Kristof, "God and Sex."

16. Chauncey, *Why Marriage*, 59–60.

17. Ellison, *Same-Sex Marriage?*, 67.

18. Ibid.; Boswell, *Same-Sex Unions*, 28–52; Jordan, *Blessing Same-Sex Unions*, 13–15.

19. Nelson, *Between Two Gardens*, 129–39.

20. Bagemihl, *Biological Exuberance*, 23–26.

21. Say, *Gays, Lesbians, and Family Values*, 19–82.

22. See Jordan, *Blessing Same-Sex Unions*, 105; Ellison, *Same-Sex Marriage?*, 73; Boswell, *Same-Sex Unions*, 111.

23. See, e.g., Warner, *Trouble with Normal*, 127–29. For a response to Warner, see Jordan, *Blessing Same-Sex Unions*, 13–16.

24. See Eskridge, *The Case for Same-Sex Marriage*; Sullivan, *Same-Sex Marriage*; Baird, *Same-Sex Marriage.*

25. Badgett, *When Gay People Get Married*, 115–50.

26. See Eskridge, *Same-Sex Marriage*; Badgett, *When Gay People Get Married*, 64–85.

27. See Ellison, *Same-Sex Marriage?*, 95–96; Warner, *Trouble with Normal.*

28. See, e.g., Nelson, *Sexuality and the Sacred*; Nelson, *Between Two Gardens*, 73–85; Mollenkott, *Is the Homosexual My Neighbor?*, 122–35; Davies, *Redefining Sexual Ethics*; Ellison, *Same Sex Marriage?*, 139–46.

29. Nelson, *Between Two Gardens*, 124.

30. Heyward, *Touching Our Strength*, 121.

31. Ibid., 125.

32. Ibid. Heyward proceeds to develop such an ethic in her book, 124–55.

33. See, e.g., Clark, *Doing the Work of Love.*

34. See, e.g., Goss, *Jesus Acted Up,* 165–68; Cheng, *Radical Love;* Lorde, "The Use of the Erotic," 73.

CHAPTER 15: "WHEN I BECAME A MAN, I PUT CHILDISH WAYS BEHIND ME"

Title. 1 Cor. 13:11.

1. Murdoch, "The Moral Decision about Homosexuality."

2. Scanzoni and Mollenkott's 1978 book *Is the Homosexual My Neighbor?* is an excellent and still timely introduction to how coming to understand and accept sexual diversity is part of the Christian spiritual journey. It cites biblical stories and fundamental principles of love and concern, and speaks in a gentle voice of gay and lesbian people's experiences.

3. BT Ketuvot 32b, BT Bava Kamma 83b.

4. BT Sanhedrin 71a.

5. It is unclear who actually coined this maxim. The Archbishop of Canterbury supposedly called it the goal of religion. In the film *Inherit the Wind,* Gene Kelly's E. K. Hornbeck says it's the role of newspapers. It seems that writer Finley Peter Dunne may have said it first, of newspapers—but he meant it satirically.

6. Chellew-Hodge, *Bulletproof Faith,* 41.

7. Rogers, *Jesus, the Bible, and Homosexuality,* 15.

8. My own story is much less traumatic than many others. For harrowing accounts of growing up gay in traditional religious communities in the South, see Sears, *Growing Up Gay in the South.*

9. "Anti-Gay Hate Crimes: Doing the Math." According to statistics kept by the FBI from 2005 to 2010, gays are 2.4 times more likely to suffer a violent hate crime attack than Jews, 2.6 times more likely than blacks, 13.8 times more likely than Latinos, and 41.5 times more likely than whites.

10. One Orthodox rabbi recently told another rabbi that it would be a "mitzvah" (commandment, good deed) for gay kids to kill themselves. Greenberg, "The Cost of Standing Idly By."

11. See Fox, *Alexander the Great,* 40–41; Cartledge, *Alexander the Great,* 54–55, 228–29.

12. See Cantarella, *Bisexuality,* 58–69; Murray, *Homosexualities,* 34–43.

13. Brooten, *Love Between Women,* 29–41; Murray, *Homosexualities,* 204–207; Harvey, *Gay Mystics,* 13–15. Sappho was one of the most widely read poets in the ancient world. Most of her work was later destroyed by censors.

14. Rowse, *Homosexuals in History,* 3, 32–36, 91–98.

15. See Field, *Sarah Churchill, Duchess of Marlborough;* Donoghue, *Passions Between Women,* 1.

16. See Crompton, *Homosexuality and Civilization,* 355–360. These facts about Christina have been known since Margaret Goldsmith's *Christina of Sweden,* published in 1933. A mostly sanitized version of Queen Christina's story was told in the film *Queen Christina* (1933) starring Greta Garbo.

17. See Saslow, *Ganymede in the Renaissance;* Crompton, *Homosexuality and Civilization,* 269–78; Rowse, *Homosexuals in History,* 17–23; Murray, *Homosexualities,* 142; Harvey, *Gay Mystics,* 104–7; Greenberg, *The Construction of Homosexuality,* 309–10.

18. See Serge Bramly, *Leonardo;* Rowse, *Homosexuals in History,* 10–17.

19. Murray, *Homosexualities,* 153–54; Smith, *Homosexual Desire in Shakespeare's England,* 74.

20. See Crompton, *Byron and Greek Love;* Fone, *Columbia Anthology of Gay Literature,* 219; MacCarthy, *Byron,* 499–501.

21. Robb, *Strangers,* 220–23; Andersen, *Hans Christian Andersen,* 153–55.

22. See Katz, *Love Stories,* 33–41, 164–77. Letters are reprinted in Bergman, *Gay American Autobiography,* 15–26. On the photographs with Doyle and other men, see Folsom, "Whitman's Calamus Photographs," 193–219.

23. Letters are quoted in Wiley, *Tchaikovsky;* Poznansky, *Tchaikovsky;* Rowse, *Homosexuals in History,* 136–40.

24. The letters are reprinted, with analysis, in Duberman, "Writhing Bedfellows," 85.

25. Rapp, "George Washington Carver."

26. Chauncey, *Why Marriage,* 14. On homosexuality in the nineteenth century, see Robb, *Strangers,* 19–31; Katz, *Love Stories.*

27. Boswell, *Same-Sex Unions,* 146–90. On the iconic pair of Serge and Bacchus, see 146–54.

28. See Roth, "'My Beloved Is Like a Gazelle,'" 143–65, reprinted in *Homosexuality and Religion and Philosophy,* 271–293.

29. See Murray, *Homosexualities,* 25–28, 43–51; Murray and Roscoe, *Islamic Homosexualities,* 14–44.

30. See Schalow, "Male Love in Early Modern Japan," 118–28; Wawrytko, "Homosexuality in Chinese and Japanese Religions," 210–215; Crompton, *Homosexuality and Civilization,* 411–443.

31. See Murray, *Homosexualities,* 77–96; Crompton, *Homosexuality and Civilization,* 419–23.

32. Ng, "Homosexuality and the State in Late Imperial China," 76–89; Conner, *Blossom of Bone,* 49–59; Wawrytko, "Homosexuality in Chinese and Japanese Religions," 200–203; Crompton, *Homosexuality and Civilization,* 213–44. When Christian missionaries arrived in China, many Chinese

nobles were shocked to discover that anyone disapproved of homosexuality. Wawrytko, "Homosexuality in Chinese and Japanese Religions," 202.

33. See Roscoe, *Changing Ones,* 222–47; Williams, *Spirit and the Flesh,* 17–109. Perhaps the original study of this phenomenon was Edward Carpenter's "On the Connection between Homosexuality and Divination," originally published in 1908 in *The Intermediate Sex.*

34. See Nanda, *Neither Man nor Woman;* Reddy, *With Respect to Sex.*

35. Conner, *Blossom of Bone,* 99–125; Roscoe, "Priests of the Goddess," 295–330.

36. See Halperin, *One Hundred Years,* 9. On cross-cultural typologies of homosexual relationships, see Murray, *Homosexualities* (categorizing relations as age-stratified, gender-stratified, or egalitarian).

37. Unks, *Gay Teen,* 5.

38. Mark Twain, *Huckleberry Finn,* chapter 31.

CHAPTER 16: "EVERYONE WHOSE SPIRIT MOVED HIM BROUGHT AN OFFERING TO GOD"

Title. Exod. 35:21.

1. McNeill, *Taking a Chance on God,* xix. See also Mollenkott, *Omnigender,* 2–3.

2. See Mollenkott, *Sensuous Spirituality,* 69–88.

3. Roger Williams, "The Bloudy Tenent, of Persecution," quoted in Miller, *Roger Williams,* 98.

CHAPTER 17: "AND I HAVE FILLED HIM WITH THE SPIRIT OF GOD . . . TO DEVISE SUBTLE WORKS IN GOLD, SILVER, AND BRASS"

Title. Exod. 31:3–4.

1. Carl Jung, *Collected Works,* vol. 9, part 1, 87, quoted in McCleary, *Special Illumination,* 20. On Jungian psychology and homosexuality, see Hopcke, *Same-Sex Love and the Path to Wholeness.* On the idea of a special receptivity, see Harvey, *Gay Mystics.*

2. For introductions to queer theology, see Loughlin, *Queer Theology;* Stuart, *Gay and Lesbian Theologies;* Cheng, *Radical Love.*

3. Heyward, *Touching Our Strength,* 3.

4. Kelly, *Seduced by Grace,* 4–20; 48–49; Nelson, *Between Two Gardens;* Goss, *Jesus Acted Up,* 69–72; Mollenkott, *Sensuous Spirituality,* 107–21; Boisvert, *Out on Holy Ground,* 45. Some writers have pointed out that the erotic has never been so distant from Christian life—it has only been sublimated; see, e.g., Rambuss, *Closet Devotions;* Althaus-Reid, *The Queer God,* 30–33; Althaus-Reid and Isherwood, *Sexual Theologian.*

5. Heyward, *Touching Our Strength,* 3, 25, 24.

6. Ibid., 21, 20–36.

7. Ibid., 99

8. Ibid., 90.

9. Ibid., 74.

10. Ibid.

11. McNeill, *Taking a Chance on God,* xxi.

12. Ibid., 28–74, 179–80.

13. Ibid., 201, 137–43, 201.

14. Wilson, *Our Tribe,* 70–87.

15. Sweasey, *From Queer to Eternity,* 26–50.

16. See Monroe, "Reverend Irene Monroe: Writer, Speaker, Theologian."

17. Spencer, *Gay and Gaia,* 118–20.

18. Alpert, *Like Bread on the Seder Plate,* 37–111.

19. See, e.g., Wilson, *Our Tribe,* 125–53; Piazza, *Gay by God,* 191–200; Goss, *Jesus Acted Up,* 61–85; Boisvert, *Out on Holy Ground,* 77–80.

20. Mollenkott, "Reading the Bible from Low and Outside," in *Taking Back the Word,* Goss, ed., 14–19.

21. Mollenkott, *Omnigender,* 81–118.

22. See Althaus-Reid and Isherwood, *Trans/Formations;* Tanis, *Trans-Gendered;* Dzmura, *Balancing on the Mechitza.*

23. See Conner, *Blossom of Bone,* 40–43; Greenberg, *Construction of Homosexuality,* 40–56.

24. See Conner, *Blossom of Bone;* Johnson, *Gay Spirituality;* Thompson, *Gay Spirit.*

25. de la Huerta, *Coming Out Spiritually,* 7–44.

26. Johnson, *Gay Spirituality.*

27. Quoted in Thompson, *Gay Soul,* 20. See, generally, Hay, *Radically Gay.*

28. Brentlinger, *Gay Christian 101,* 1.

29. Boisvert, *Out on Holy Ground,* 41.

30. Kelly, *Seduced by Grace,* 96.

CHAPTER 18: "FOR NOTHING IN CREATION CAN SEPARATE YOU FROM THE LOVE OF GOD"

Title. Rom. 8:39.

Bibliography

Aarons, Leroy. *Prayers for Bobby: A Mother's Coming to Terms with the Suicide of Her Gay Son.* San Francisco: HarperOne, 1996.

Ackerman, Susan. *When Heroes Love: The Ambiguity of Eros in the Stories of Gilgamesh and David.* New York: Columbia University Press, 2005.

Alison, James. *Faith beyond Resentment: Fragments Catholic and Gay.* New York: Crossroad Publishing, 2001.

Alpert, Rebecca T. "Do Justice, Love Mercy, Walk Humbly: Reflections on Micah and Gay Ethics." In *Take Back the Word,* eds. Goss and West, 170–78.

————. *Like Bread on the Seder Plate: Jewish Lesbians and the Transformation of Tradition.* New York: Columbia University Press, 1998.

Althaus-Reid, Marcella. *The Queer God.* New York: Routledge, 2003.

Althaus-Reid, Marcella, and Lisa Isherwood. *Trans/Formations.* London: SCM Press, 2009.

Althaus-Reid, Marcella, and Lisa Isherwood, eds. *The Sexual Theologian: Essays on Sex, God, and Politics.* New York: T & T Clark, 2005.

American Psychological Association. *Lesbian and Gay Parenting.* Washington, DC: American Psychological Association, 2005.

Andersen, Jens. *Hans Christian Andersen: A New Life.* New York: Overlook Press, 2006.

"Anti-Gay Hate Crimes: Doing the Math." Southern Poverty Law Center Intelligence Report No. 140, Winter 2010. www.splcenter.org/.

Associated Press. "Psychologists Reject Gay 'Therapy.'" *New York Times,* August 9, 2009.

Augustine. *Confessions.* Translated by R.S. Pine-Coffin. New York: Penguin, 1961.

Avis, Paul D. L. *Eros and the Sacred.* Harrisburg, PA: Morehouse Publishing, 1990.

Badgett, M. V. Lee. *When Gay People Get Married: What Happens When So-*

cieties Legalize Same-Sex Marriage. New York: New York University Press, 2009.

Bagemihl, Bruce. *Biological Exuberance: Animal Homosexuality and Natural Diversity.* New York: St. Martin's Press, 2000.

Baird, Robert M., and Stuart E. Rosenbaum, eds. *Same-Sex Marriage: The Moral and Legal Debate.* Amherst, MA: Prometheus Books, 2004.

Bakker, Jay. *Fall to Grace: A Revolution of God, Self, and Society.* Nashville: Faithwords, 2011.

Balch, David. *Homosexuality, Science, and the "Plain Sense" of Scripture.* Grand Rapids, MI: Eerdmans, 2000.

Balka, Christie, and Andy Rose, eds. *Twice Blessed: On Being Lesbian or Gay and Jewish.* Boston: Beacon Press, 1989.

Ball, Carlos. *The Morality of Gay Rights: An Exploration in Political Philosophy.* London: Routledge, 2002.

Banerjee, Neela. "Gay and Evangelical, Seeking Paths of Acceptance." *New York Times,* December 12, 2006.

"Barney Frank Reveals Gay Agenda." *Advocate,* December 22, 2010.

Barzan, Robert. *Sex and Spirit: Exploring Gay Men's Spirituality.* Brooklyn, NY: White Crane Press, 1995.

Bell, Robin. "Homosexual Men and Women." *British Medical Journal* 318, no. 7181 (1999). www.bmj.com/content/318/7181/452.full/.

Bergman, David, ed. *Gay American Autobiography: Writings from Whitman to Sedaris.* Madison: University of Wisconsin Press, 2009.

Black, Patrick. "The Broken Wings of Eros: Christian Ethics and the Denial of Desire." *Theological Studies* 64, no. 1 (2003): 106–26.

Boisvert, Donald J. *Out on Holy Ground: Meditations on Gay Men's Spirituality.* Cleveland: Pilgrim Press, 2000.

Bos, Henny, and Theo Sandfort. "Children's Gender Identity in Lesbian and Heterosexual Two-Parent Families." *Sex Roles* 62 (2010): 114.

Boswell, John. *Christianity, Social Tolerance, and Homosexuality.* Chicago: University of Chicago Press, 1987.

——. "Concepts, Experience, and Sexuality." In *Que(e)rying Religion,* eds. Comstock and Henking, 116–29.

——. *Same-Sex Unions in Premodern Europe.* New York: Vintage Press, 1995.

Boyarin, Daniel. *Carnal Israel: Reading Sex in Talmudic Culture.* Berkeley: University of California Press, 1995.

Boyd, Malcolm. *Are You Running with Me, Jesus?* Cambridge, MA: Cowley Publications, 2006.

——. *Take Off the Masks.* Brooklyn, NY: White Crane Books, 2007.

Bramly, Serge. *Leonardo: Discovering the Life of Leonardo da Vinci.* New York: HarperCollins, 1991.

Brawley, Robert, ed. *Biblical Ethics and Homosexuality: Listening to Scripture.* Louisville: Presbyterian Publishing, 1996.

Brentlinger, Rick. *Gay Christian 101: Spiritual Self-Defense for Gay Christians.* Pace, FL: Salient Press, 2007.

Bronski, Michael. *A Queer History of the United States.* Boston: Beacon Press, 2011.

Brooten, Bernadette J. *Love Between Women: Early Christian Responses to Female Homoeroticism.* Chicago: University of Chicago Press, 1998.

Brown, Judith. *Immodest Acts: The Life of a Lesbian Nun in Renaissance Italy.* New York: Oxford University Press, 1986.

———. "Lesbian Sexuality in Medieval and Modern Europe." In *Hidden from History,* eds. Duberman et al., 67–75.

Cantarella, Eva. *Bisexuality in the Ancient World.* Translated by Cormac O Cuilleanain. New Haven: Yale University Press, 1992.

Carden, Michael. *Sodomy: The History of a Christian Biblical Myth.* London: Equinox Publishing, 2004.

Carpenter, Edward. *The Intermediate Sex: A Study of Some Transitional Types of Men and Women.* Frankston, TX: TGS Publishing, 2009.

Carr, David. *The Erotic Word: Sexuality, Spirituality, and the Bible.* New York: Oxford University Press, 2005.

Cartledge, Paul. *Alexander the Great: The Hunt for a New Past.* New York: Vintage, 2005.

Cervantes, Vincent. "My Ex-Gay Experience Part 2." www.youtube.com/watch?v=vY6vXQooPzM.

Chapman, Patrick. *Thou Shalt Not Love: What Evangelicals Really Say to Gays.* Fort Collins, CO: Haiduk Press, 2008.

Chauncey, George. *Why Marriage: The History Shaping Today's Debate Over Gay Equality.* New York: Basic Books, 2005.

Chellew-Hodge, Candace. *Bulletproof Faith: A Spiritual Survival Guide for Gay and Lesbian Christians.* San Francisco: Jossey-Bass, 2008.

Cheng, Patrick. *Radical Love: An Introduction to Queer Theology.* New York: Seabury Books, 2011.

Clark, J. Michael. "Coming Out: Discovering Empowerment, Balance, and Wholeness." In *Homophobia and the Judaeo-Christian Tradition,* eds. Stemmeler and Clark, 191–208.

———. *Doing the Work of Love: Men and Commitment in Same-Sex Couples.* Harriman, TN: Men's Studies Press, 1999.

Cleaver, Richard. *Know My Name: A Gay Liberation Theology.* Louisville: Westminster John Know, 1995.

Cobb, Michael. *God Hates Fags: The Rhetorics of Religious Violence.* New York: New York University Press, 2006.

Comstock, Gary David. *Gay Theology Without Apology.* Eugene, OR: Wipf and Stock, 2009.

Comstock, Gary David, and Susan Henking, eds. *Que(e)rying Religion: A Critical Anthology.* New York: Continuum Press, 1997.

Conner, Randy P. *Blossom of Bone: Reclaiming the Connections between Homoeroticism and the Sacred.* San Francisco: HarperOne, 1993.

Countryman, L. William. *Dirt, Greed, and Sex: Sexual Ethics in the New Testament and Their Relation for Today.* Minneapolis: Augsburg Fortress Press, 2007.

"The Creation of Exodus International." www.youtube.com/watch?v= zraXAiOtdFw.

Crompton, Louis. *Byron and Greek Love: Homophobia in 19th-Century England.* London: Gay Men's Press, 1998.

———. *Homosexuality and Civilization.* Cambridge, MA: Belknap Press, 2006.

Dallas, Joe. *The Gay Gospel: How Pro-Gay Advocates Misread the Bible.* Eugene, OR: Harvest House, 2007.

D'Angelo, Mary Rose. "Women Partners in the New Testament." *Journal of Feminist Studies in Religion* 6, no. 1 (Spring 1990): 65–86.

D'Augelli, Anthony, Scott Hershberger, and Neil Pilkington. "Suicidality Patterns and Sexual Orientation-Related Factors among Lesbian, Gay, and Bisexual Youths." *Suicide and Life-Threatening Behavior* 31, no. 3 (Fall 2001): 250–64.

Davies, Susan B., ed. *Redefining Sexual Ethics: A Sourcebook of Essays, Stories, and Poems.* Cleveland: Pilgrim Press, 1991.

Davis, Christie. "Religious Boundaries and Sexual Morality." In *Que(e)rying Religion,* eds. Comstock and Henking, 39–60.

De Hoop, Raymond. "Saul the Sodomite." In *Sodom's Sin,* eds. Noort and Tigchelaar, 17–26.

de la Huerta, Christian. *Coming Out Spiritually: The Next Step.* New York: Tarcher Press, 1999.

DeSilva, David A. "Paul and the Stoa: A Comparison." *Journal of the Evangelical Theological Society* 38, no. 4 (1995): 549–64.

di Leonardo, Micaela. "Warrior Virgins and Boston Marriages: Spinsterhood in History and Culture." In *Que(e)rying Religion,* eds. Comstock and Henking, 138–55.

DiNovo, Cheri. *Que(e)rying Evangelism: Growing a Community from the Outside In.* Cleveland: Pilgrim Press, 2005.

Donoghue, Emma. *Passions between Women: British Lesbian Culture, 1668–1801.* London: Scarlet Press, 1994.

Dover, K.J. "Greek Homosexuality and Initiation." In *Que(e)rying Religion,* eds. Comstock and Henking.

Dreyfuss, Robert. "The Holy War on Gays." *Rolling Stone,* March 18, 1999.

Drinkwater, Gregg, Joshua Lesser, and David Shneer, eds. *Torah Queeries: Weekly Commentary on the Hebrew Bible.* New York: New York University Press, 2009.

Duberman, Martin. "Writhing Bedfellows: 1826. Two Young Men from Antebellum South Carolina's Ruling Elite Share 'Extravagant Delight.'" *Journal of Homosexuality* 6, nos. 1–2 (1980/81): 85–101.

Duberman, Martin, Martha Vicinus, and George Chauncey, eds. *Hidden from History: Reclaiming the Gay and Lesbian Past.* New York: Plume, 1990.

Duncan, Celena M. "The Book of Ruth." In *Take Back the Word,* eds. Goss and West.

Dwyer, John F. *Those 7 References: A Study of 7 References to Homosexuality in the Bible.* Charleston, SC: BookSurge Publishing, 2007.

Dynes, Wayne R., and Stephen Donaldson, eds. *Homosexuality and Religion and Philosophy.* New York: Garland Publishing, 1992.

Dzmura, Noach. *Balancing on the Mechitza: Transgender in the Jewish Community.* Berkeley, CA: North Atlantic Books, 2010.

Edberg, Eric. "Bearing False Witness." *Life, the Cello, and Everything* (blog), November 5, 2006. http://ericedberg.wordpress.com/2006/11/05/bearing-false-witness/.

Edwards, George. *Gay/Lesbian Liberation: A Biblical Perspective.* Cleveland: Pilgrim Press, 1984.

Ellison, Marvin. "Homosexuality and Protestantism." In *Homosexuality and World Religions,* ed. Swidler, 149–79.

———. *Same-Sex Marriage? A Christian Ethical Analysis.* Cleveland: Pilgrim Press, 2004.

Ellison, Marvin, and Kelly Brown Douglas, eds. *Sexuality and the Sacred: Sources for Theological Reflection.* Louisville: Westminster John Knox, 2010.

Erkkila, Betsy, and Jay Grossman, eds. *Breaking Bounds: Whitman and American Cultural Studies.* New York: Oxford University Press, 1996.

Eskridge, William. *The Case for Same-Sex Marriage: From Sexual Liberty to Civilized Commitment.* New York: Free Press, 1996.

———, and Darren R. Spedale. *Gay Marriage: For Better or for Worse? What We've Learned from the Evidence.* New York: Oxford University Press, 2007.

Evangelicals Concerned. www.ecinc.org.

"Ex-Gay Survivors on Tyra," April 12, 2007. www.youtube.com/watch?v=S-J5T6wsnEQ.

Faderman, Lillian. "Surpassing the Love of Men." In *Sexuality and the Sacred,* eds. Ellison and Douglas, 179–81.

———. *Surpassing the Love of Men: Romantic Friendship and Love between Women from the Renaissance to the Present.* New York: Harper, 1998.

Falsani, Cathleen. "Is Evangelical Christianity Having a Great Gay Awak-

ening?" *Huffington Post,* January 13, 2011. www.huffingtonpost.com/
cathleen-falsani/the-great-gay-awakening_b_808235.html.

Family Research Council. "Washington Update: A Word from Our Media
Center." www.frc.org/get.cfm?i=WU10E03 (last accessed January 30,
2011).

Farley, Margaret. *Just Love: A Framework for Christian Sexual Ethics.* New
York: Continuum, 2006.

Ferguson, David, Fritz Guy, and David Larson, eds. *Christianity and Homosexuality: Some Seventh-Day Adventist Perspectives.* www.sdagayperspectives
.com.

Field, Ophelia. *Sarah Churchill, Duchess of Marlborough: The Queen's Favourite.*
New York: St. Martin's Press, 2003.

Fitzgerald, Bridget. "Children of Lesbian and Gay Parents: A Review of the
Literature." *Marriage and Family Review* 29 (1999): 57–75.

Folsom, Ed. "Whitman's Calamus Photographs." In *Breaking Bounds: Whitman and American Cultural Studies,* eds. Erkkila and Grossman, 193–219.

Fone, Byrne, ed. *The Columbia Anthology of Gay Literature.* New York: Columbia University Press, 2001.

"Former Ex-Gay Leaders Apologize." www.youtube.com/watch?v=aDiYe
JbsQo.

Fox, Robin Lane. *Alexander the Great.* New York: Penguin, 2004.

Frank, Barney. "Rep. Barney Frank on the Radical Homosexual Agenda."
www.youtube.com/watch?v=Ooh5Vtke3OA.

Frontain, Raymond J., ed. *Reclaiming the Sacred: The Bible in Gay and Lesbian
Culture.* Binghamton, NY: Haworth Press, 1997.

Fruth, Barbara, and Gottfried Hohmann. "Social Grease for Females?
Same-Sex Genital Contacts in Wild Bonobos." In *Homosexual Behaviour
in Animals,* eds. Sommer and Vasey, 294–315.

Gagnon, Robert. *The Bible and Homosexual Practice: Texts and Hermeneutics.*
Nashville: Abingdon Press, 2002.

Gallagher, John, ed. *Homosexuality and the Magisterium: Documents from the
Vatican and U.S. Bishops.* Mount Rainier, MD: New Ways Ministry, 1986.

Garofalo, Robert, R. Cameron Wolf, Lawrence S. Wissow, Elizabeth R.
Woods, and Elizabeth Goodman. "Sexual Orientation and Risk of Suicide Attempts among a Representative Sample of Youth." *Archives of Pediatrics and Adolescent Medicine* 153 (1999): 487–93.

Gartrell, Nanette, Henny Bos, and Naomi Goldberg. "Adolescents of the
U.S. National Longitudinal Lesbian Family Study: Sexual Orientation,
Sexual Behavior, and Sexual Risk Exposure." *Archives of Sexual Behavior*
(2010). DOI: 10.1007/s10508-010-9692-2. www.springerlink.com/content/
d967883qp3255733/.

Glaser, Chris. *Coming Out as Sacrament.* Louisville: Westminster John Knox, 1998.

———. *Coming Out to God: Prayers for Lesbians, Gay Men, Their Families, and Friends.* Louisville: Presbyterian Publishing Corp., 1991.

———. *Uncommon Calling: A Gay Christian's Struggle to Serve the Church.* New York: HarperCollins, 1988.

Gomes, Peter. *The Good Book: Reading the Bible with Mind and Heart.* New York: William Morrow and Company, 1996.

Goodstein, Laurie. "Presbyterians Approve Ordination of Gay People." *New York Times,* May 10, 2011.

Goss, Robert. *Jesus Acted Up: A Gay and Lesbian Manifesto.* New York: HarperCollins, 1994.

———. *Queering Christ: Beyond Jesus Acted Up.* Cleveland: Pilgrim Press, 2002.

Goss, Robert, and Mona West. *Take Back the Word.* Cleveland: Pilgrim Press, 2000.

Gramick, Jeannine, and Pat Furey. *The Vatican and Homosexuality: Reactions to the "Letters to the Bishops of the Catholic Church on the Pastoral Care of Homosexual Persons".* New York: Crossroad Publishing, 1988.

Gramick, Jeannine, and Robert Nugent. *Voices of Hope: A Collection of Positive Catholic Writings on Gay & Lesbian Issues.* Mount Rainier, MD: New Ways Ministry, 1995.

Grant, Colin. "For the Love of God: Agape." *Journal of Religious Ethics* 24, no. 1 (1996): 3–21.

Greenberg, David F. *The Construction of Homosexuality.* Chicago: University of Chicago Press, 1990.

Greenberg, Steven. "The Cost of Standing Idly By." *Jewish Week,* October 12, 2010.

———. *Wrestling with God and Men: Homosexuality in the Jewish Tradition.* Madison: University of Wisconsin Press, 2005.

Gudorf, Christine. "The Bible and Science on Sexuality." In *Homosexuality, Science, and the "Plain Sense" of Scripture,* ed. Balch, 121–41.

Halperin, David. *One Hundred Years of Homosexuality and Other Essays on Greek Love.* London: Routledge, 1989.

Hannant, Olive Elaine. *God Comes Out: A Queer Homiletic.* Cleveland: Pilgrim Press, 2007.

Harvey, Andrew. *The Essential Gay Mystics.* New York: HarperCollins, 1998.

Hay, Harry. *Radically Gay: Gay Liberation in the Words of Its Founder.* Boston: Beacon Press, 1997.

Haynes, Stephen R. *Noah's Curse: The Biblical Justification of American Slavery.* New York: Oxford University Press, 2007.

Hays, Richard. "Relations Natural and Unnatural: A Response to John Boswell's Exegesis on Romans 1." *Journal of Religious Ethics* 14, no. 1 (1986): 184–215.

Helminiak, Daniel. *What the Bible Really Says About Homosexuality.* Sacramento: Alamo Square Press, 2000.

Herdt, Gilbert. *Same Sex, Different Cultures: Exploring Gay and Lesbian Lives.* New York: Basic Books, 1997.

Herek, Gregory M., ed. *Stigma and Sexual Orientation: Understanding Prejudice Against Lesbians, Gay Men, and Bisexuals.* Thousand Oaks, CA: Sage, 1998.

Herodotus. *The Histories.* Translated by George Rawlinson. London: J. M. Dent, 1992.

Heyward, Carter. *Our Passion for Justice: Images of Power, Sexuality and Liberation.* Cleveland: Pilgrim Press, 1984.

———. *Touching Our Strength: The Erotic as Power and the Love of God.* San Francisco: Harper, 1989.

Holtz, Raymond C. *Listen to the Stories: Gay and Lesbian Catholics Talk about Their Lives and the Church.* New York: Garland, 1991.

Hopcke, Robert H., ed. *Same-Sex Love and the Path to Wholeness.* Boston: Shambhala, 1993.

Horner, Thomas. *Jonathan Loved David: Homosexuality in Biblical Times.* Louisville: Westminster John Knox, 1978.

Hume, Basil. *The Mystery of Love.* Brewster, MA: Paraclete Press, 2001.

Hunt, Mary. "Lovingly Lesbian: Toward a Feminist Theology of Friendship." In *Sexuality and the Sacred,* eds. Ellison and Douglas, 169–82.

Jennings, Theodore W. *Jacob's Wound: Homoerotic Narrative in the Literature of Ancient Israel.* New York: Continuum, 2005.

———. *The Man Jesus Loved.* Cleveland: Pilgrim Press, 2009.

Johnson, Toby. *Gay Spirituality: Gay Identity and the Transformation of Human Consciousness.* Maple Shade, NJ: White Crane Books, 2004.

Johnston, Maury. *Gays Under Grace: A Gay Christian's Response to Homosexuality.* Nashville: Winston-Derek Publishers, 1991.

Jordan, Mark D. *Blessing Same-Sex Unions: The Perils of Queer Romance and the Confusions of Christian Marriage.* Chicago: University of Chicago Press, 2005.

———. *The Invention of Sodomy in Christian Theology.* Chicago: University of Chicago Press, 1998.

———. *The Silence of Sodom: Homosexuality in Modern Catholicism.* Chicago: University of Chicago Press, 2000.

Jung, Patricia Beattie, ed. *Sexual Diversity and Catholicism: Toward the Development of Moral Theology.* Collegeville, MN: Liturgical Press, 2001.

Katz, Jonathan Ned. *The Invention of Heterosexuality.* Chicago: University of Chicago Press, 2007.

————. *Love Stories: Sex between Men before Homosexuality.* Chicago: University of Chicago Press, 2003.

Kelly, Michael Bernard. *Seduced by Grace: Contemporary Spirituality, Gay Experience, and Christian Faith.* Melbourne: Clouds of Magellan, 2007.

King, Christopher. "A Love as Fierce as Death." In *Take Back the Word,* eds. Robert Goss and Mona West, 126–42.

Kotrschal, Kurt, Josef Hemetsberger, and Brigitte Weiss. "Making the Best of a Bad Situation: Homosexuality in Male Greylag Geese." In *Homosexual Behaviour in Animals,* eds. Volker Sommer and Paul L. Vasey, 45–76. Cambridge, UK: Cambridge University Press, 2006.

Kristof, Nicholas D. "God and Sex." *New York Times,* October 23, 2004.

Kugle, Scott. *Homosexuality in Islam: Islamic Reflection on Gay, Lesbian, and Transgender Muslims.* Oxford, UK: Oneworld, 2010.

Laeuchli, Samuel. *Power and Sexuality: The Emergence of Canon Law at the Synod of Elvira.* Philadelphia: Temple University Press, 1972.

Lancaster, Roger. *The Trouble with Nature: Sex in Science and Popular Culture.* Berkeley: University of California Press, 2003.

Langbein, Laura, and Mark Yost Jr. "Same-Sex Marriage and Negative Externalities." *Social Science Quarterly* 90 (2009): 292–308.

Laumann, Edward O., John H. Gagnon, Robert T. Michael, and Stuart Michaels. *The Social Organization of Sexuality: Sexual Practices in the United States.* Chicago: University of Chicago Press, 1994.

LeVay, Simon. *Gay, Straight, and the Reason Why: The Science of Sexual Orientation.* New York: Oxford University Press, 2010.

Ligert, Leanne McCall, and Maren Tirabassi, eds. *Transgendering Faith: Identity, Sexuality, and Spirituality.* Cleveland: Pilgrim Press, 2004.

Liuzzi, Peter J. *With Listening Hearts: Understanding the Voices of Lesbian and Gay Catholics.* Mahwah, NJ: Paulist Press, 2001.

Lorde, Audre. "The Use of the Erotic: Erotic as Power." In *Sexuality and the Sacred,* eds. Ellison and Douglas, 75–79.

Loughlin, Gerard, ed. *Queer Theology: Rethinking the Western Body.* Malden, MA: Wiley-Blackwell Publishing, 2007.

MacCarthy, Fiona. *Byron: Life and Legend.* London: Faber and Faber, 2004.

Maher, Michael, Jr. *Being Gay and Lesbian in a Catholic High School: Beyond the Uniform.* Binghamton, NY: Haworth, 2001.

Malik, Faris. "The Ancient Roman and Talmudic Definition of Natural Eunuchs." Paper presented at the conference "Eunuchs in Antiquity and Beyond," Cardiff University, July 27, 1999. www.well.com/user/aquarius/cardiff.htm.

Martin, Dale. "Arsenokoites and Malakos: Meanings and Consequences." In *Biblical Ethics and Homosexuality: Listening to Scripture,* edited by Robert Brawley, 117–36. Louisville: Presbyterian Publishing, 1996.

Matthews, Victor H. "Hospitality and Hostility in Genesis 19 and Judges 19." *Biblical Theology Bulletin* 22, no. 1 (1992): 3–11.

McCleary, Rollan. *A Special Illumination: Authority, Inspiration, and Heresy in Gay Spirituality.* London: Equinox Publishing, 2004.

McGuire, Brian Patrick. *Brother and Lover: Aelred of Rievaulx.* New York: Crossroad Publishing, 1994.

McNeill, John. *The Church and the Homosexual.* Boston: Beacon Press, 1993.

————. *Freedom, Glorious Freedom: The Spiritual Journey to the Fullness of Life for Gays, Lesbians, and Everybody Else.* Boston: Beacon Press, 1995.

————. *Taking a Chance on God: Liberating Theology for Gays, Lesbians, and Their Lovers, Families, and Friends.* Boston: Beacon Press, 1996.

Michaelson, Jay. "Anti-Legalism and Anti-Judaism." In Michaelson, *Jews and the Law.* New Orleans: Quid Pro Books, 2012.

————. "Chaos, Law, and God: The Religious Meanings of Homosexuality." *Michigan Journal of Gender and Law* 15 (2008): 41–119.

————. "It's the Purity, Stupid: Reading Leviticus in Context: Parashat Metzora." In *Torah Queeries,* eds. Drinkwater et al., 145–50.

————. "On the Religious Significance of Homosexuality; or, Queering God, Torah and Israel." In *The Passionate Torah,* ed. Ruttenberg, 212–28.

Miller, James. "The Practices of Romans 1:26: Homosexual or Heterosexual?" *Novum Testamentum* 37, no. 1 (1995): 1–11.

Miller, Neil. *Out of the Past: Gay and Lesbian History from 1869 to the Present.* New York: Vintage, 1995.

Miner, Rev. Jeff, and John Tyler Connoley. *The Children Are Free: Reexamining the Biblical Evidence on Same-Sex Relationships.* Indianapolis: Found Pearl Press, 2002.

Mollenkott, Virginia Ramey. *Omnigender: A Trans-Religious Approach.* Cleveland: Pilgrim Press, 2007.

————. *Sensuous Spirituality: Out from Fundamentalism.* Cleveland: Pilgrim Press, 2008.

Mollenkott, Virginia Ramey, and Letha Scanzoni. *Is the Homosexual My Neighbor? Another Christian View.* New York: Harper and Row, 1978.

Monroe, Irene. "Reverend Irene Monroe: Writer, Speaker, Theologian." Irene Monroe website. www.irenemonroe.com.

Mooallem, Jon. "Can Animals Be Gay?" *New York Times Sunday Magazine,* March 31, 2010.

Moon, Dawne. *God, Sex, and Politics: Homosexuality and Everyday Theologies.* Chicago: University of Chicago Press, 2004.

Moore, Gareth. *A Question of Truth: Christianity and Homosexuality.* New York: Continuum Press, 2003.

Morchauser, Scott. "'Hospitality,' Hostiles, and Hostages: On the Legal Background to Genesis 19.1–9." *Journal for the Study of the Old Testament* 27, no. 4 (2003): 461–85.

More Light Presbyterians (website). www.mlp.org.

"MSNBC Fires Shock Host Michael Savage After He Tells Caller, 'Get AIDS and Die, You Pig.'" Democracy Now website, July 8, 2003. www .democracynow.org/2003/7/8/msnbc_fires_shock_host_michael_savage.

Murdoch, Iris. "The Moral Decision about Homosexuality." *The Ladder,* December 1964. Also published in *Man and Society* 7 (1964).

Murray, Stephen O. *Homosexualities.* Chicago: University of Chicago Press, 2002.

Murray, Stephen O., and Will Roscoe, eds. *Boy-Wives and Female Husbands: Studies in African Homosexualities.* New York: Palgrave, 1998.

———. *Islamic Homosexualities: Culture, History, and Literature.* New York: New York University Press, 1997.

Nanda, Serena. *Neither Man nor Woman: The Hijras of India.* Stamford, CT: Wadsworth Publishing, 1999.

Nardelli, Jean-Fabrice. *Homosexuality and Liminality in the Gilgamesh and Samuel.* Amsterdam: Adolf Hakkert, 2007.

Nelson, James B. *Between Two Gardens: Reflections on Sexuality and Religious Experience.* Eugene, OR: Wipf and Stock, 2008.

———, and Sandra Longfellow, eds. *Sexuality and the Sacred: Sources for Theological Reflection.* Louisville: Westminster John Knox, 1994.

Newman, Louis E. "Constructing a Jewish Sexual Ethic." In *Sexual Orientation and Human Rights,* eds. Olyan and Nussbaum, 46–48.

Ng, Vivian. "Homosexuality and the State in Late Imperial China." In *Hidden from History,* eds. Duberman et al., 76–89.

Nissinen, Martti. *Homoeroticism in the Biblical World: A Historical Perspective.* Minneapolis: Augsburg Fortress Press, 2004.

Noort, Ed, and Eibert Tigchelaar, eds. *Sodom's Sin: Genesis 18–19 and Its Interpretations.* Boston: Brill Academic, 2004.

Nygren, Anders. *Eros et Agape: la notion chrétienne de l'amour et ses transformations.* Paris: Aubier, 1944.

Olyan, Saul. "'And with a Man You Shall Not Lie the Lying Down of a Woman': On the Meaning and Significance of Leviticus 18:22 and 20:13." In *Que(e)rying Religion,* eds. Comstock and Henking, 398–414.

Olyan, Saul, and Martha Nussbaum, eds. *Sexual Orientation and Human Rights in American Religious Discourse.* New York: Oxford University Press, 1998.

Ostriker, Alicia. *For the Love of God: The Bible as an Open Book.* Piscataway, NJ: Rutgers University Press, 2009.

Patterson, Charlotte L. "Children of Lesbian and Gay Parents." *Current Directions in Psychological Science* 15 (2006): 241–44.

Patterson, Linda J. *Hate Thy Neighbor: How the Bible is Misused to Condemn Homosexuality.* West Conshohocken, PA: Infinity Publishing, 2009.

Paul VI. Congregation for the Doctrine of the Faith. "Declaration on Certain Questions Concerning Sexual Ethics–*Persona Humana.*" December 29, 1975.

Perez, Joe. *Soulfully Gay: How Harvard, Sex, Drugs, and Integral Philosophy Drove Me Crazy and Brought Me Back to God.* Boston: Integral Books, 2007.

Perry, Troy. *The Lord Is My Shepherd and He Knows I'm Gay.* Wichita, KS: Liberty Press, 1987.

Perry v. Schwarzenegger, 704 F. Supp. 2d 921 N.D. Cal. 2010.

Petersen, William. "Can ΑΡΣΕΝΟΚΟΙΤΑΙ Be Translated by 'Homosexuals'? 1 Cor. 6:9; 1 Tim. 1:10." *Vigiliae Christianae* 40, no. 2 (1986).

Piazza, Michael. *Gay by God: How to be Lesbian or Gay and Christian.* Dallas: Sources of Hope Publishing, 2008.

Plaskow, Judith. "Sexual Orientation and Human Rights: A Progressive Jewish Perspective." In *Sexual Orientation and Human Rights in American Religious Discourse,* eds. Olyan and Nussbaum, 29–45.

Poznansky, Alexander. *Tchaikovsky: The Quest for the Inner Man.* Stamford, CT: Schirmer Books, 2000.

"Psychologists Reject Gay 'Therapy.'" *New York Times,* August 9, 2009.

Quero, Martin Hugo Cordova. "Friendship with Benefits: A Queer Reading of Aelred of Rivaulx and His Theology of Friendship." In *The Sexual Theologian,* eds. Althaus-Reid and Isherwood, 26–46.

Rambuss, Richard. *Closet Devotions.* Durham, NC: Duke University Press, 1998.

Rapp, Linda. "George Washington Carver." *GLBTQ: An Encyclopedia of Gay, Lesbian, Bisexual, and Transgender Culture.* www.glbtq.com/social -sciences/carver_gw,4.html.

Reddy, Gayatri. *With Respect to Sex: Negotiating Hijra Identity in South India.* Chicago: University of Chicago Press, 2005.

Rich, Adrienne. *Blood, Bread, and Poetry: Selected Prose, 1979–1985.* New York: Norton, 1994.

———. "Compulsory Heterosexuality and Lesbian Existence." *Signs: Journal of Women in Culture and Society* 5 (1980): 631–60.

Robb, Graham. *Strangers: Homosexual Love in the Nineteenth Century.* New York: W. W. Norton, 2004.

Robinson, Gene. *In the Eye of the Storm: Swept to the Center by God.* New York: Seabury Books, 2008.

Robinson, Jack Clark. "Jesus, the Centurion, and His Lover." *Gay and Lesbian Review* 14, no. 6 (2007): 70–72.

Roden, Frederick S. "What a Friend We Have in Jesus: Same-Sex Biblical Couples in Victorian Literature." In *Reclaiming the Sacred,* ed. Frontain, 115–36.

Rogers, Jack. *Jesus, the Bible, and Homosexuality: Explode the Myths, Heal the Church.* Louisville: Westminster John Knox, 2009.

Roscoe, Will. *Changing Ones: Third and Fourth Genders in Native North America.* New York: Palgrave, 2000.

———. "Priests of the Goddess: Gender Transgression in Ancient Religion." *History of Religions* 35, no. 3 (1996): 195–230.

Roth, Norman. " 'My Beloved Is Like a Gazelle': Imagery of the Beloved Boy in Religious Hebrew Poetry." *Hebrew Annual Review* 8 (1984): 143–65.

Rotheram-Borus, Mary J., Joyce Hunter, and Margaret Rosario. "Suicidal Behavior and Gay-Related Stress among Gay and Bisexual Male Adolescents." *Journal of Adolescent Research* 9 (1994): 498–508.

Roughgarden, Joan. *Evolution's Rainbow: Diversity, Gender, and Sexuality in Nature and People.* Berkeley: University of California Press, 2009.

Rowse, A.L. *Homosexuals in History.* Cambridge, MA: De Capo Press, 1997.

Ruttenberg, Danya, ed. *The Passionate Torah: Sex and Judaism.* New York: New York University Press, 2009.

Saslow, James M. *Ganymede in the Renaissance: Homosexuality in Art and Society.* New Haven: Yale University Press, 1986.

Say, Elizabeth, and Mark Kowalewski. *Gays, Lesbians & Family Values.* Cleveland: Pilgrim Press, 1998.

Schalow, Paul Gordon. "Male Love in Early Modern Japan: A Literary Depiction of the 'Youth.' " In *Hidden from History,* eds. Duberman et al., 118–28.

Scroggs, Robin. *The New Testament and Homosexuality.* Minneapolis: Augsburg Fortress Press, 1983.

Sears, James T., ed. *Growing Up Gay in the South: Race, Gender, and Journeys of the Spirit.* New York: Routledge, 1991.

Shakespeare, William. *The Merchant of Venice.* New York: Simon & Schuster, 2009.

Shallenberger, David. *Reclaiming the Spirit: Gay Men and Lesbians Come to Terms with Their Religions.* New Brunswick, NJ: Rutgers University Press, 1998.

Silenzio, Vincent M. B., Juan B. Pena, Paul R. Duberstein, Julie Cerel, and Kerry L. Knox. "Sexual Orientation and Risk Factors for Suicidal Ideation and Suicide Attempts among Adolescents and Young Adults." *American Journal of Public Health* 97, no. 11 (2007): 2017–19.

Smith, Bruce R. *Homosexual Desire in Shakespeare's England: A Cultural Poetics.* Chicago: University of Chicago Press, 1995.

Sommer, Volker, and Paul L. Vasey, eds. *Homosexual Behaviour in Animals: An Evolutionary Perspective.* Cambridge, UK: Cambridge University Press, 2006.

Spencer, Daniel. *Gay and Gaia: Ethics, Ecology, and the Erotic.* Cleveland: Pilgrim Press, 1996.

Stacey, Judith. "Cruising to Familyland: Gay Hypergamy and Rainbow Kinship." *Current Sociology* 52, no. 2 (2004): 181–97.

Statement of Principles on the Place of Jews with a Homosexual Orientation in Our Community. http://statementofprinciplesnya.blogspot.com/.

Stemmeler, Michael, and J. Michael Clark, eds. *Homophobia and the Judaeo-Christian Tradition.* Memphis: Monument Press, 1990.

Stone, Andrea. "Dobson's Successor Gives Mega-Ministry New Focus." AOL News, April 24, 2010. www.aolnews.com/2010/04/24/wkd-edited -dobsons-successor-gives-mega-ministry-new-focus/.

Stone, Kenneth. *Practicing Safer Texts: Food, Sex, and Bible in Queer Perspective.* New York: T & T Clark, 2005.

Stuart, Elizabeth. *Gay and Lesbian Theologies: Repetitions with Critical Difference.* Burlington, VT: Ashgate, 2003.

———. *Just Good Friends: Towards a Lesbian and Gay Theology of Relationships.* Lincoln, RI: Andrew Mowbray, 1996.

———. *Religion Is a Queer Thing: A Guide to the Christian Faith for Lesbian, Gay, Bisexual, and Transgendered People.* Cleveland: Pilgrim Press, 1997.

Sullivan, Andrew. *Love Undetectable: Notes on Friendship, Sex, and Survival.* New York: Vintage, 1999.

———. *Virtually Normal: An Argument about Homosexuality.* New York: Vintage, 1996.

Sullivan, Andrew, ed. *Same-Sex Marriage: Pro and Con: A Reader.* New York: Vintage, 2004.

Sweasey, Peter. *From Queer to Eternity: Spirituality in the Lives of Lesbian, Gay and Bisexual People.* London: Cassell Press, 1997.

Swidler, Arlene, ed. *Homosexuality and World Religions.* Philadelphia: Trinity Press International, 1993.

Tanis, Justin. *Trans-Gendered: Theology, Ministry, and Communities of Faith.* Cleveland: Pilgrim Press, 2003.

Thompson, Mark. *Gay Soul: Finding the Heart of the Gay Spirit and Nature.* New York: HarperOne, 1995.

————. *Gay Spirit: Myth and Meaning.* New York: St. Martin's, 1988.

Tigert, Leanne McCall, and Maren C. Tirabassi, eds. *Transgendering Faith: Identity, Sexuality, and Spirituality.* Cleveland: Pilgrim Press, 2004.

Twain, Mark. *Adventures of Huckleberry Finn.* 3rd ed. Berkeley: University of California Press, 2005.

UNAIDS. *2007 AIDS Epidemic Update.* UNAIDS/07.27E/JC1322E, December 2007.

Unks, Gerald, ed. *The Gay Teen: Educational Practice and Theory for Lesbian, Gay, and Bisexual Adolescents.* New York: Routledge, 1995.

U.S. Department of Justice. *Sexually Assaulted Children: National Estimates & Characteristics.* National Incidence Studies of Missing, Abducted, Runaway & Throwaway Children, August 2008. www.crisisconnectioninc.org/pdf/child_sexual_abuse_stats.pdf.

Vaid, Urvashi. *Virtual Equality: The Mainstreaming of Gay and Lesbian Equality.* Norwell, MA: Anchor Press, 1996.

Vandermeersch, Patrick. "Sodomites, Gays, and Biblical Scholars: A Gathering Organized by Peter Damian?" In *Sodom's Sin,* eds. Noort and Tigchelaar, 149–71.

Vasey, Paul L. "The Pursuit of Pleasure: An Evolutionary History of Homosexual Behavior in Japanese Macaques." In *Homosexual Behaviour in Animals,* eds., Sommer and Vasey, 191–217.

Wade, Nicholas. "Depth of the Kindness Hormone Appears to Know Some Bounds." *New York Times,* January 10, 2011.

Warner, Michael. *The Trouble with Normal: Sex, Politics, and the Ethics of Queer Life.* Cambridge: Harvard University Press, 1999.

Watson, Philip S. *Agape and Eros.* New York: Harper & Row, 1969.

Wawrytko, Sandra. "Homosexuality in Chinese and Japanese Religions." In *Homosexuality and World Religions,* ed. Swidler, 199–230.

White, Mel. *Stranger at the Gate: To Be Gay and Christian in America.* New York: Plume, 1995.

Wiley, Roland John. *Tchaikovsky.* New York: Oxford University Press, 2009.

Williams, Walter. *The Spirit and the Flesh: Sexual Diversity in American Indian Culture.* Boston: Beacon Press, 1986.

Wilson, E. O. *Sociobiology: The New Synthesis.* Cambridge, MA: Belknap Press, 2000.

Wilson, Nancy. *Our Tribe: Queer Folks, God, Jesus, and the Bible.* Sacramento: Alamo Square Press, 2000.

Wold, Donald. *Out of Order: Homosexuality and the Bible in the Near East.* San Antonio: Cedar Leaf Press, 2009.

Wolf, James G., ed. *Gay Priests.* New York: HarperCollins, 1989.

Wright, David. "Homosexuals or Prostitutes? The Meaning of ἀρσενοκοῖται I Cor. 6:9, 1 Tim. 1:10." *Vigiliae Christianae* 38, no. 2 (1984): 125–53.

Index